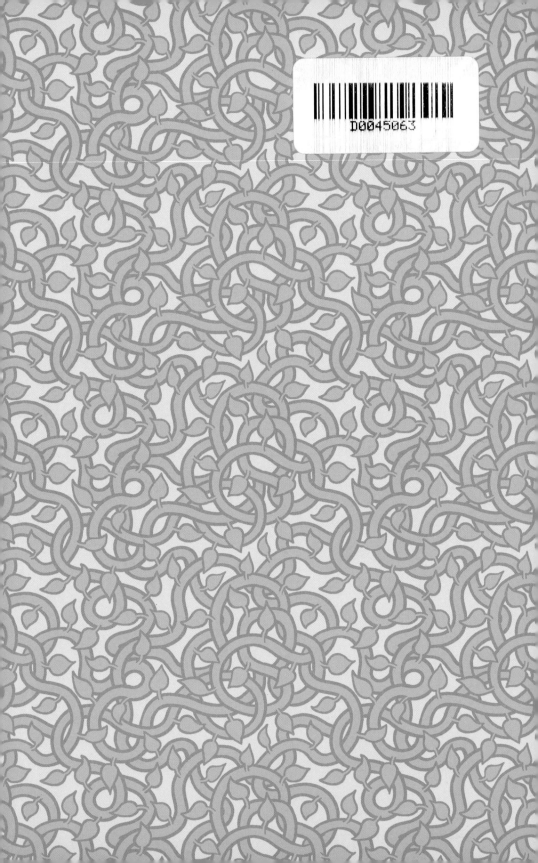

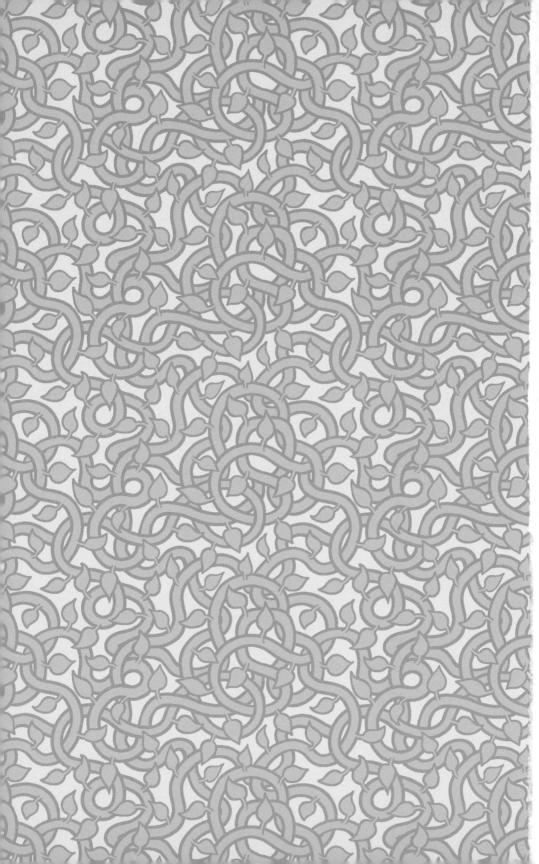

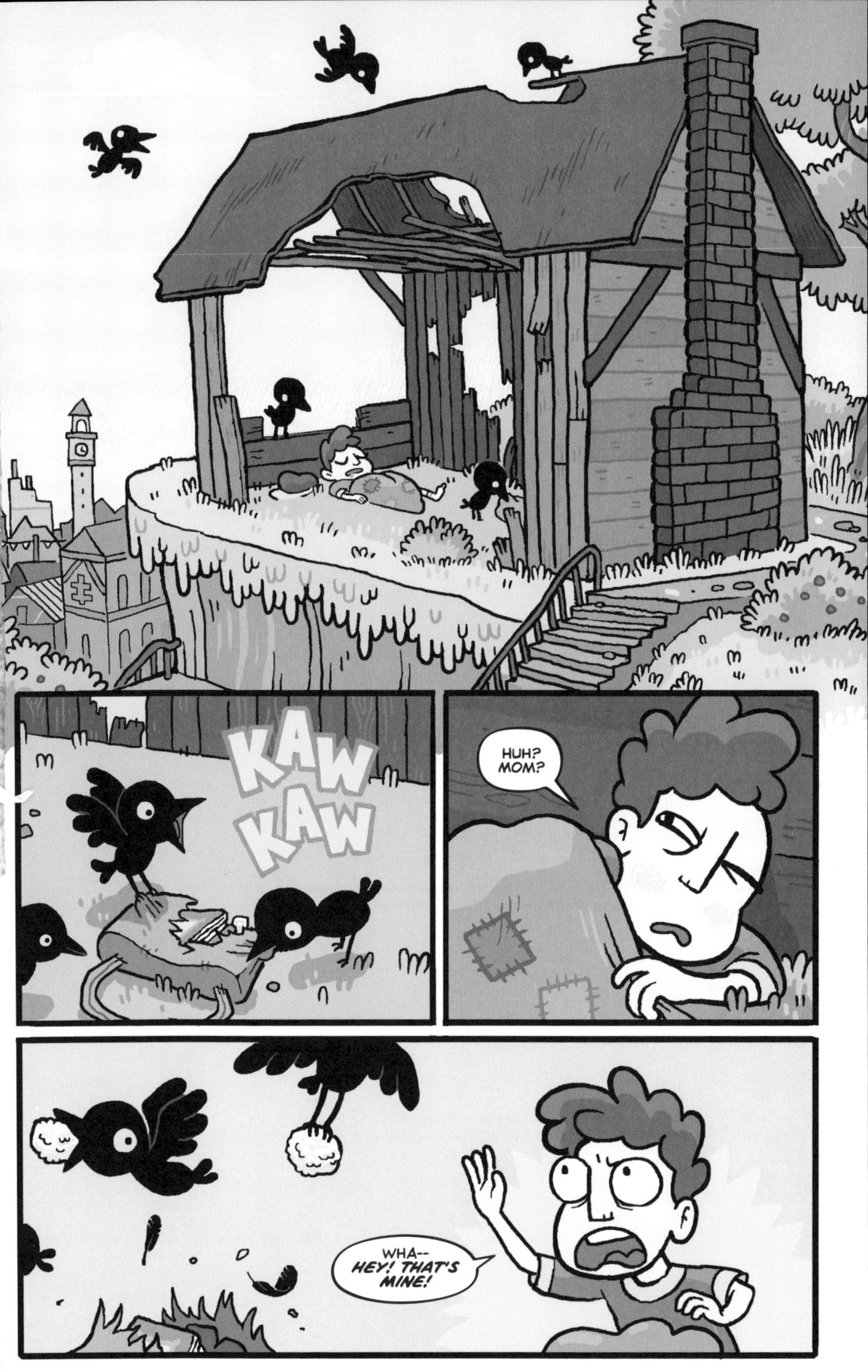
KAW
KAW
HUH? MOM?
WHA-- HEY! THAT'S MINE!

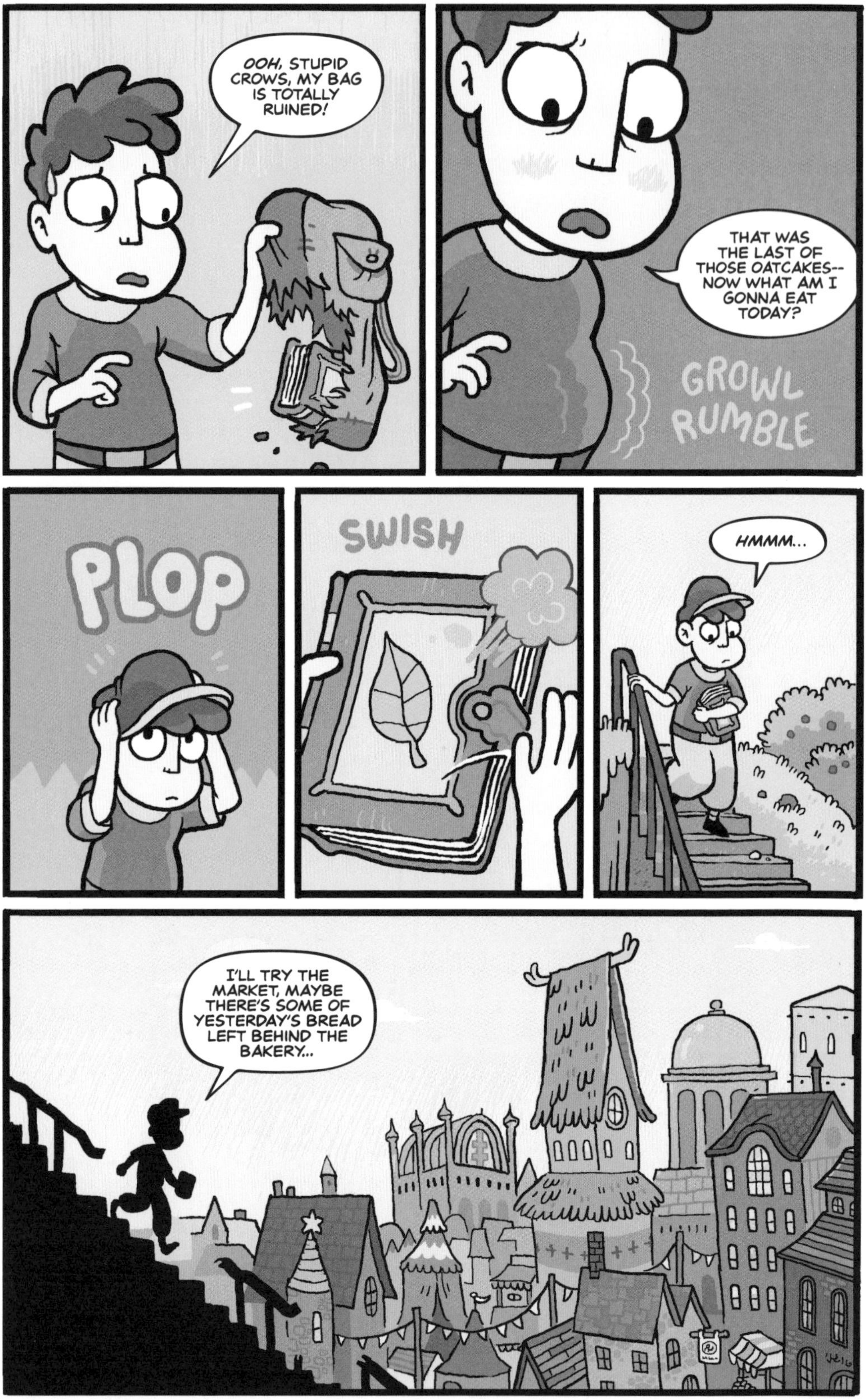
OOH, STUPID CROWS, MY BAG IS TOTALLY RUINED!
THAT WAS THE LAST OF THOSE OATCAKES-- NOW WHAT AM I GONNA EAT TODAY?
GROWL RUMBLE
PLOP
SWISH
HMMM...
I'LL TRY THE MARKET, MAYBE THERE'S SOME OF YESTERDAY'S BREAD LEFT BEHIND THE BAKERY...

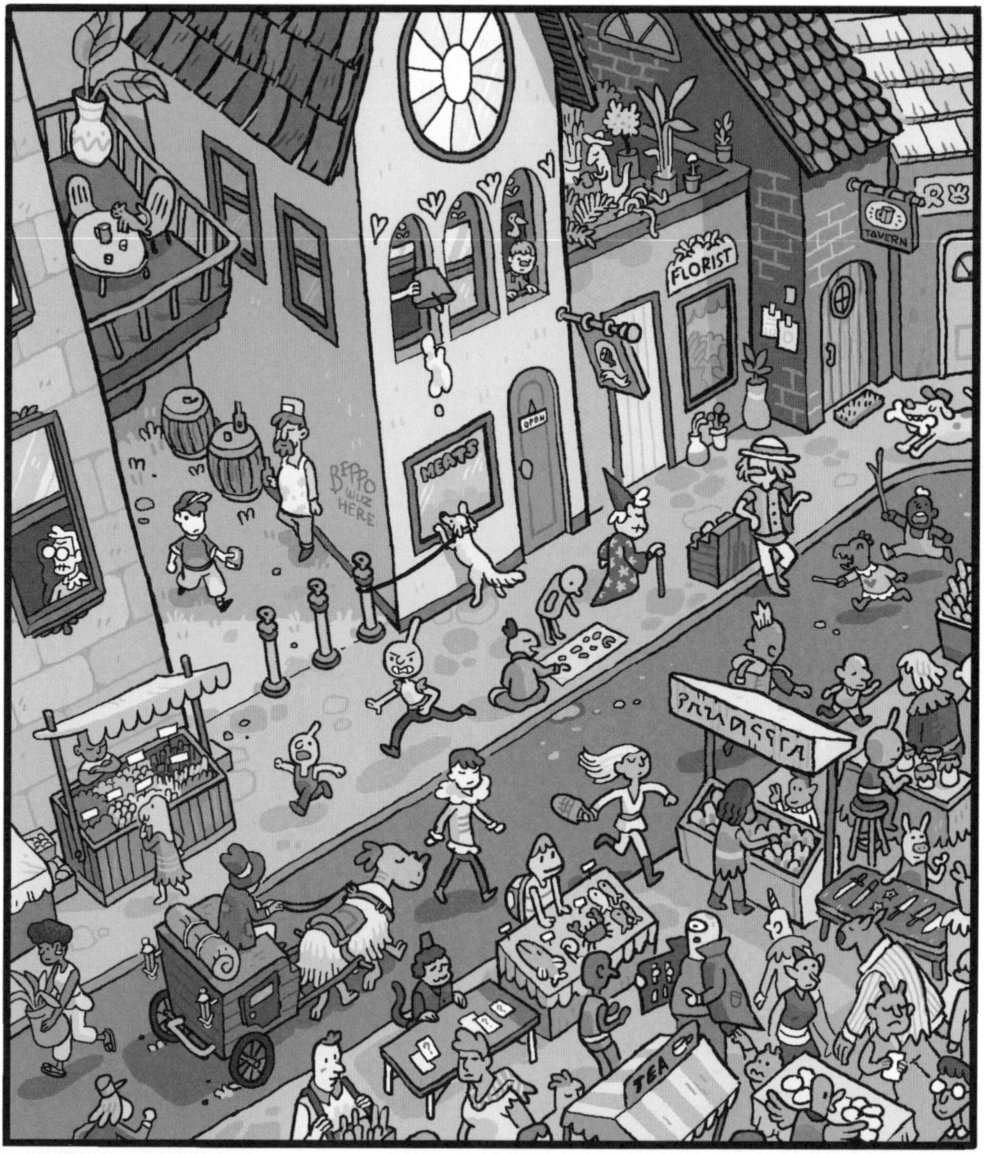
FLORIST
TAVERN
MEATS
OPEN
BEPPO WUZ HERE
TEA

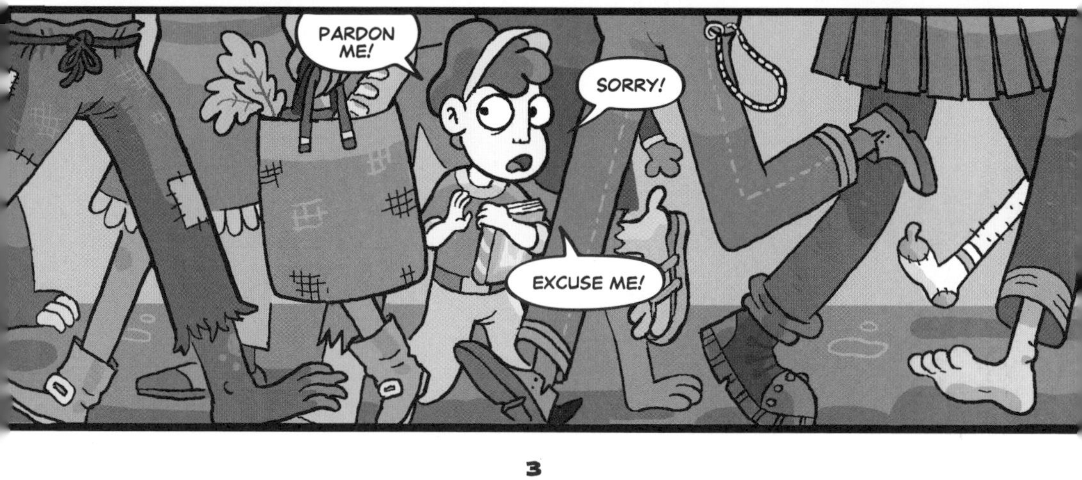
PARDON ME!
SORRY!
EXCUSE ME!

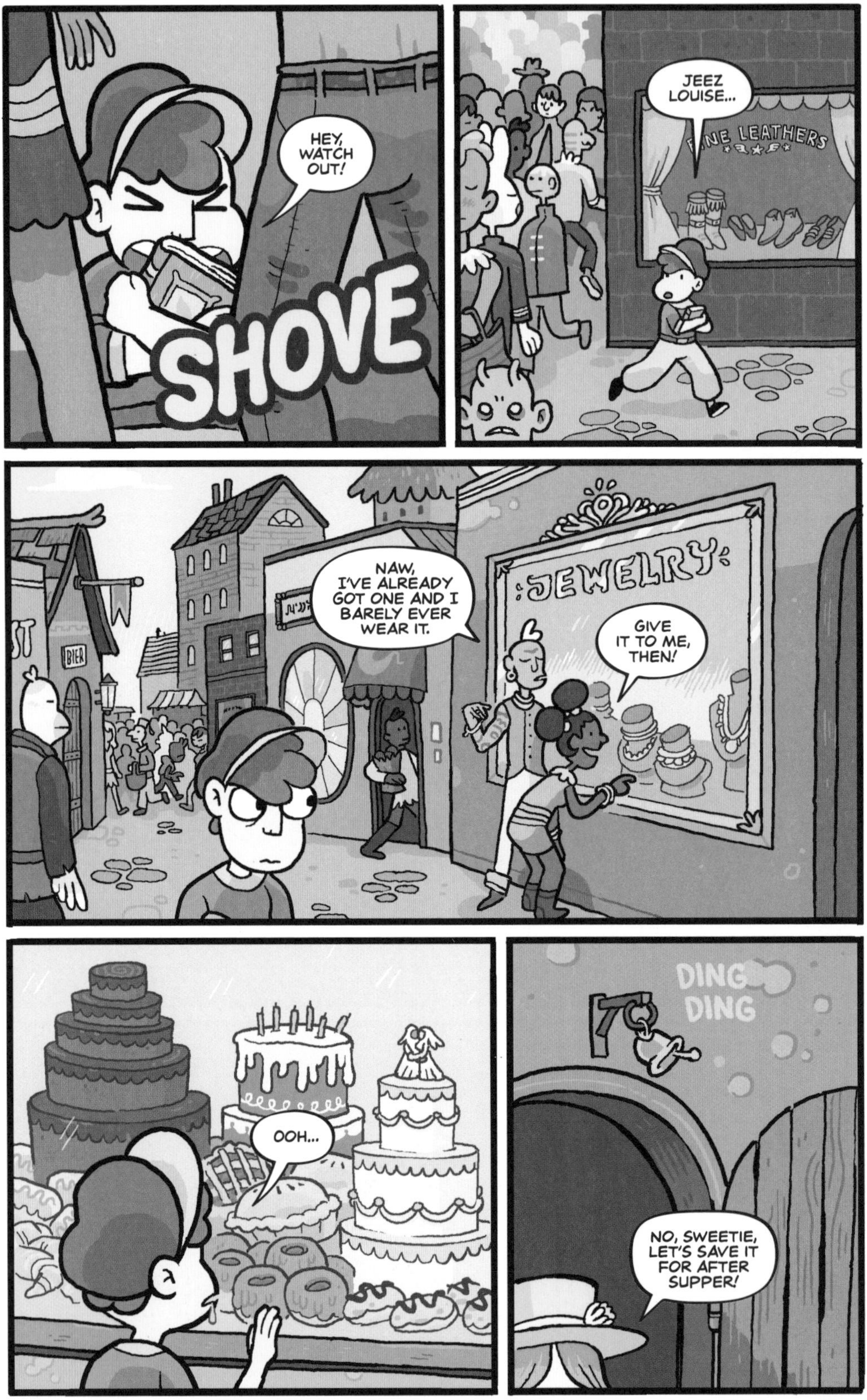
HEY, WATCH OUT!
SHOVE
JEEZ LOUISE...
FINE LEATHERS
NAW, I'VE ALREADY GOT ONE AND I BARELY EVER WEAR IT.
JEWELRY
GIVE IT TO ME, THEN!
BIER
OOH...
DING DING
NO, SWEETIE, LET'S SAVE IT FOR AFTER SUPPER!

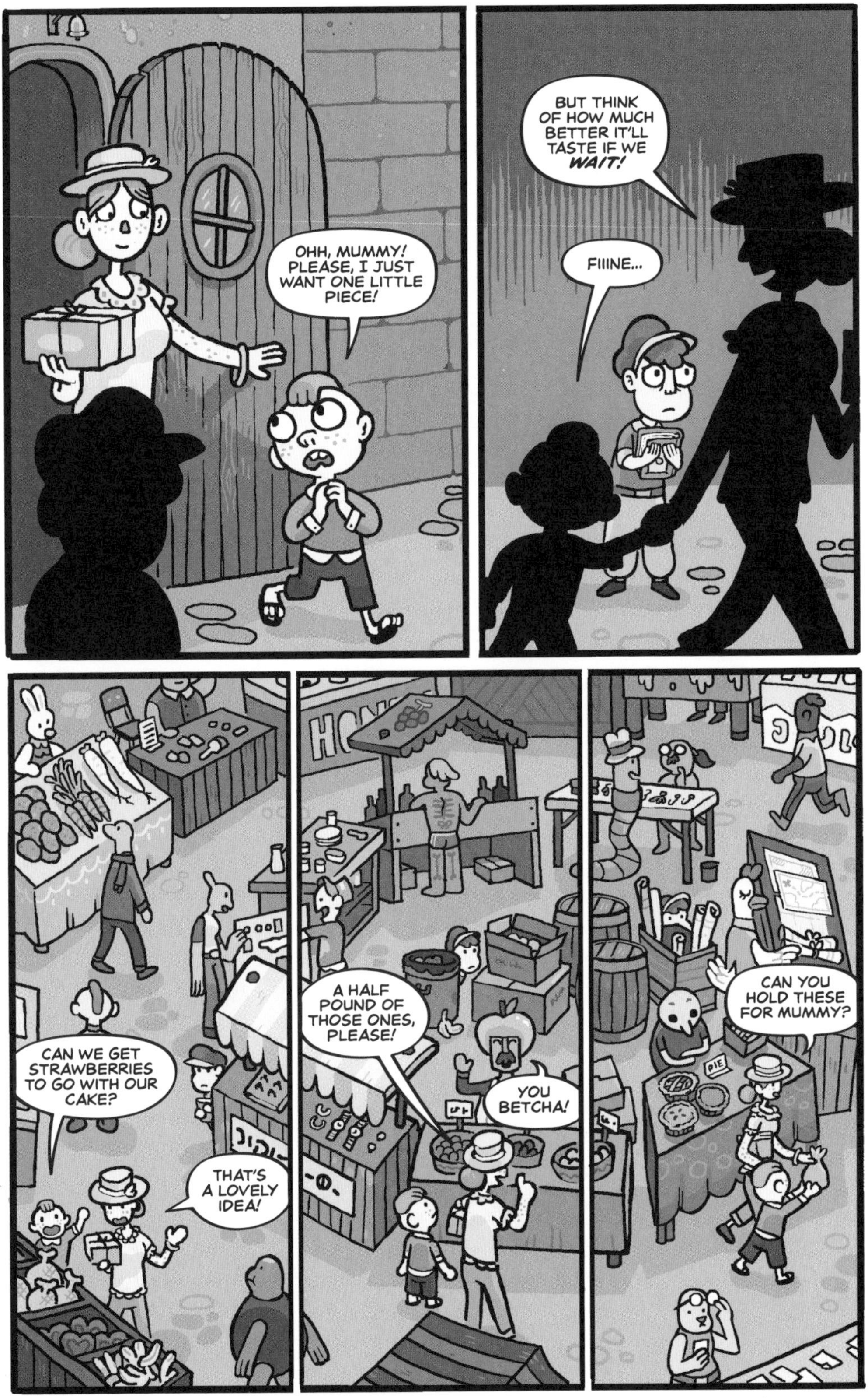
OHH, MUMMY! PLEASE, I JUST WANT ONE LITTLE PIECE!
BUT THINK OF HOW MUCH BETTER IT'LL TASTE IF WE *WAIT!*
FIIINE...
CAN WE GET STRAWBERRIES TO GO WITH OUR CAKE?
THAT'S A LOVELY IDEA!
A HALF POUND OF THOSE ONES, PLEASE!
YOU BETCHA!
CAN YOU HOLD THESE FOR MUMMY?
PIE

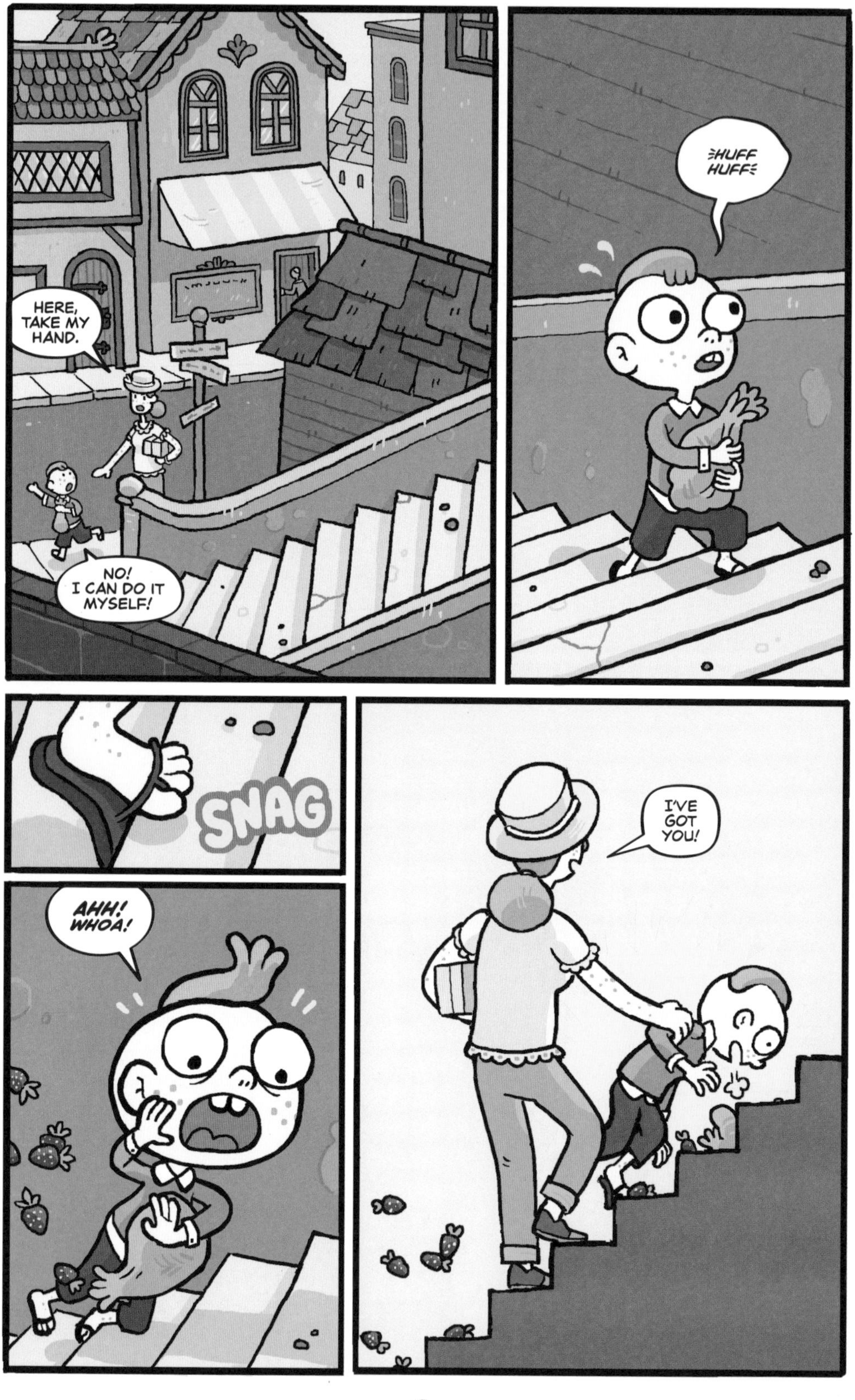
HERE, TAKE MY HAND.
NO! I CAN DO IT MYSELF!
HUFF HUFF
SNAG
AHH! WHOA!
I'VE GOT YOU!

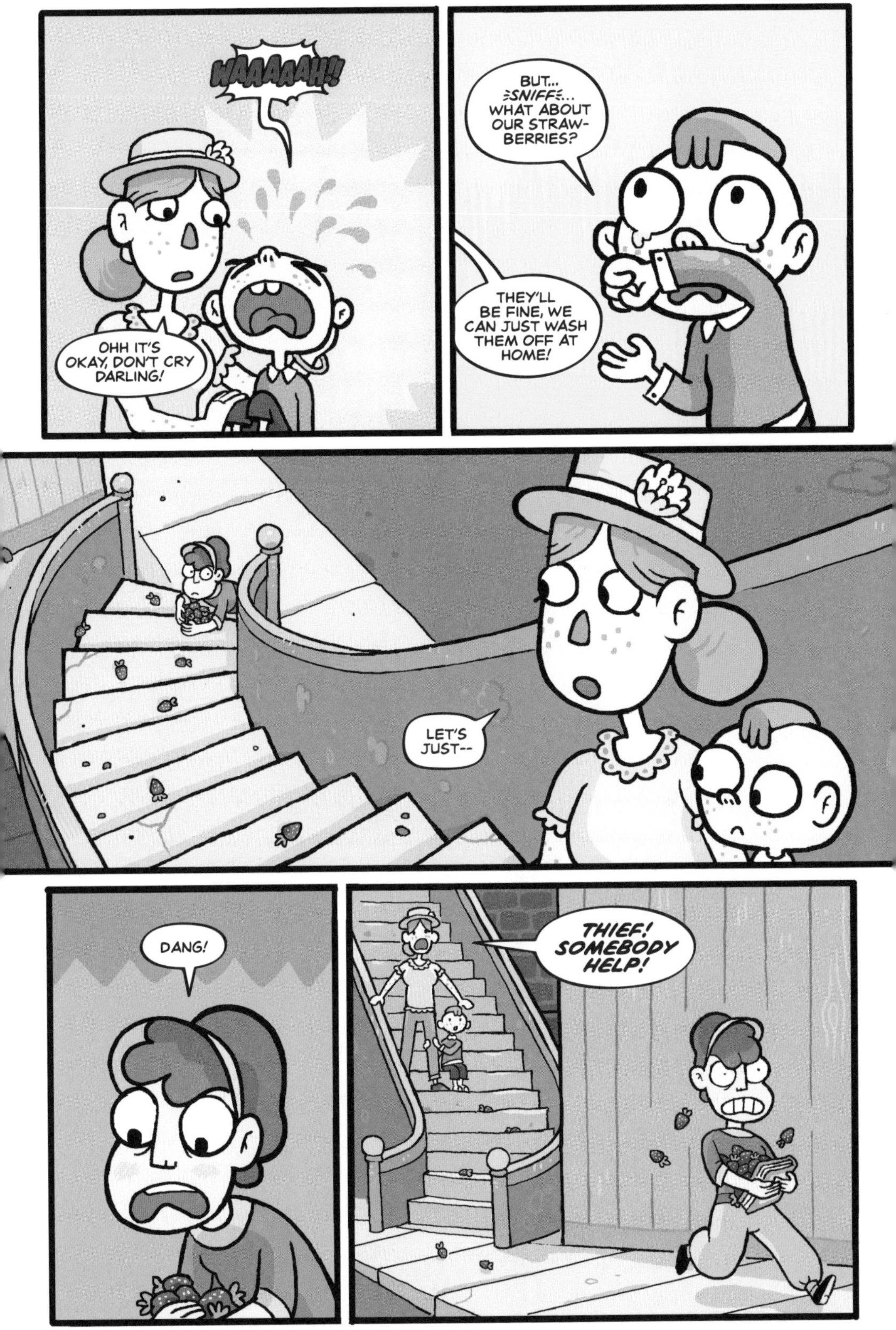
WAAAAAH!!
OHH IT'S OKAY, DON'T CRY DARLING!
BUT... SNIFF... WHAT ABOUT OUR STRAW-BERRIES?
THEY'LL BE FINE, WE CAN JUST WASH THEM OFF AT HOME!
LET'S JUST--
DANG!
THIEF! SOMEBODY HELP!

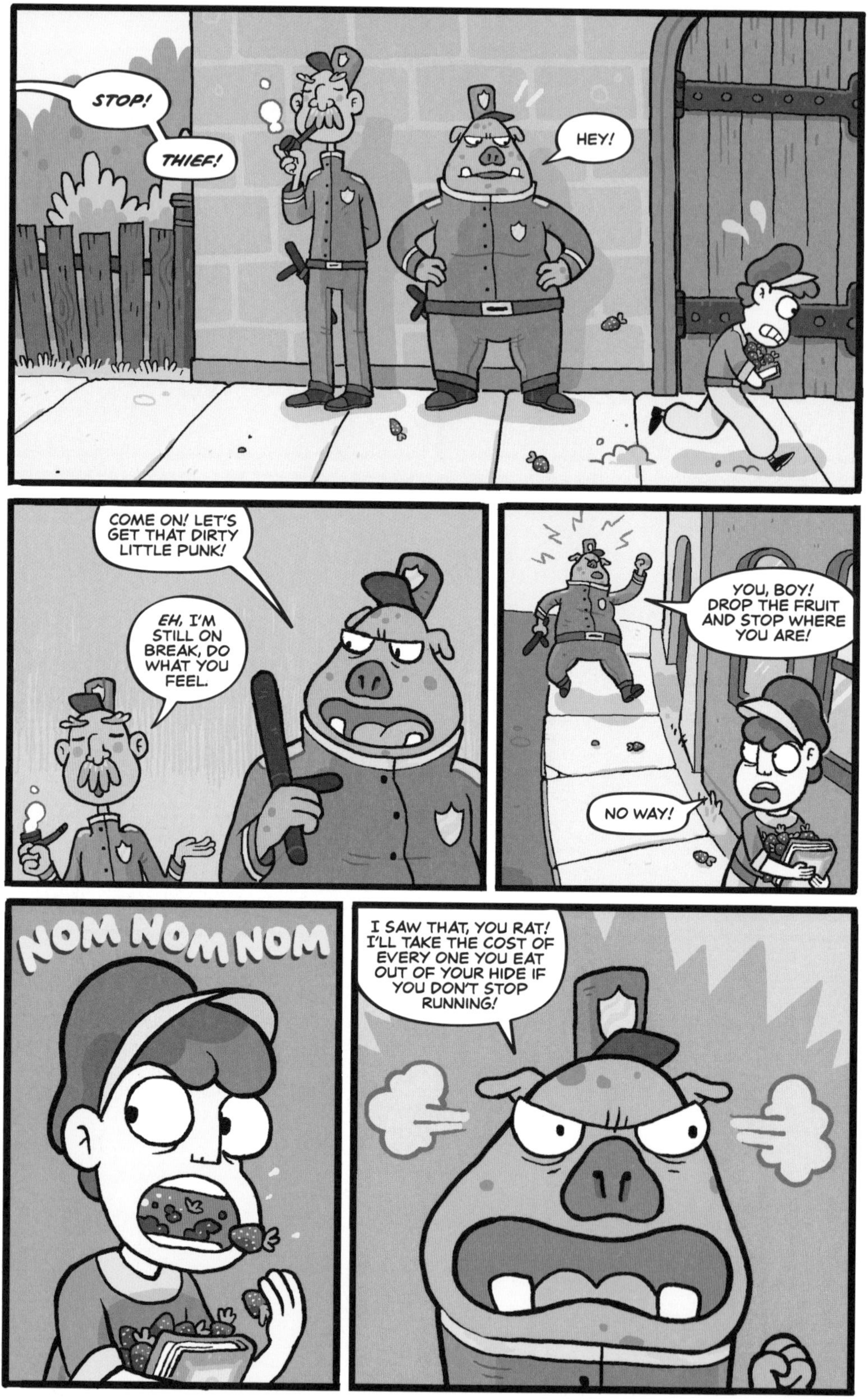
STOP!
THIEF!
HEY!
COME ON! LET'S GET THAT DIRTY LITTLE PUNK!
EH, I'M STILL ON BREAK, DO WHAT YOU FEEL.
YOU, BOY! DROP THE FRUIT AND STOP WHERE YOU ARE!
NO WAY!
NOM NOM NOM
I SAW THAT, YOU RAT! I'LL TAKE THE COST OF EVERY ONE YOU EAT OUT OF YOUR HIDE IF YOU DON'T STOP RUNNING!

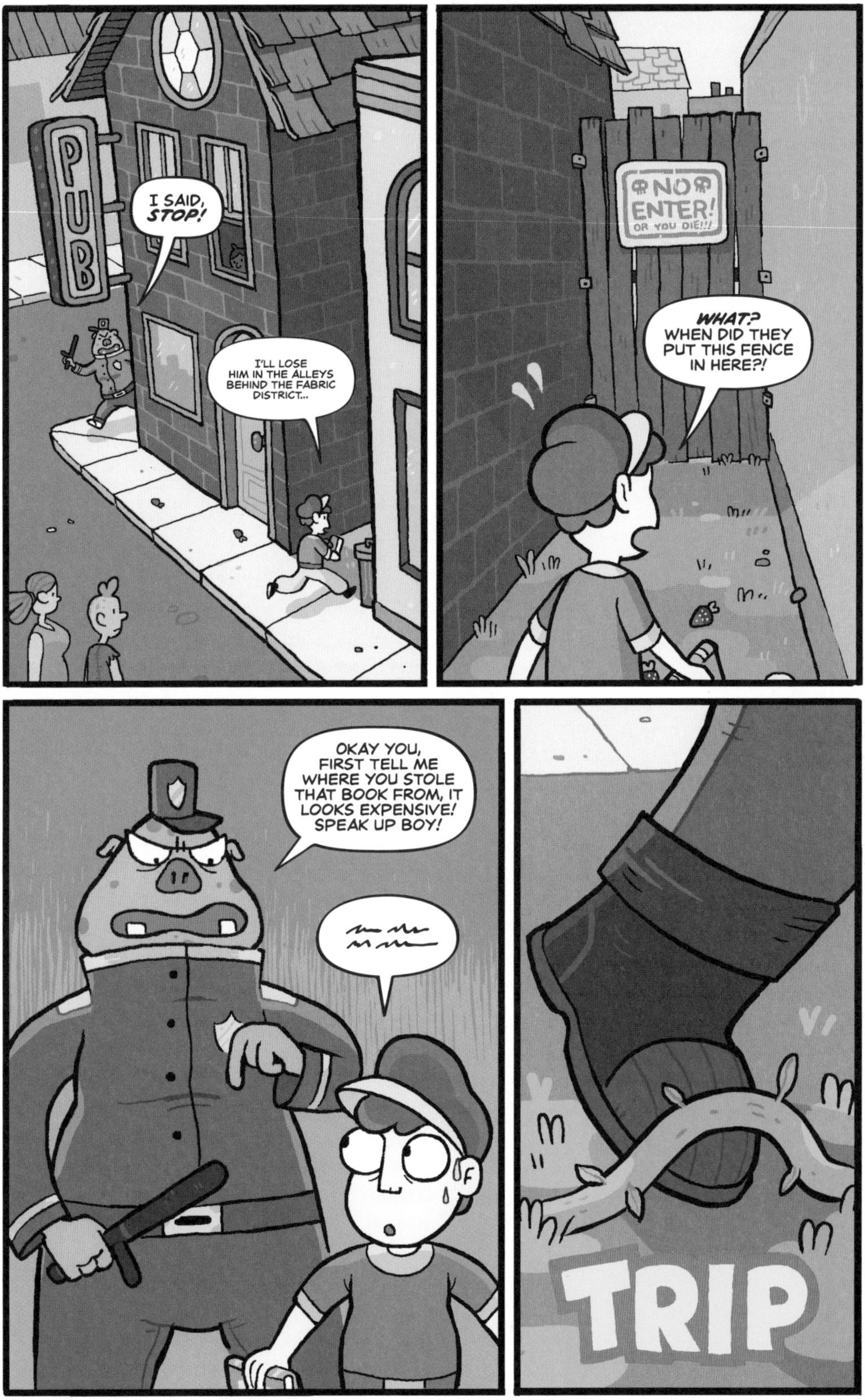
PUB
I SAID, *STOP!*
I'LL LOSE HIM IN THE ALLEYS BEHIND THE FABRIC DISTRICT...
NO ENTER! OR YOU DIE!!!
WHAT? WHEN DID THEY PUT THIS FENCE IN HERE?!
OKAY YOU, FIRST TELL ME WHERE YOU STOLE THAT BOOK FROM, IT LOOKS EXPENSIVE! SPEAK UP BOY!
TRIP

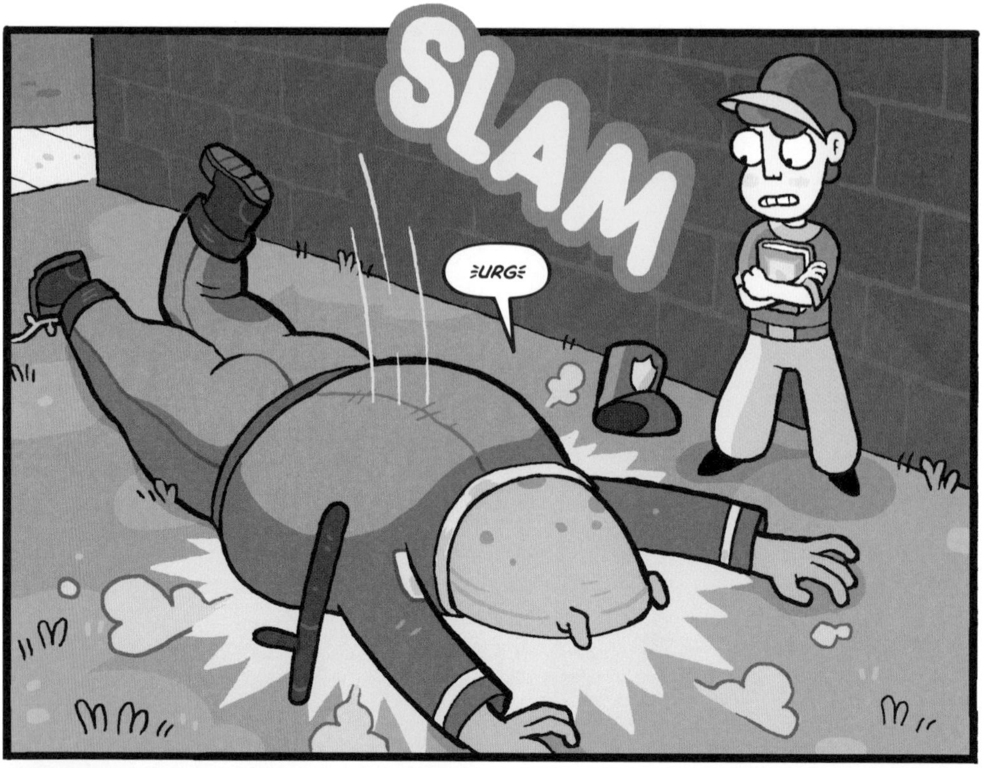
SLAM
URG
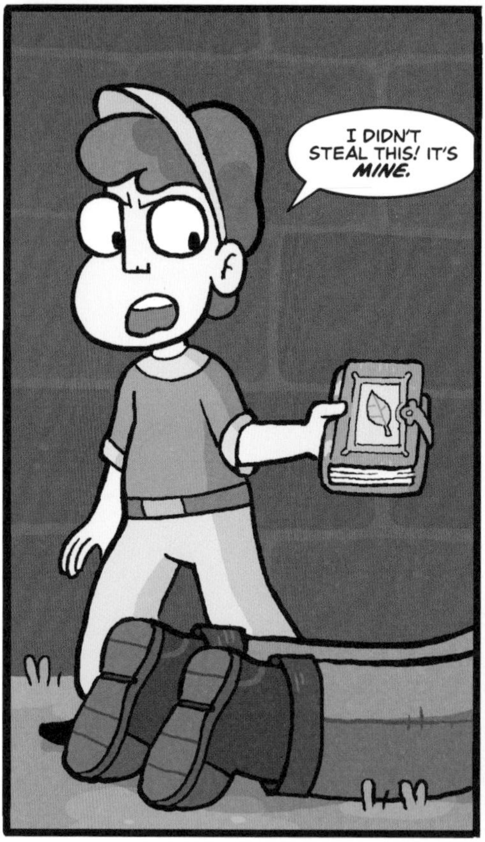
I DIDN'T STEAL THIS! IT'S ***MINE.***
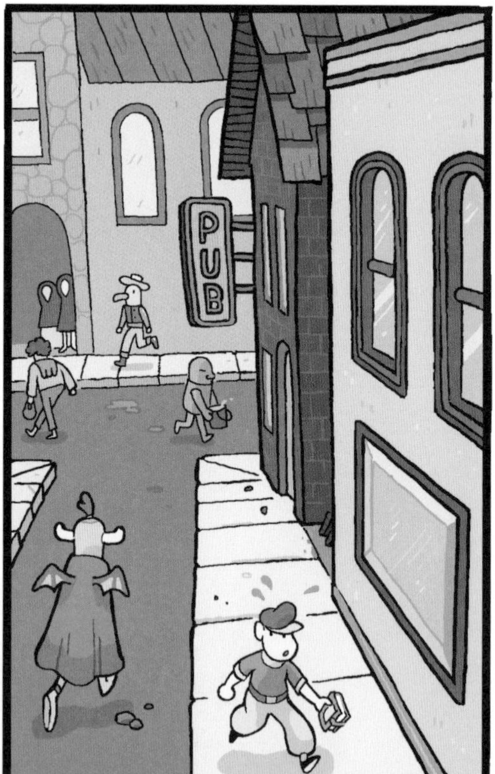
PUB

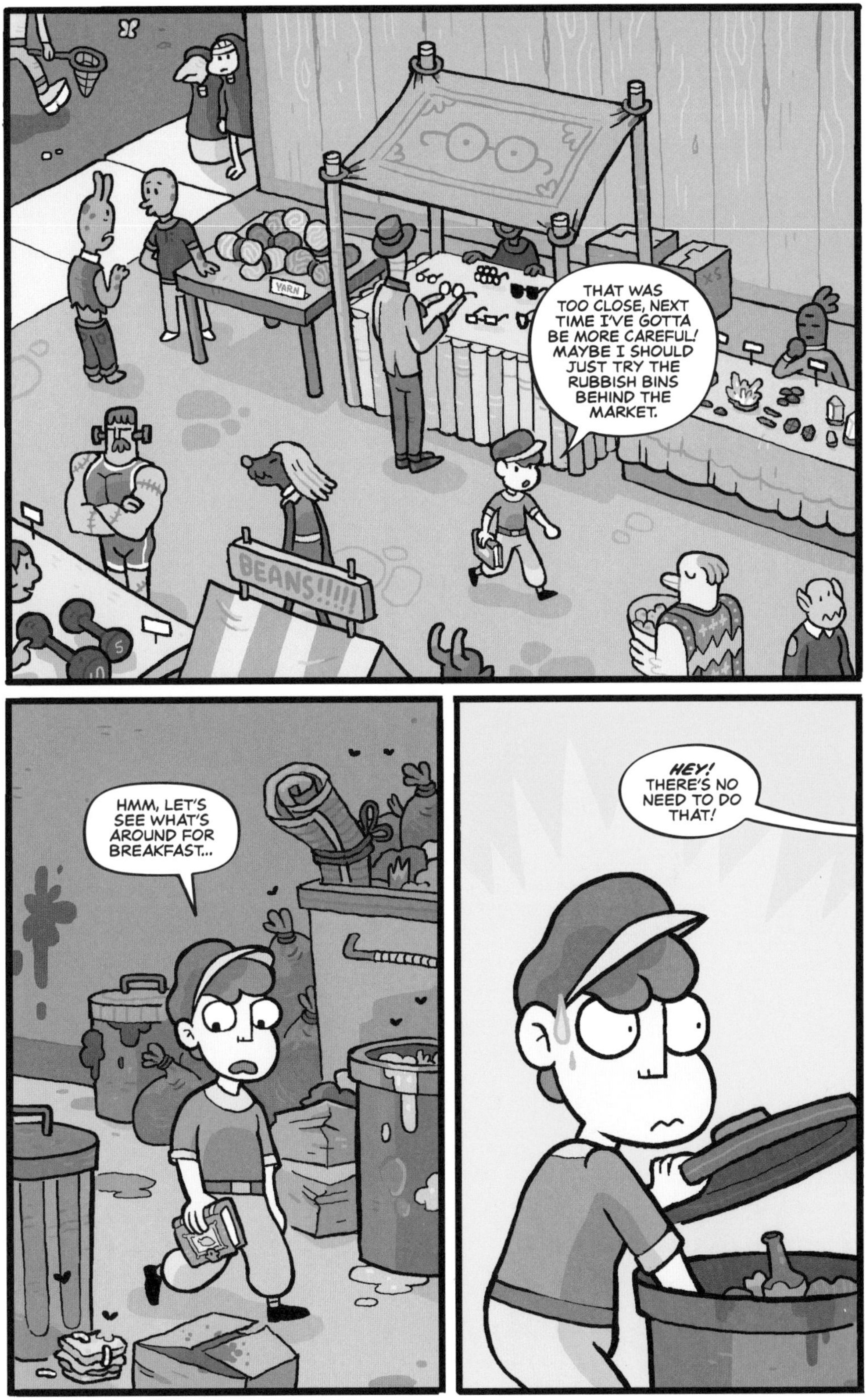
THAT WAS TOO CLOSE, NEXT TIME I'VE GOTTA BE MORE CAREFUL! MAYBE I SHOULD JUST TRY THE RUBBISH BINS BEHIND THE MARKET.
YARN
BEANS!!!!!
HMM, LET'S SEE WHAT'S AROUND FOR BREAKFAST...
HEY! THERE'S NO NEED TO DO THAT!

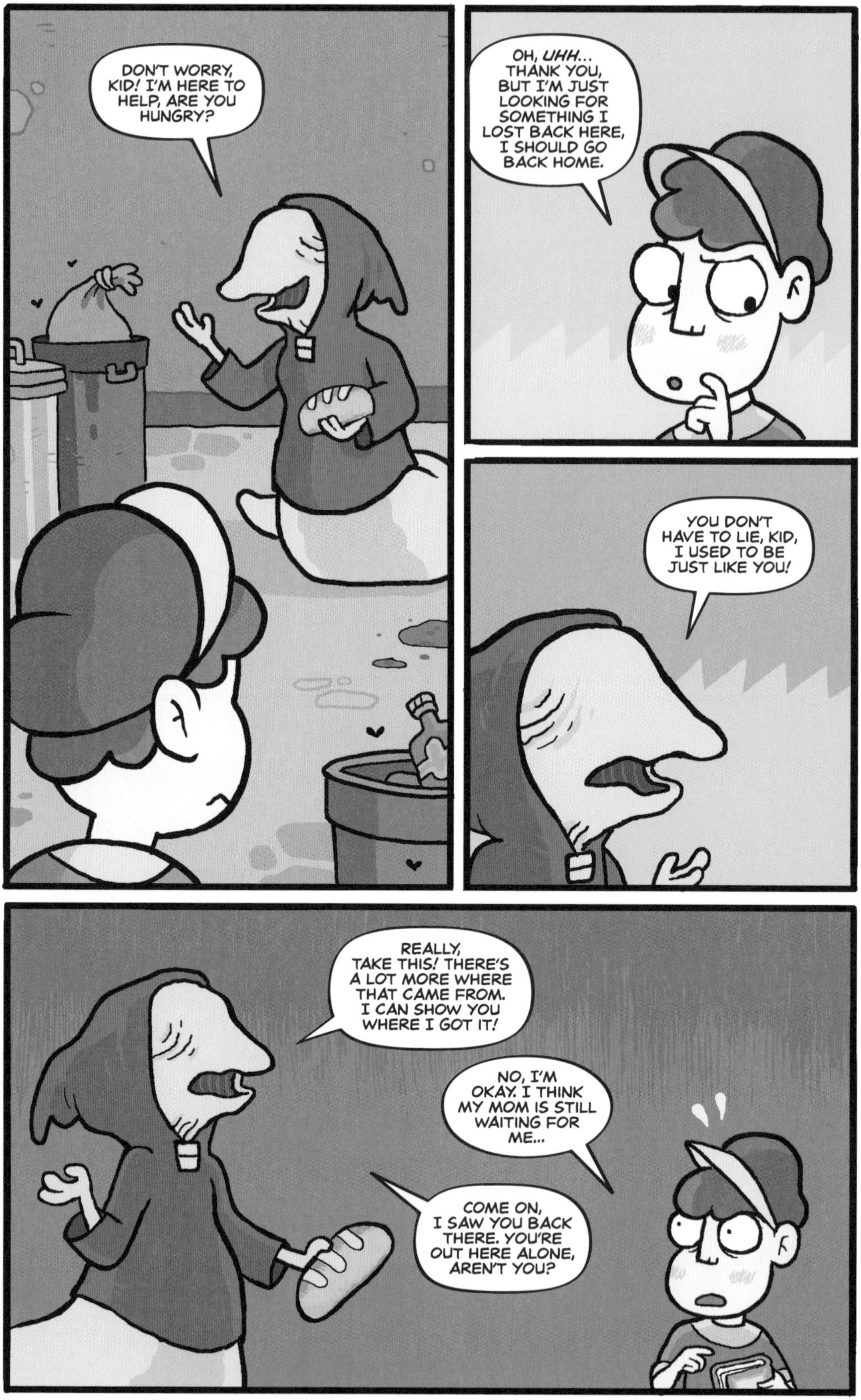
DON'T WORRY, KID! I'M HERE TO HELP, ARE YOU HUNGRY?
OH, *UHH*... THANK YOU, BUT I'M JUST LOOKING FOR SOMETHING I LOST BACK HERE, I SHOULD GO BACK HOME.
YOU DON'T HAVE TO LIE, KID, I USED TO BE JUST LIKE YOU!
REALLY, TAKE THIS! THERE'S A LOT MORE WHERE THAT CAME FROM. I CAN SHOW YOU WHERE I GOT IT!
NO, I'M OKAY. I THINK MY MOM IS STILL WAITING FOR ME...
COME ON, I SAW YOU BACK THERE. YOU'RE OUT HERE ALONE, AREN'T YOU?

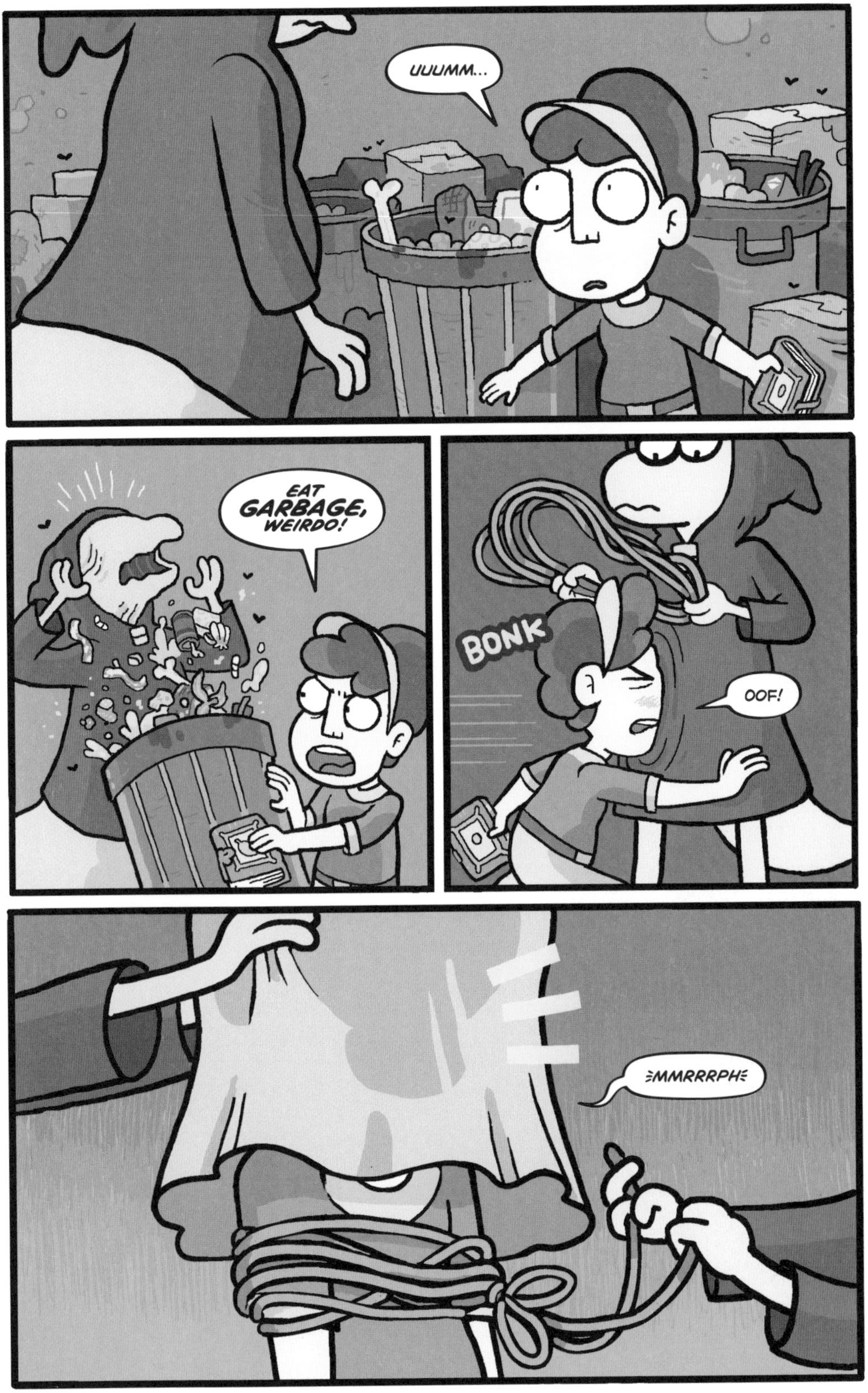
UUUMM...
EAT GARBAGE, WEIRDO!
BONK
OOF!
MMRRRPH

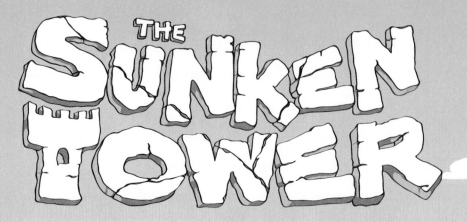

THE SUNKEN TOWER

WRITTEN, ILLUSTRATED, AND COLORED BY
TAIT HOWARD

AN ONI PRESS PUBLICATION

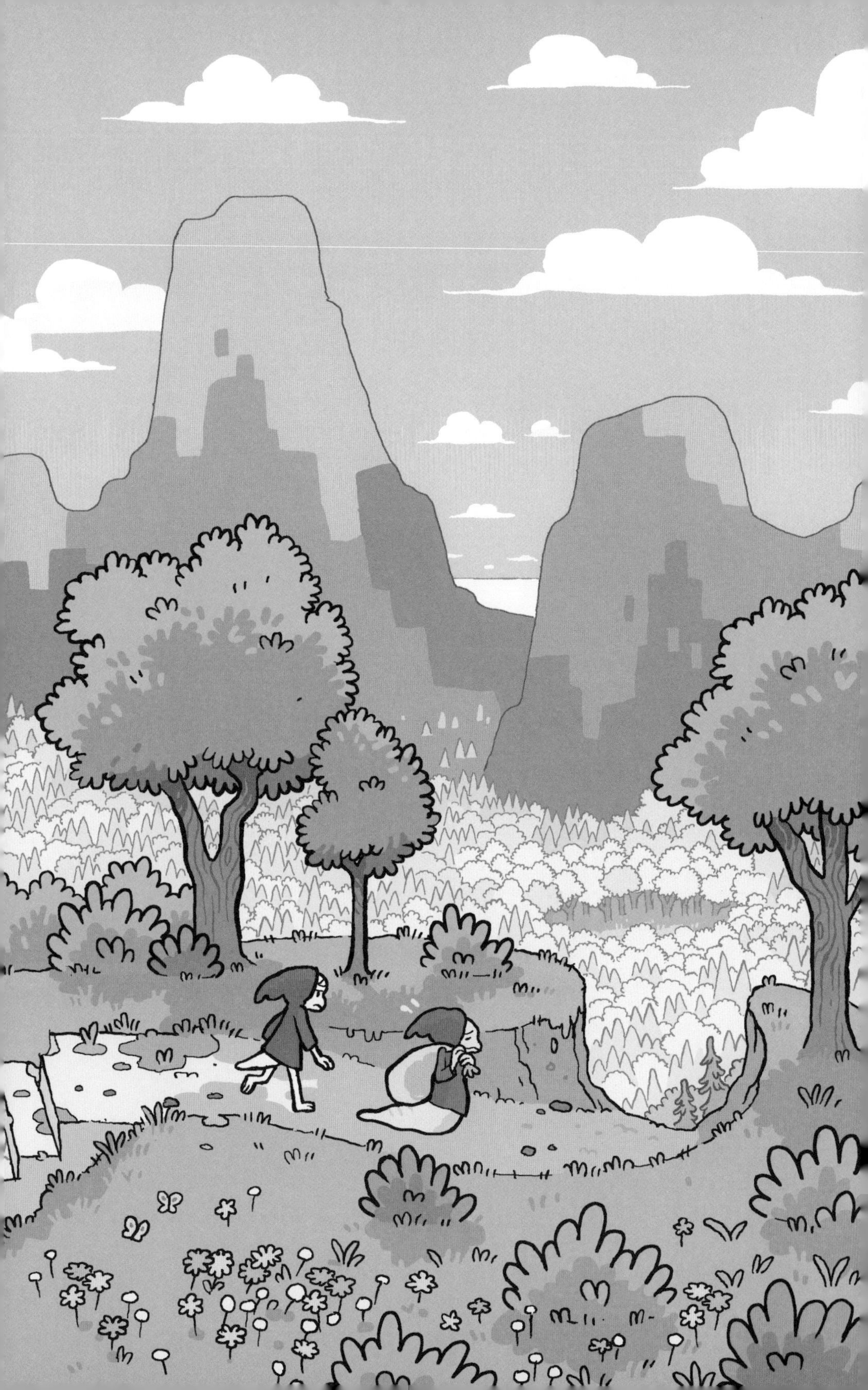

For my mom and dad, who taught me how to make things.
& Georgie, who helped me make this book... twice. —TH

LETTERED BY
ADITYA BIDIKAR

DESIGNED BY
SONJA SYNAK

ORIGINAL SERIES EDITED BY
CALEB GOELLNER

COLLECTION EDITED BY
ROBIN HERRERA

Published by Oni-Lion Forge Publishing Group, LLC
Digital Version Published By Stela

JAMES LUCAS JONES,
president & publisher

HILARY THOMPSON,
graphic designer

SARAH GAYDOS,
editor in chief

ANGIE KNOWLES,
digital prepress lead

CHARLIE CHU,
e.v.p. of creative & business development

SHAWNA GORE,
senior editor

BRAD ROOKS,
director of operations

ROBIN HERRERA,
senior editor

AMBER O'NEILL,
special projects manager

AMANDA MEADOWS,
senior editor

HARRIS FISH,
events manager

JASMINE AMIRI,
editor

MARGOT WOOD,
director of marketing & sales

GRACE BORNHOFT,
editor

JEREMY ATKINS,
director of brand communications

ZACK SOTO,
editor

DEVIN FUNCHES,
sales & marketing manager

STEVE ELLIS,
vice president of games

TARA LEHMANN,
marketing & publicity associate

BEN EISNER,
game developer

TROY LOOK,
director of design & production

MICHELLE NGUYEN,
executive assistant

KATE Z. STONE,
senior graphic designer

JUNG LEE,
logistics coordinator

SONJA SYNAK,
graphic designer

JOE NOZEMACK,
publisher emeritus

First Edition: March 2020

ISBN 978-1-62010-687-7

Printed in China.

1 2 3 4 5 6 7 8 9 10

Library of Congress Control Number: 2019940881

onipress.com | lionforge.com
facebook.com/onipress | facebook.com/lionforge
twitter.com/onipress | twitter.com/lionforge
instagram.com/onipress | instagram.com/lionforge

@ TAITCOMICS

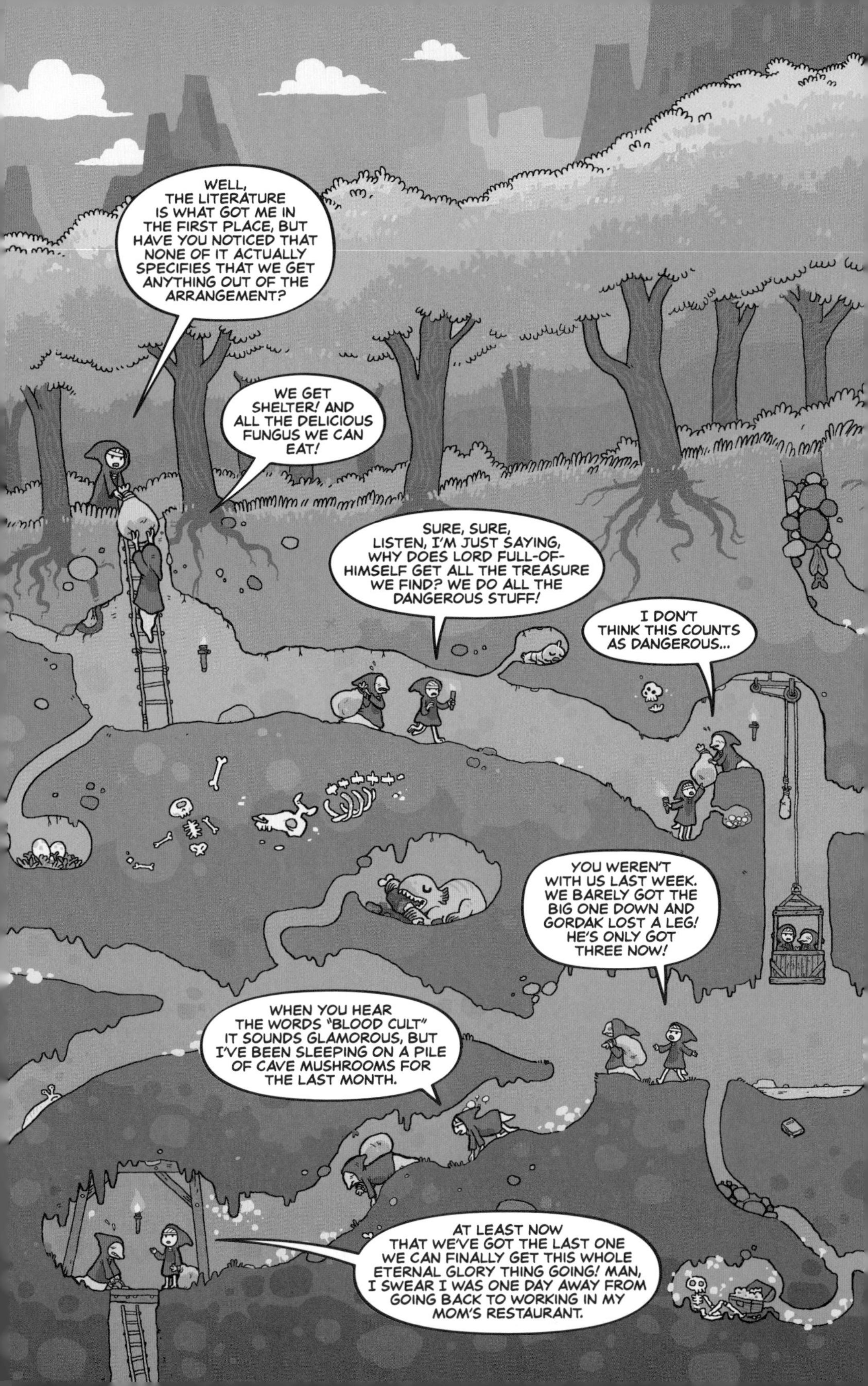
WELL, THE LITERATURE IS WHAT GOT ME IN THE FIRST PLACE, BUT HAVE YOU NOTICED THAT NONE OF IT ACTUALLY SPECIFIES THAT WE GET ANYTHING OUT OF THE ARRANGEMENT?
WE GET SHELTER! AND ALL THE DELICIOUS FUNGUS WE CAN EAT!
SURE, SURE, LISTEN, I'M JUST SAYING, WHY DOES LORD FULL-OF-HIMSELF GET ALL THE TREASURE WE FIND? WE DO ALL THE DANGEROUS STUFF!
I DON'T THINK THIS COUNTS AS DANGEROUS...
YOU WEREN'T WITH US LAST WEEK. WE BARELY GOT THE BIG ONE DOWN AND GORDAK LOST A LEG! HE'S ONLY GOT THREE NOW!
WHEN YOU HEAR THE WORDS "BLOOD CULT" IT SOUNDS GLAMOROUS, BUT I'VE BEEN SLEEPING ON A PILE OF CAVE MUSHROOMS FOR THE LAST MONTH.
AT LEAST NOW THAT WE'VE GOT THE LAST ONE WE CAN FINALLY GET THIS WHOLE ETERNAL GLORY THING GOING! MAN, I SWEAR I WAS ONE DAY AWAY FROM GOING BACK TO WORKING IN MY MOM'S RESTAURANT.

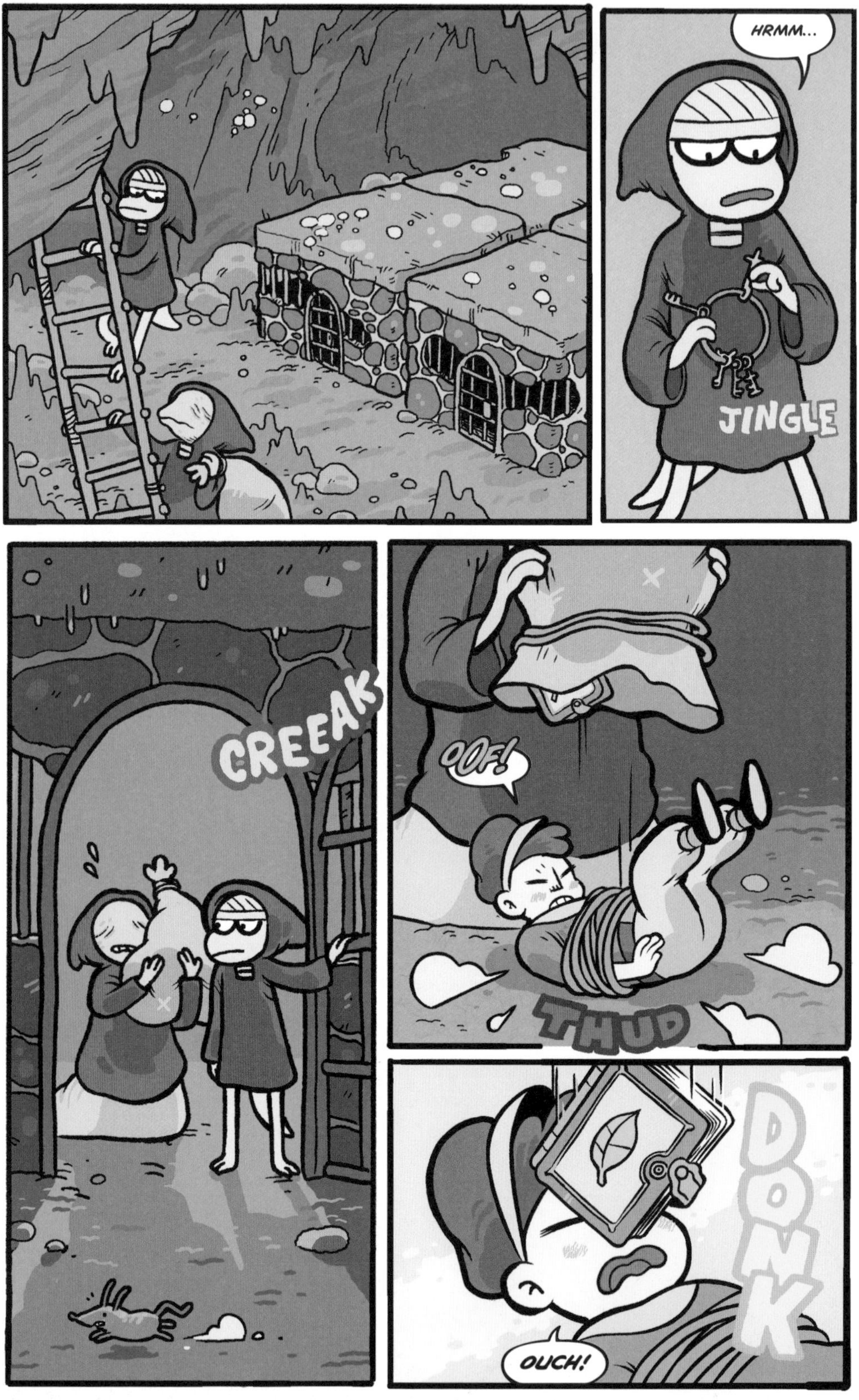
HRMM...
JINGLE
CREEAK
OOF!
THUD
DONK
OUCH!

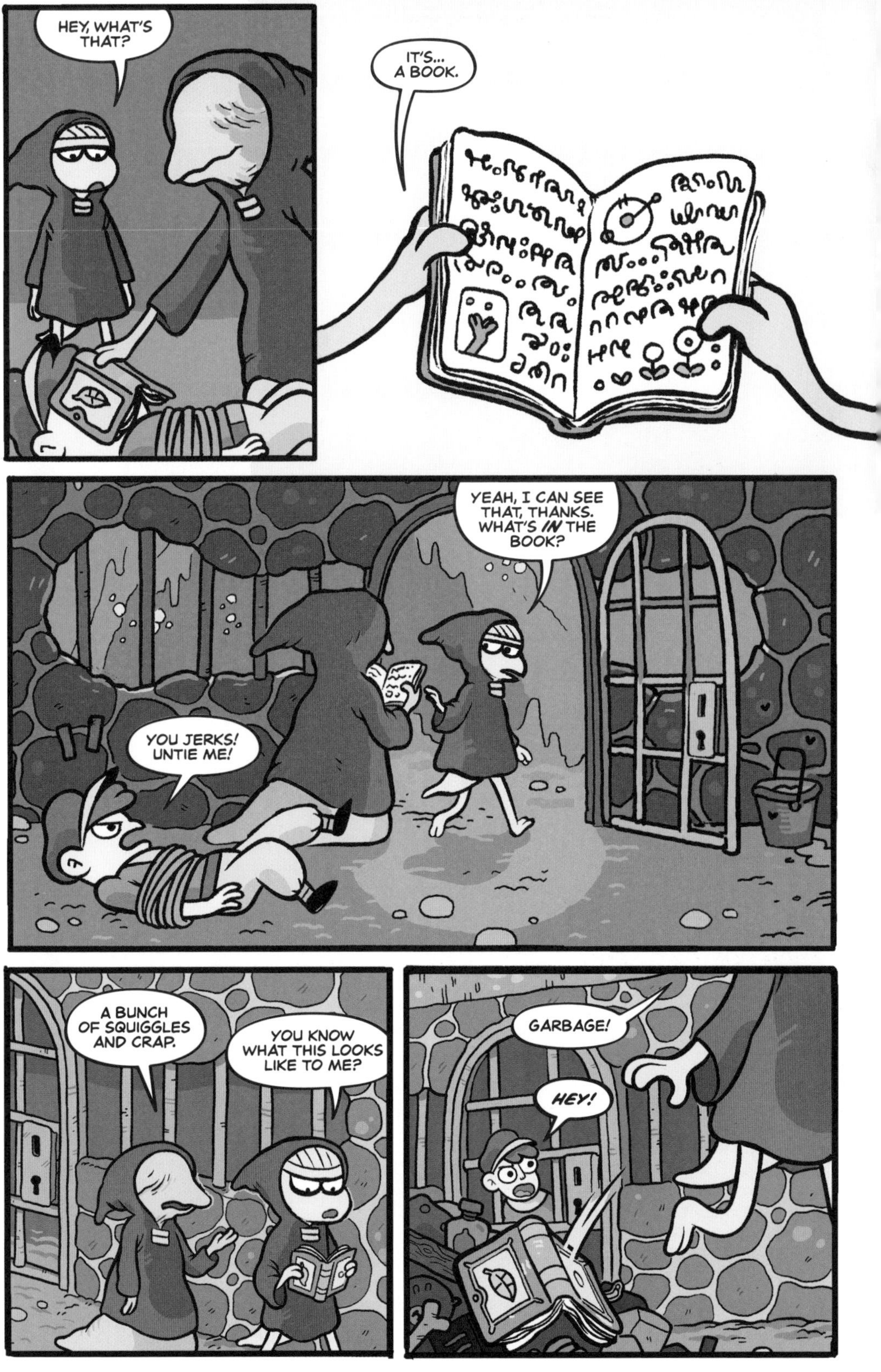
HEY, WHAT'S THAT?
IT'S... A BOOK.
YEAH, I CAN SEE THAT, THANKS. WHAT'S *IN* THE BOOK?
YOU JERKS! UNTIE ME!
A BUNCH OF SQUIGGLES AND CRAP.
YOU KNOW WHAT THIS LOOKS LIKE TO ME?
GARBAGE!
HEY!

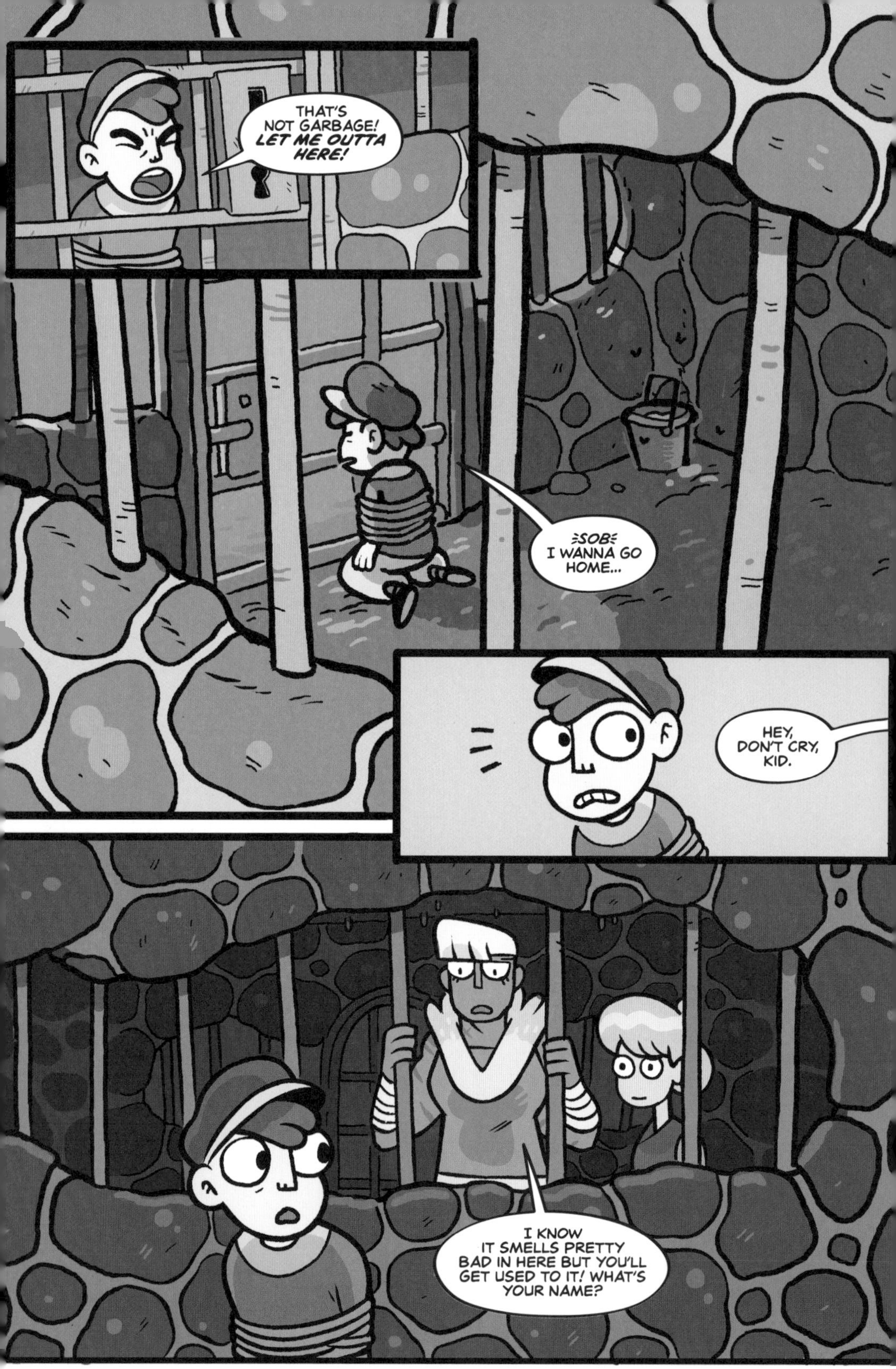
THAT'S NOT GARBAGE! ***LET ME OUTTA HERE!***
SOB I WANNA GO HOME...
HEY, DON'T CRY, KID.
I KNOW IT SMELLS PRETTY BAD IN HERE BUT YOU'LL GET USED TO IT! WHAT'S YOUR NAME?

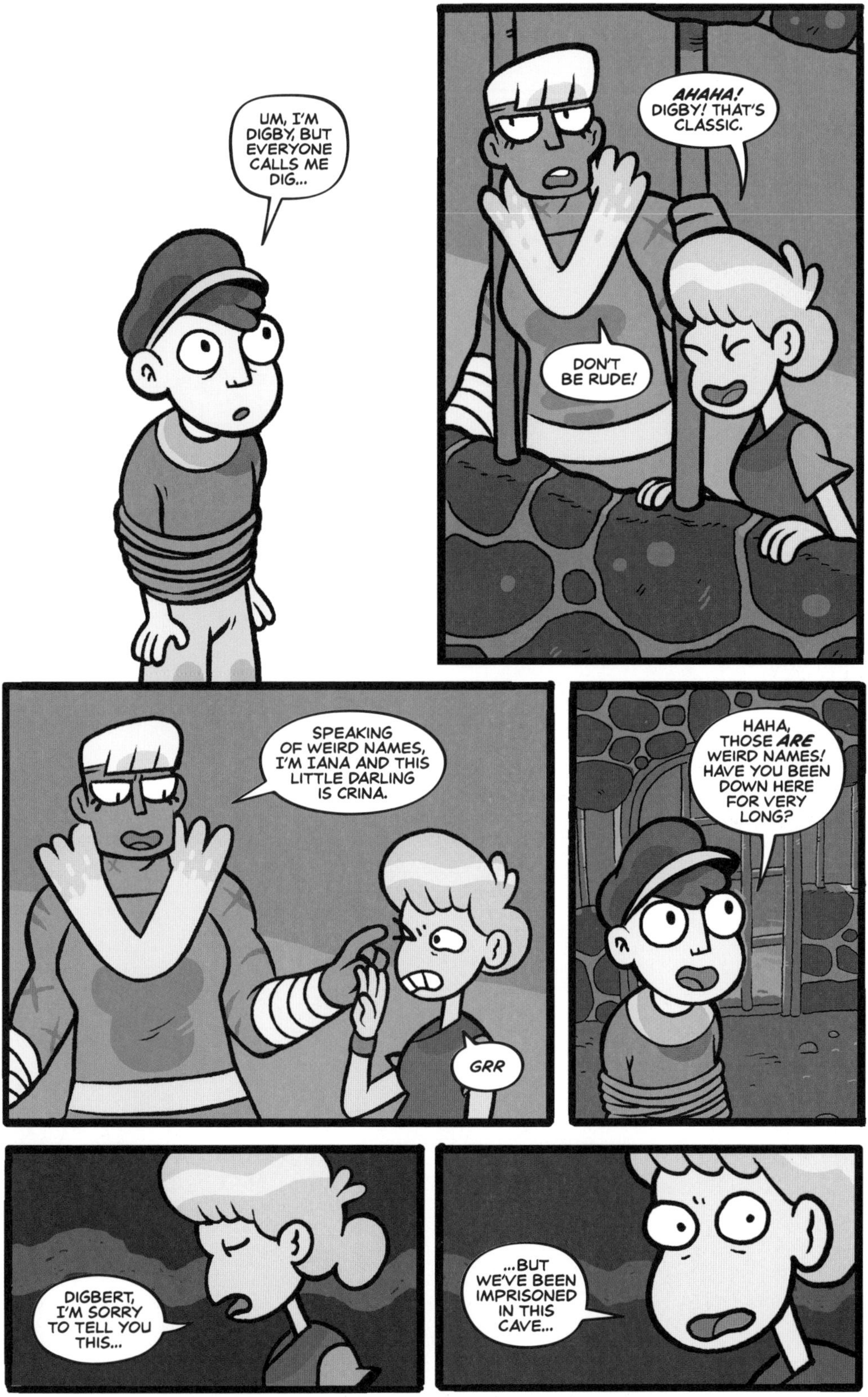
UM, I'M DIGBY, BUT EVERYONE CALLS ME DIG...
AHAHA! DIGBY! THAT'S CLASSIC.
DON'T BE RUDE!
SPEAKING OF WEIRD NAMES, I'M IANA AND THIS LITTLE DARLING IS CRINA.
GRR
HAHA, THOSE ARE WEIRD NAMES! HAVE YOU BEEN DOWN HERE FOR VERY LONG?
DIGBERT, I'M SORRY TO TELL YOU THIS...
...BUT WE'VE BEEN IMPRISONED IN THIS CAVE...

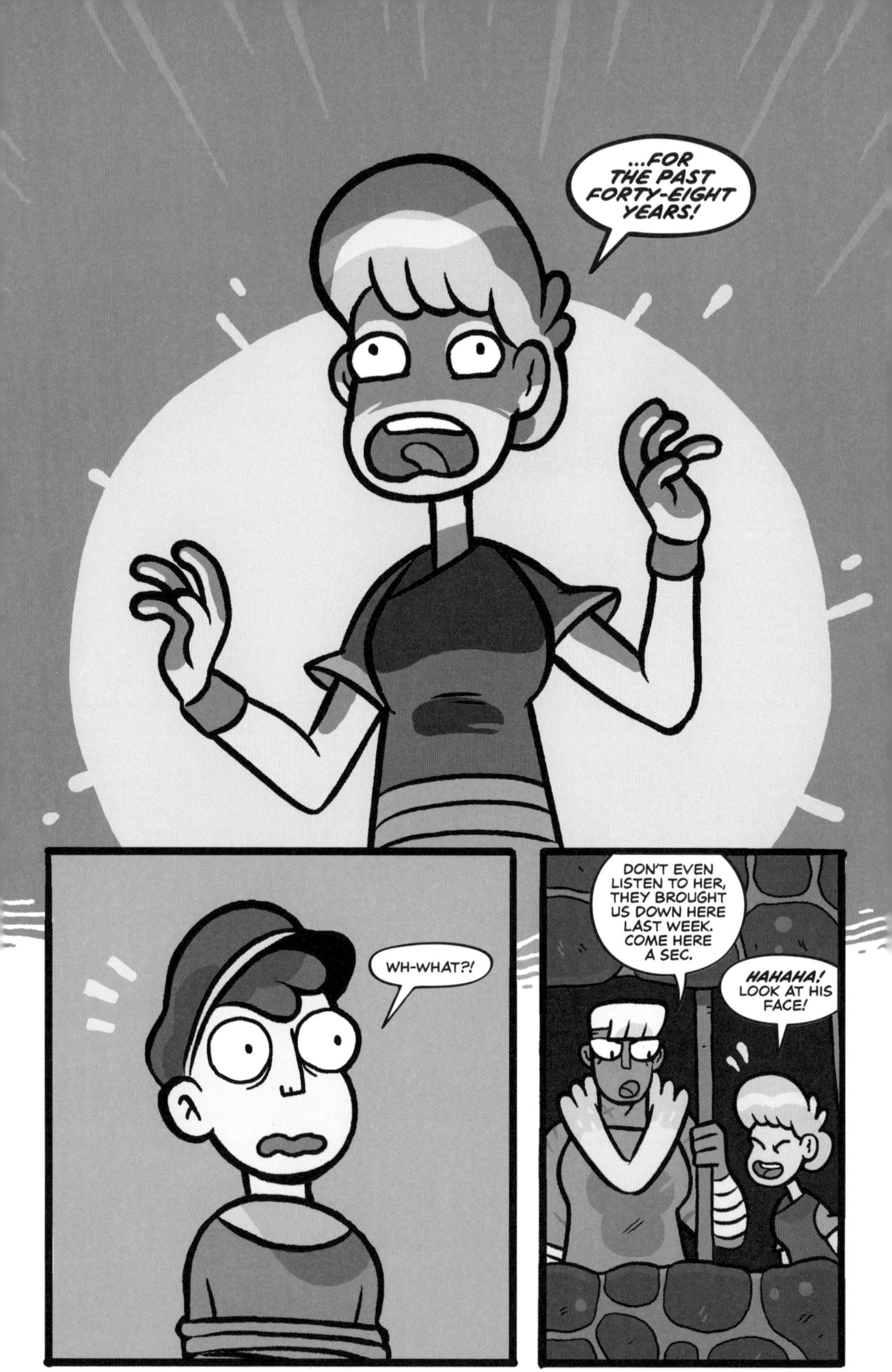
...FOR THE PAST FORTY-EIGHT YEARS!
WH-WHAT?!
DON'T EVEN LISTEN TO HER, THEY BROUGHT US DOWN HERE LAST WEEK. COME HERE A SEC.
HAHAHA! LOOK AT HIS FACE!

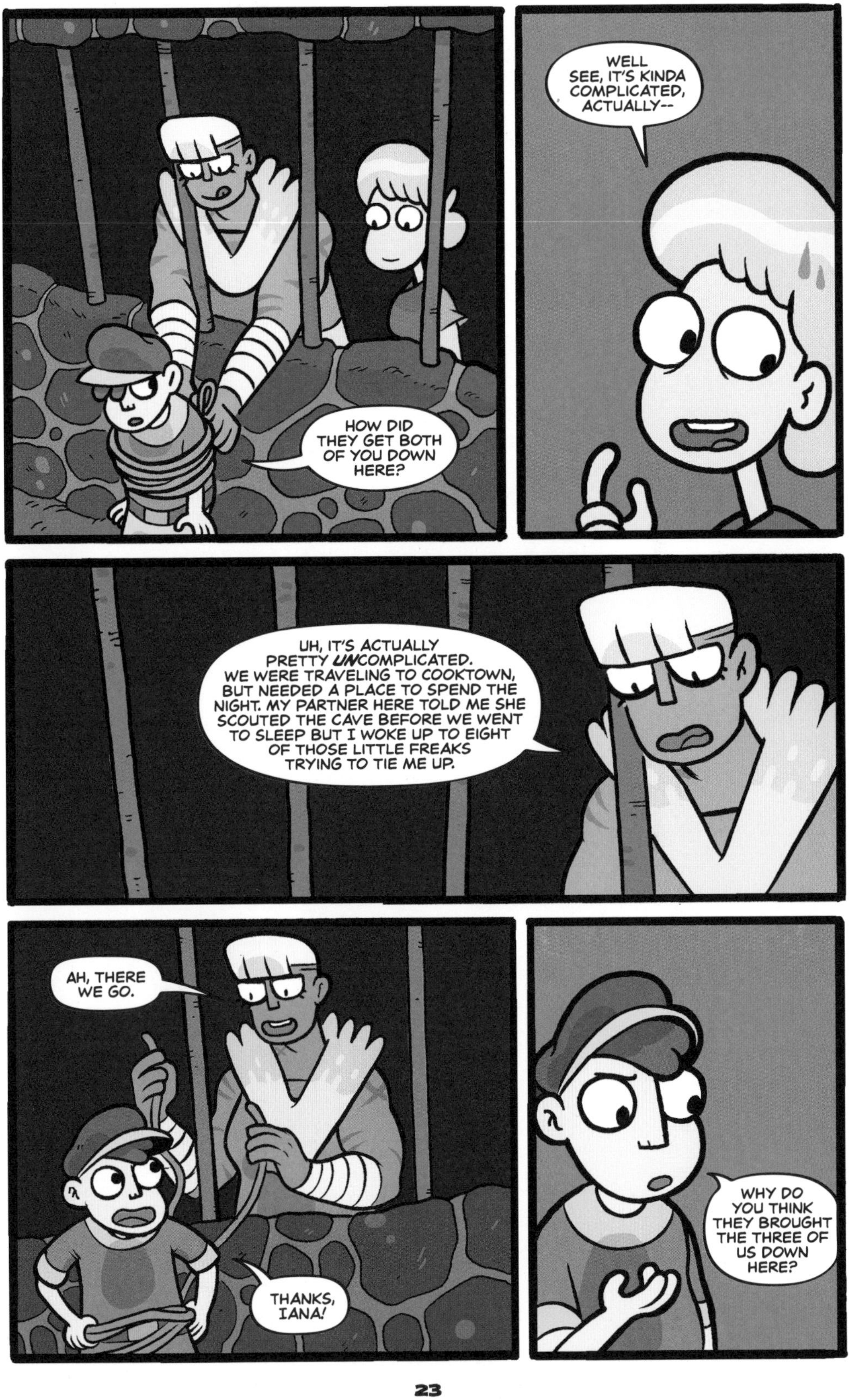
HOW DID THEY GET BOTH OF YOU DOWN HERE?
WELL SEE, IT'S KINDA COMPLICATED, ACTUALLY--
UH, IT'S ACTUALLY PRETTY *UN*COMPLICATED. WE WERE TRAVELING TO COOKTOWN, BUT NEEDED A PLACE TO SPEND THE NIGHT. MY PARTNER HERE TOLD ME SHE SCOUTED THE CAVE BEFORE WE WENT TO SLEEP BUT I WOKE UP TO EIGHT OF THOSE LITTLE FREAKS TRYING TO TIE ME UP.
AH, THERE WE GO.
THANKS, IANA!
WHY DO YOU THINK THEY BROUGHT THE THREE OF US DOWN HERE?

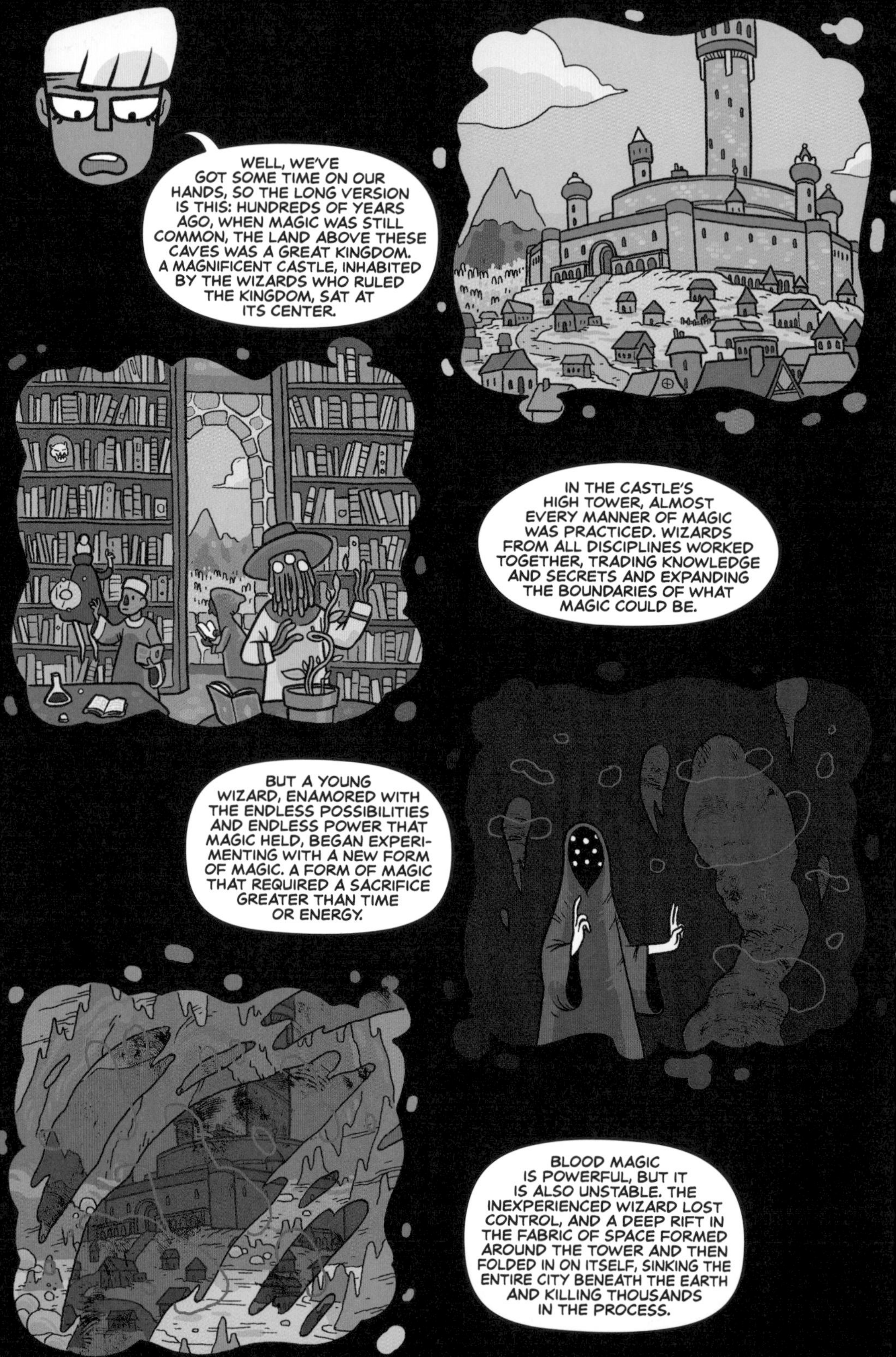
WELL, WE'VE GOT SOME TIME ON OUR HANDS, SO THE LONG VERSION IS THIS: HUNDREDS OF YEARS AGO, WHEN MAGIC WAS STILL COMMON, THE LAND ABOVE THESE CAVES WAS A GREAT KINGDOM. A MAGNIFICENT CASTLE, INHABITED BY THE WIZARDS WHO RULED THE KINGDOM, SAT AT ITS CENTER.
IN THE CASTLE'S HIGH TOWER, ALMOST EVERY MANNER OF MAGIC WAS PRACTICED. WIZARDS FROM ALL DISCIPLINES WORKED TOGETHER, TRADING KNOWLEDGE AND SECRETS AND EXPANDING THE BOUNDARIES OF WHAT MAGIC COULD BE.
BUT A YOUNG WIZARD, ENAMORED WITH THE ENDLESS POSSIBILITIES AND ENDLESS POWER THAT MAGIC HELD, BEGAN EXPERIMENTING WITH A NEW FORM OF MAGIC. A FORM OF MAGIC THAT REQUIRED A SACRIFICE GREATER THAN TIME OR ENERGY.
BLOOD MAGIC IS POWERFUL, BUT IT IS ALSO UNSTABLE. THE INEXPERIENCED WIZARD LOST CONTROL, AND A DEEP RIFT IN THE FABRIC OF SPACE FORMED AROUND THE TOWER AND THEN FOLDED IN ON ITSELF, SINKING THE ENTIRE CITY BENEATH THE EARTH AND KILLING THOUSANDS IN THE PROCESS.

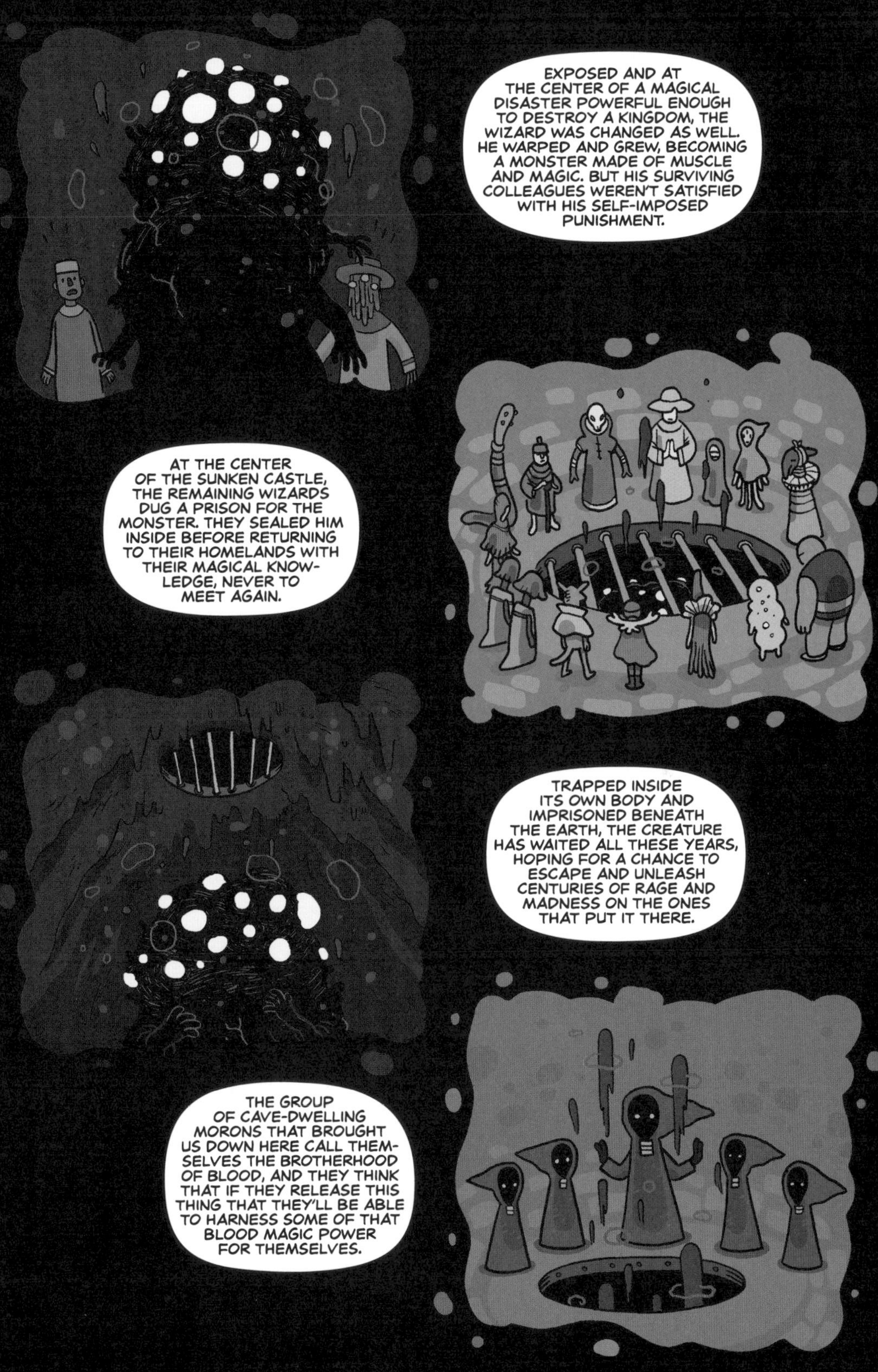
EXPOSED AND AT THE CENTER OF A MAGICAL DISASTER POWERFUL ENOUGH TO DESTROY A KINGDOM, THE WIZARD WAS CHANGED AS WELL. HE WARPED AND GREW, BECOMING A MONSTER MADE OF MUSCLE AND MAGIC. BUT HIS SURVIVING COLLEAGUES WEREN'T SATISFIED WITH HIS SELF-IMPOSED PUNISHMENT.
AT THE CENTER OF THE SUNKEN CASTLE, THE REMAINING WIZARDS DUG A PRISON FOR THE MONSTER. THEY SEALED HIM INSIDE BEFORE RETURNING TO THEIR HOMELANDS WITH THEIR MAGICAL KNOW-LEDGE, NEVER TO MEET AGAIN.
TRAPPED INSIDE ITS OWN BODY AND IMPRISONED BENEATH THE EARTH, THE CREATURE HAS WAITED ALL THESE YEARS, HOPING FOR A CHANCE TO ESCAPE AND UNLEASH CENTURIES OF RAGE AND MADNESS ON THE ONES THAT PUT IT THERE.
THE GROUP OF CAVE-DWELLING MORONS THAT BROUGHT US DOWN HERE CALL THEM-SELVES THE BROTHERHOOD OF BLOOD, AND THEY THINK THAT IF THEY RELEASE THIS THING THAT THEY'LL BE ABLE TO HARNESS SOME OF THAT BLOOD MAGIC POWER FOR THEMSELVES.

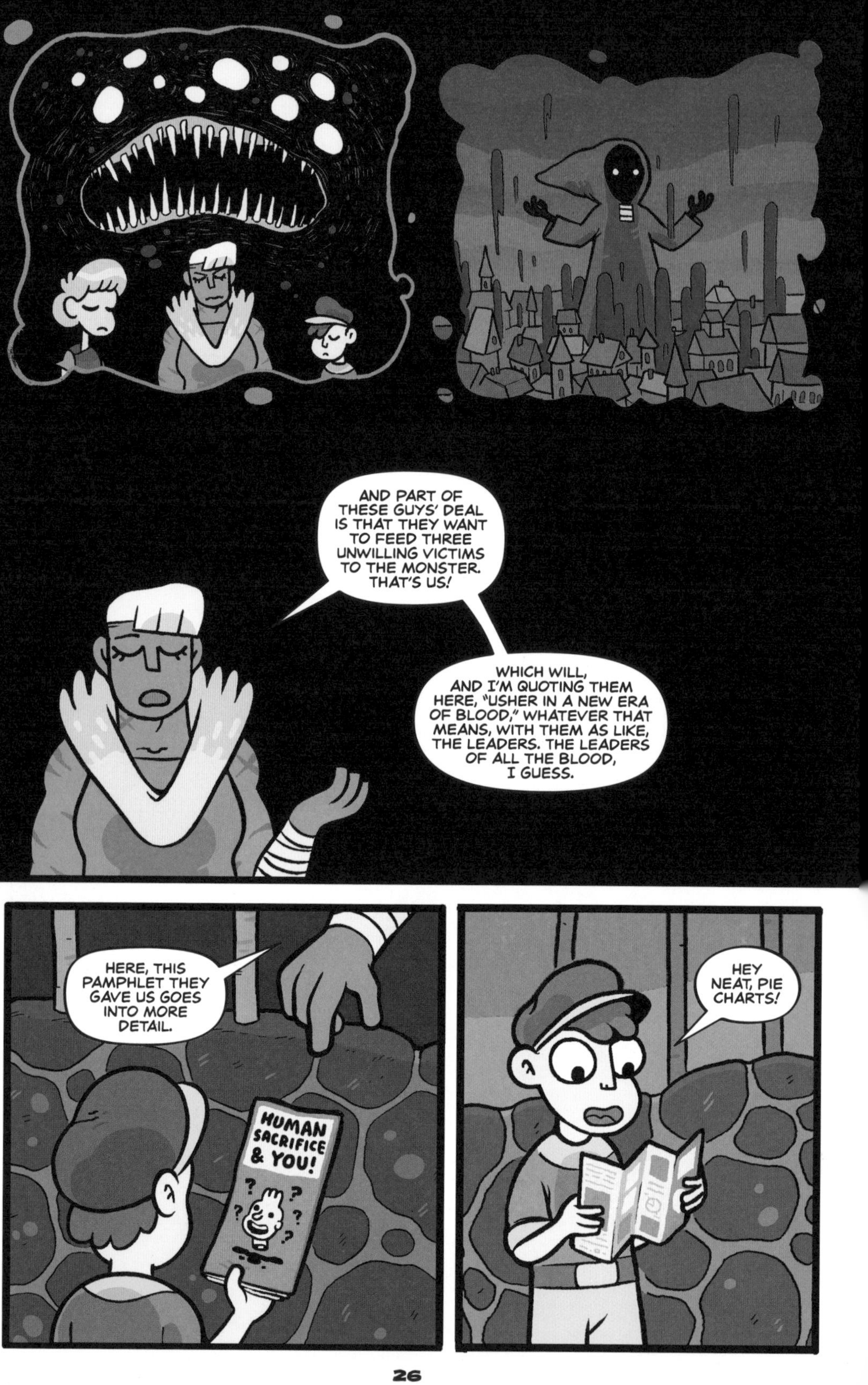
AND PART OF THESE GUYS' DEAL IS THAT THEY WANT TO FEED THREE UNWILLING VICTIMS TO THE MONSTER. THAT'S US!
WHICH WILL, AND I'M QUOTING THEM HERE, "USHER IN A NEW ERA OF BLOOD," WHATEVER THAT MEANS, WITH THEM AS LIKE, THE LEADERS. THE LEADERS OF ALL THE BLOOD, I GUESS.
HERE, THIS PAMPHLET THEY GAVE US GOES INTO MORE DETAIL.
HUMAN SACRIFICE & YOU!
HEY NEAT, PIE CHARTS!

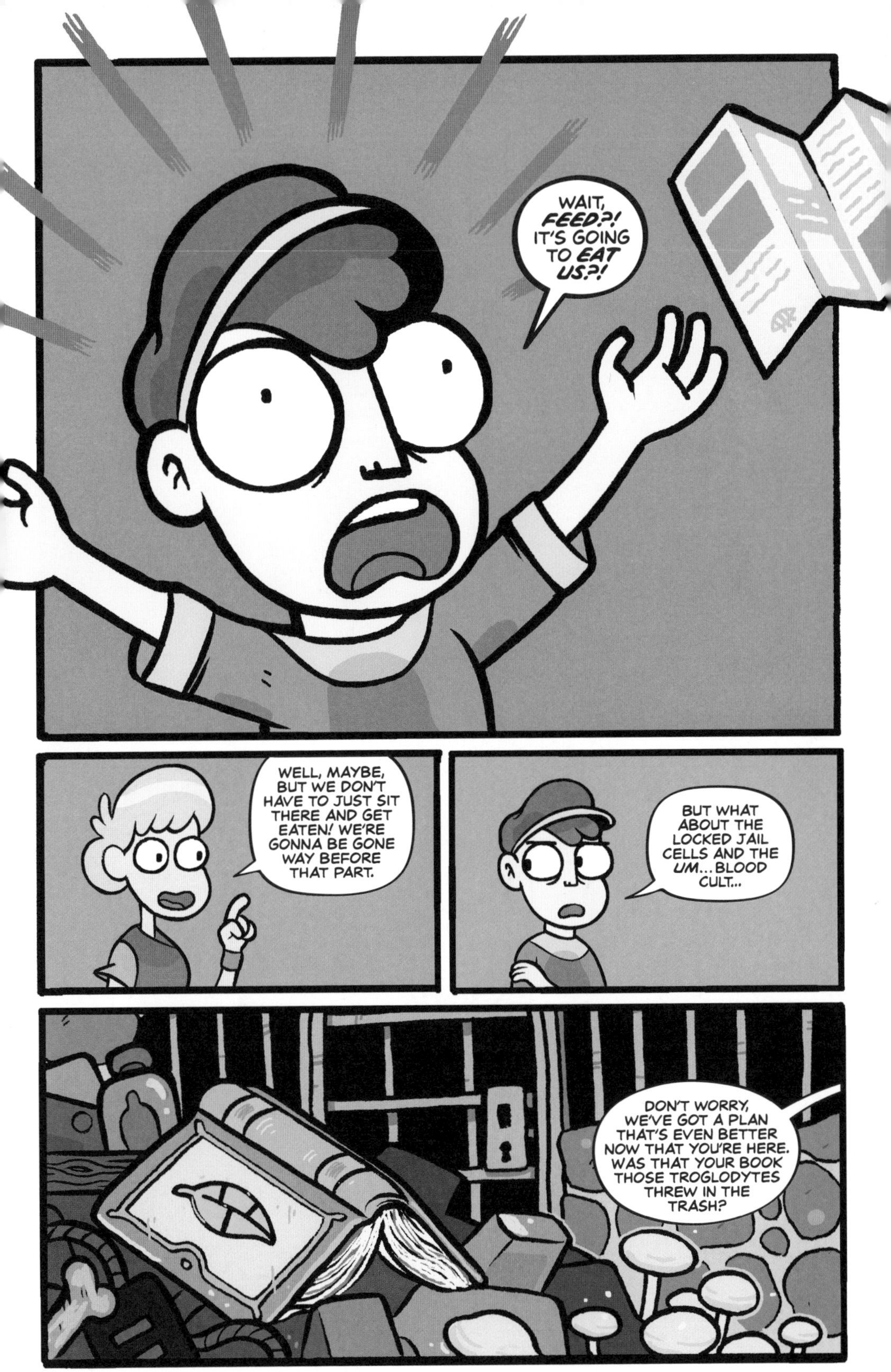
WAIT, FEED?! IT'S GOING TO EAT US?!
WELL, MAYBE, BUT WE DON'T HAVE TO JUST SIT THERE AND GET EATEN! WE'RE GONNA BE GONE WAY BEFORE THAT PART.
BUT WHAT ABOUT THE LOCKED JAIL CELLS AND THE UM... BLOOD CULT...
DON'T WORRY, WE'VE GOT A PLAN THAT'S EVEN BETTER NOW THAT YOU'RE HERE. WAS THAT YOUR BOOK THOSE TROGLODYTES THREW IN THE TRASH?

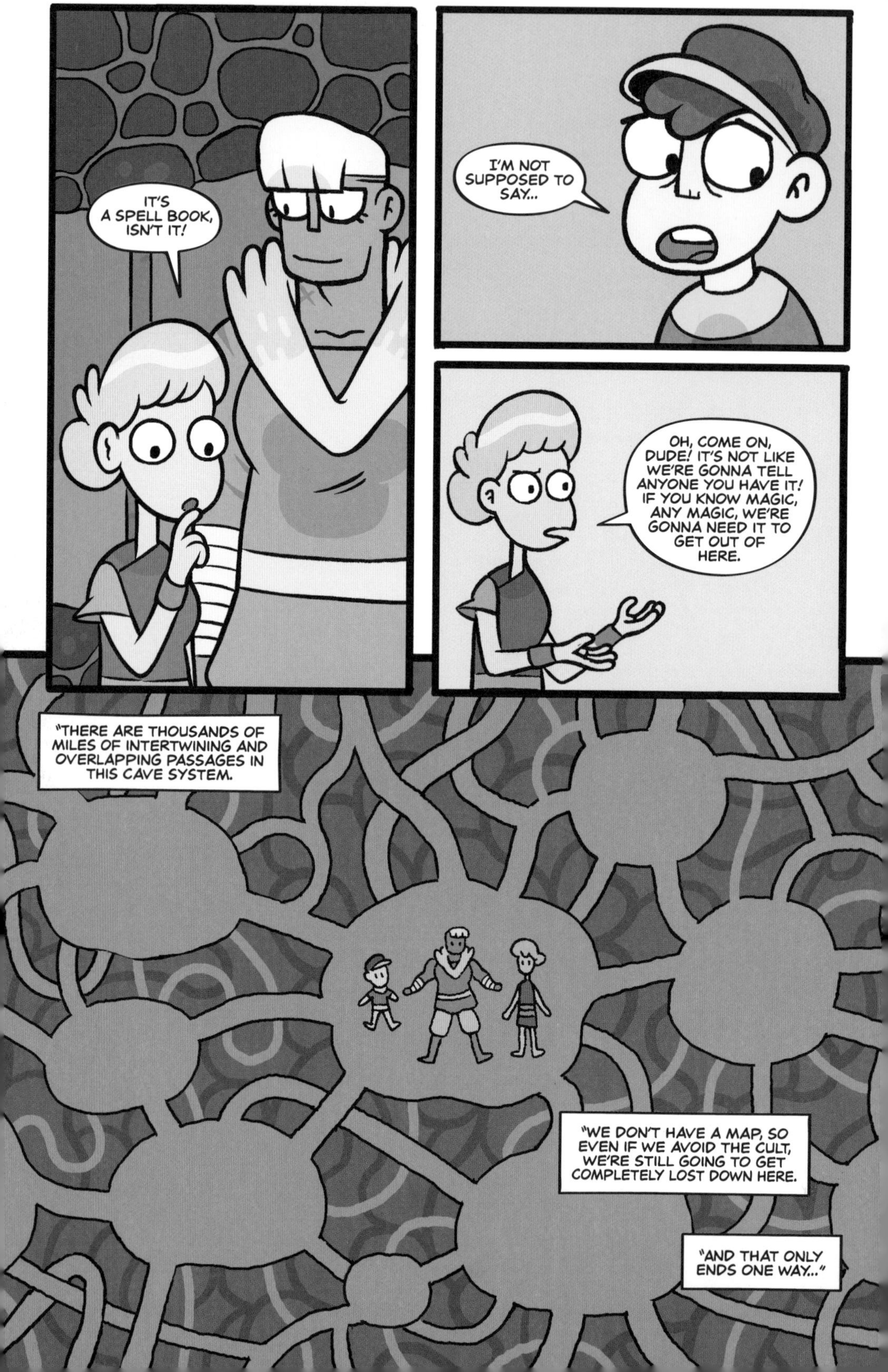
IT'S A SPELL BOOK, ISN'T IT!
I'M NOT SUPPOSED TO SAY...
OH, COME ON, DUDE! IT'S NOT LIKE WE'RE GONNA TELL ANYONE YOU HAVE IT! IF YOU KNOW MAGIC, ANY MAGIC, WE'RE GONNA NEED IT TO GET OUT OF HERE.
"THERE ARE THOUSANDS OF MILES OF INTERTWINING AND OVERLAPPING PASSAGES IN THIS CAVE SYSTEM.
"WE DON'T HAVE A MAP, SO EVEN IF WE AVOID THE CULT, WE'RE STILL GOING TO GET COMPLETELY LOST DOWN HERE.
"AND THAT ONLY ENDS ONE WAY..."

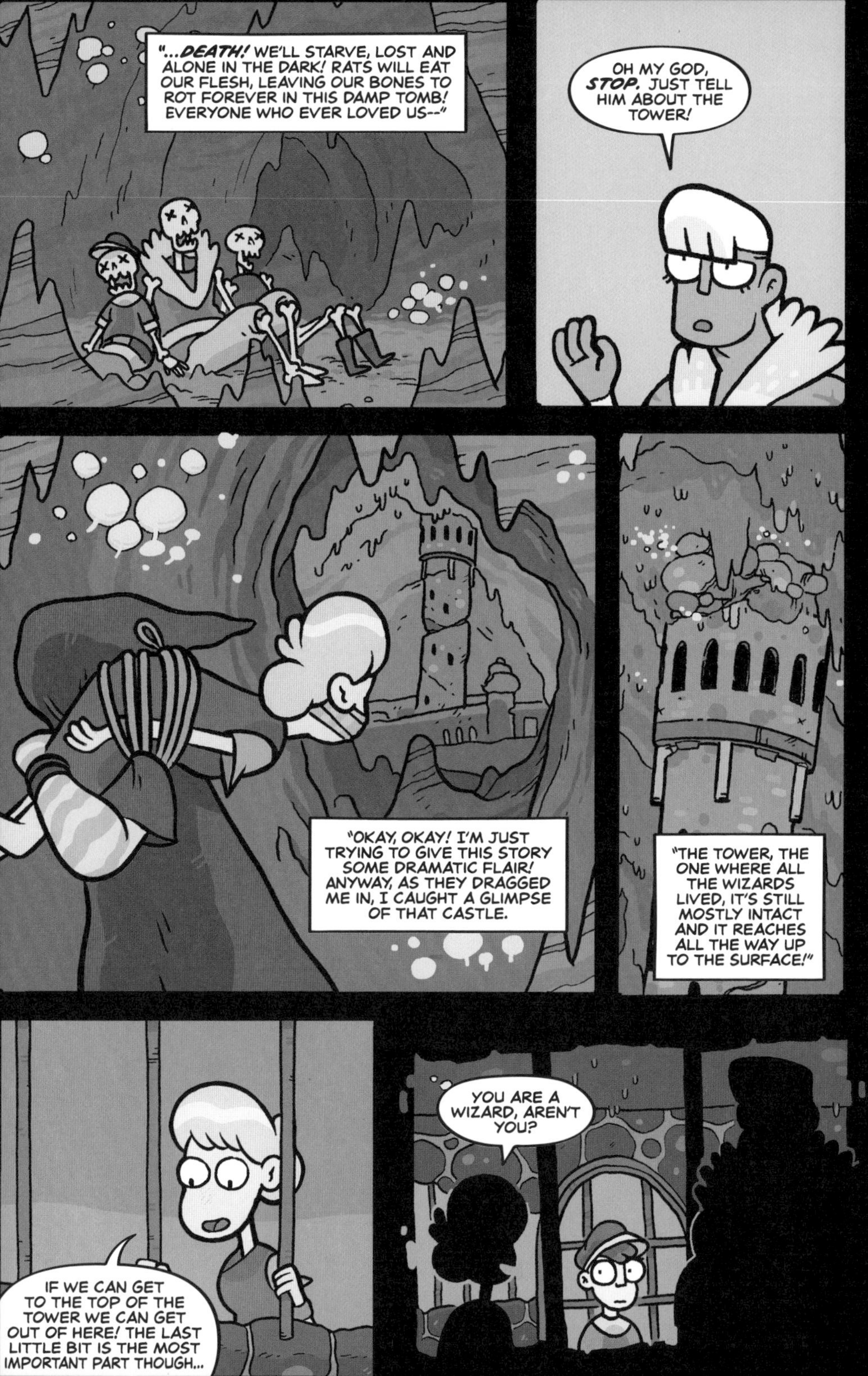
"...DEATH! WE'LL STARVE, LOST AND ALONE IN THE DARK! RATS WILL EAT OUR FLESH, LEAVING OUR BONES TO ROT FOREVER IN THIS DAMP TOMB! EVERYONE WHO EVER LOVED US--"
OH MY GOD, STOP. JUST TELL HIM ABOUT THE TOWER!
"OKAY, OKAY! I'M JUST TRYING TO GIVE THIS STORY SOME DRAMATIC FLAIR! ANYWAY, AS THEY DRAGGED ME IN, I CAUGHT A GLIMPSE OF THAT CASTLE.
"THE TOWER, THE ONE WHERE ALL THE WIZARDS LIVED, IT'S STILL MOSTLY INTACT AND IT REACHES ALL THE WAY UP TO THE SURFACE!"
IF WE CAN GET TO THE TOP OF THE TOWER WE CAN GET OUT OF HERE! THE LAST LITTLE BIT IS THE MOST IMPORTANT PART THOUGH...
YOU ARE A WIZARD, AREN'T YOU?

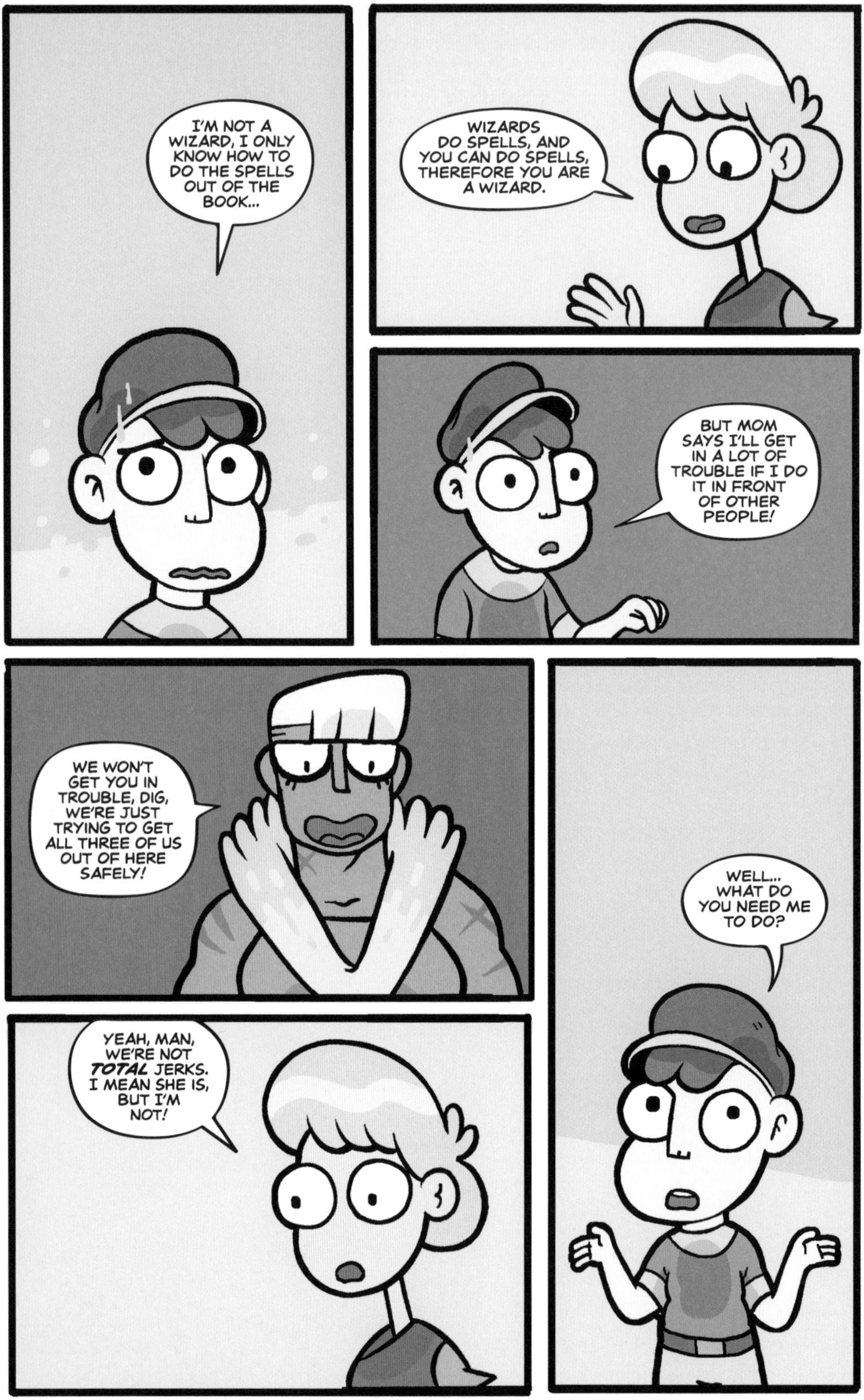
I'M NOT A WIZARD, I ONLY KNOW HOW TO DO THE SPELLS OUT OF THE BOOK...
WIZARDS DO SPELLS, AND YOU CAN DO SPELLS, THEREFORE YOU ARE A WIZARD.
BUT MOM SAYS I'LL GET IN A LOT OF TROUBLE IF I DO IT IN FRONT OF OTHER PEOPLE!
WE WON'T GET YOU IN TROUBLE, DIG, WE'RE JUST TRYING TO GET ALL THREE OF US OUT OF HERE SAFELY!
YEAH, MAN, WE'RE NOT *TOTAL* JERKS. I MEAN SHE IS, BUT I'M NOT!
WELL... WHAT DO YOU NEED ME TO DO?

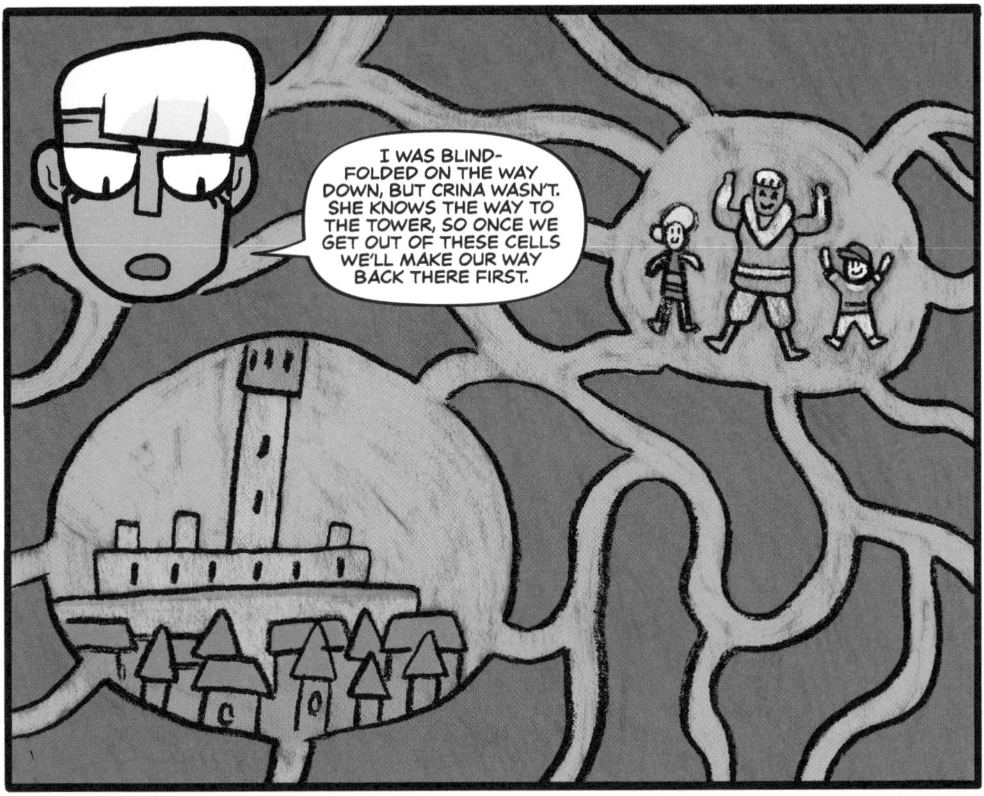
I WAS BLIND-FOLDED ON THE WAY DOWN, BUT CRINA WASN'T. SHE KNOWS THE WAY TO THE TOWER, SO ONCE WE GET OUT OF THESE CELLS WE'LL MAKE OUR WAY BACK THERE FIRST.
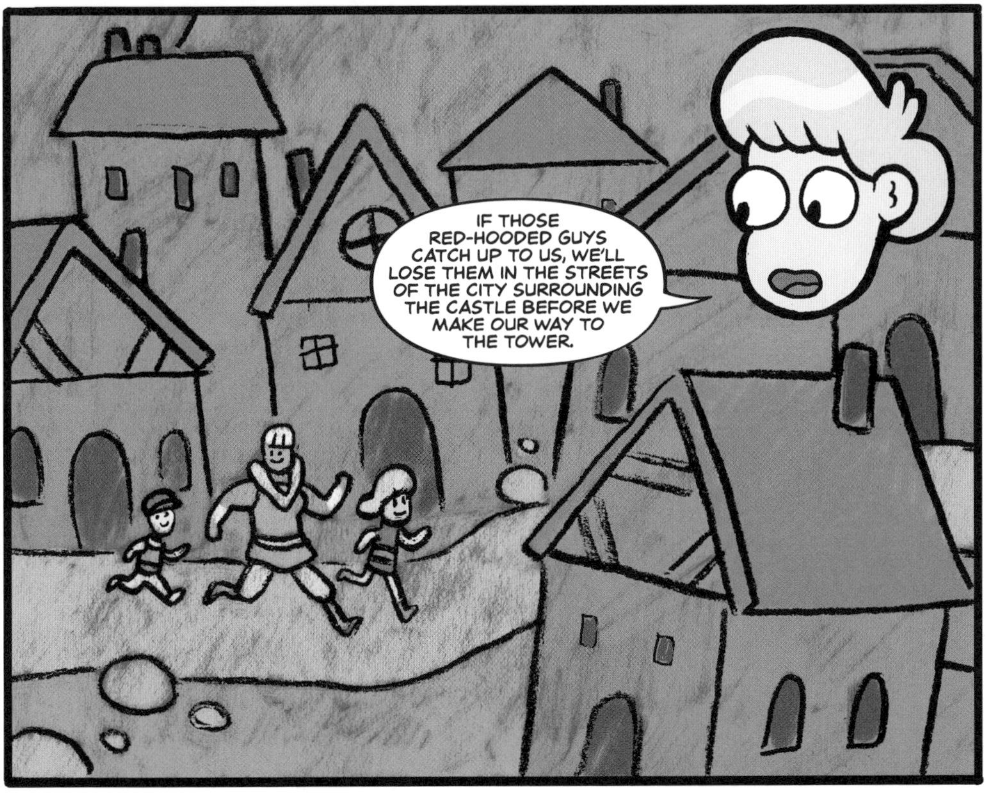
IF THOSE RED-HOODED GUYS CATCH UP TO US, WE'LL LOSE THEM IN THE STREETS OF THE CITY SURROUNDING THE CASTLE BEFORE WE MAKE OUR WAY TO THE TOWER.

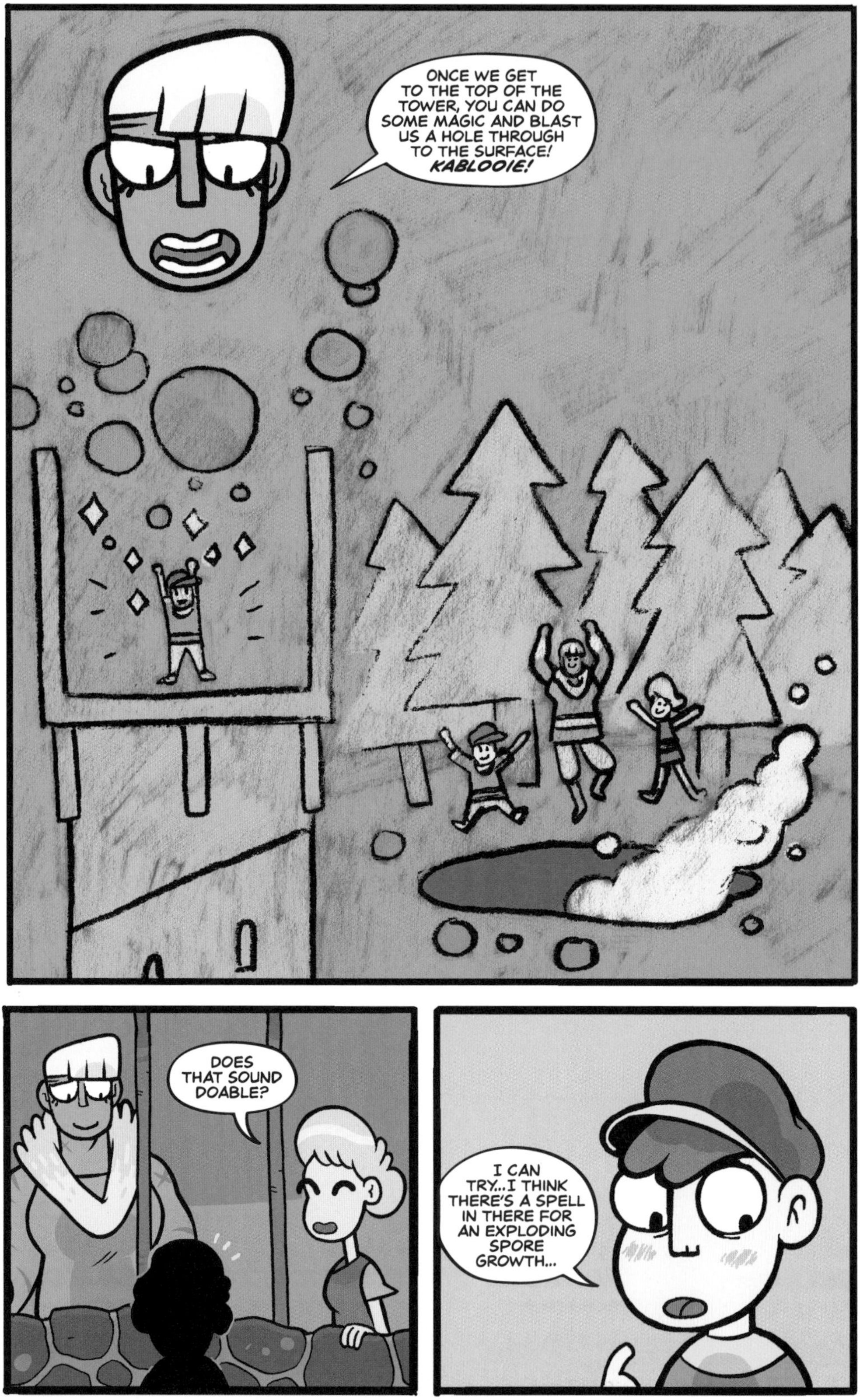
ONCE WE GET TO THE TOP OF THE TOWER, YOU CAN DO SOME MAGIC AND BLAST US A HOLE THROUGH TO THE SURFACE! KABLOOIE!
DOES THAT SOUND DOABLE?
I CAN TRY...I THINK THERE'S A SPELL IN THERE FOR AN EXPLODING SPORE GROWTH...

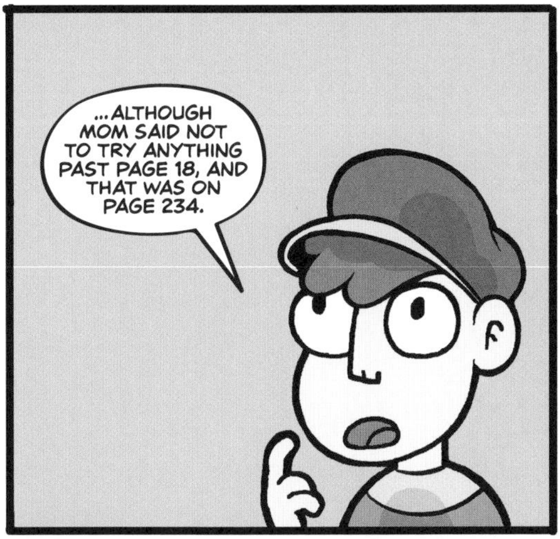
...ALTHOUGH MOM SAID NOT TO TRY ANYTHING PAST PAGE 18, AND THAT WAS ON PAGE 234.
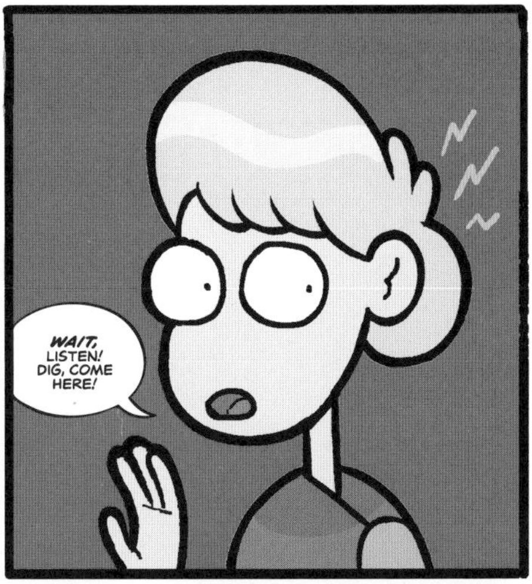
WAIT, LISTEN! DIG, COME HERE!
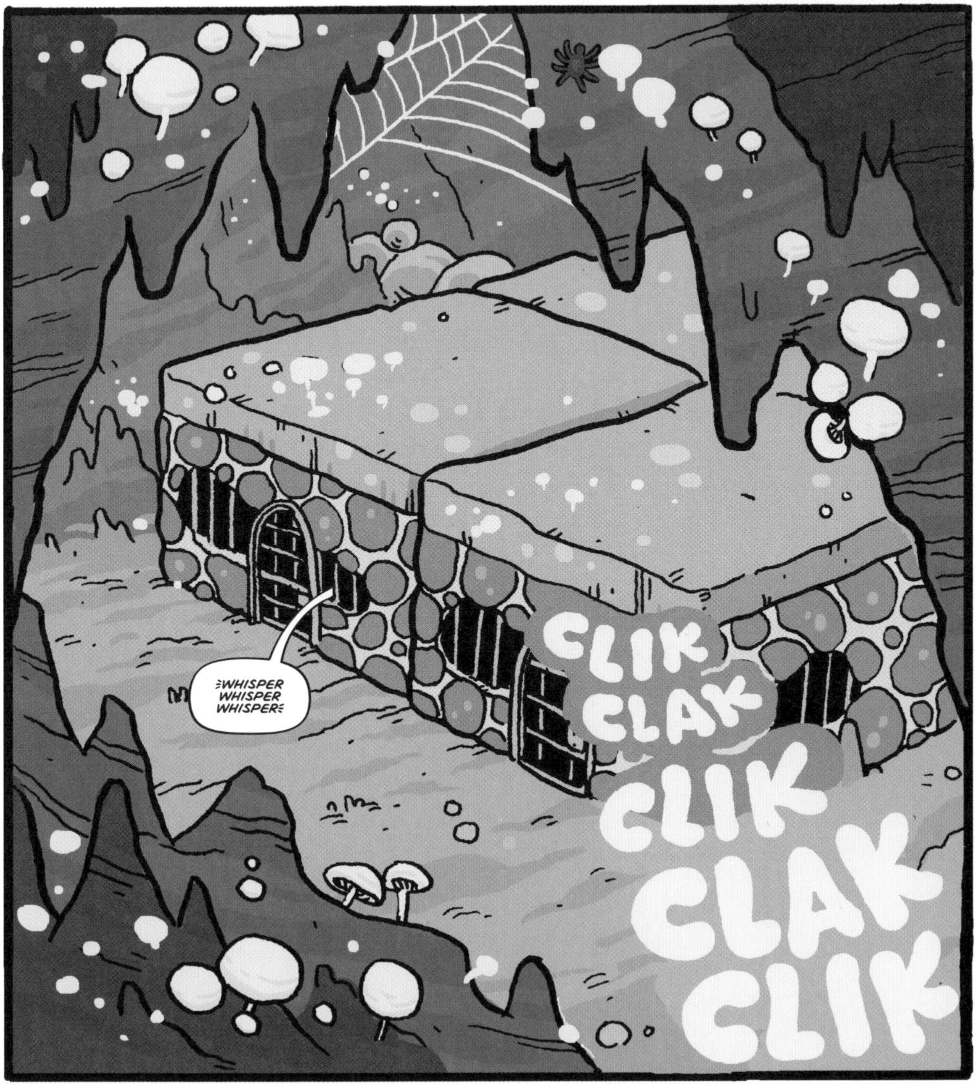
WHISPER WHISPER WHISPER
CLIK CLAK
CLIK CLAK CLIK

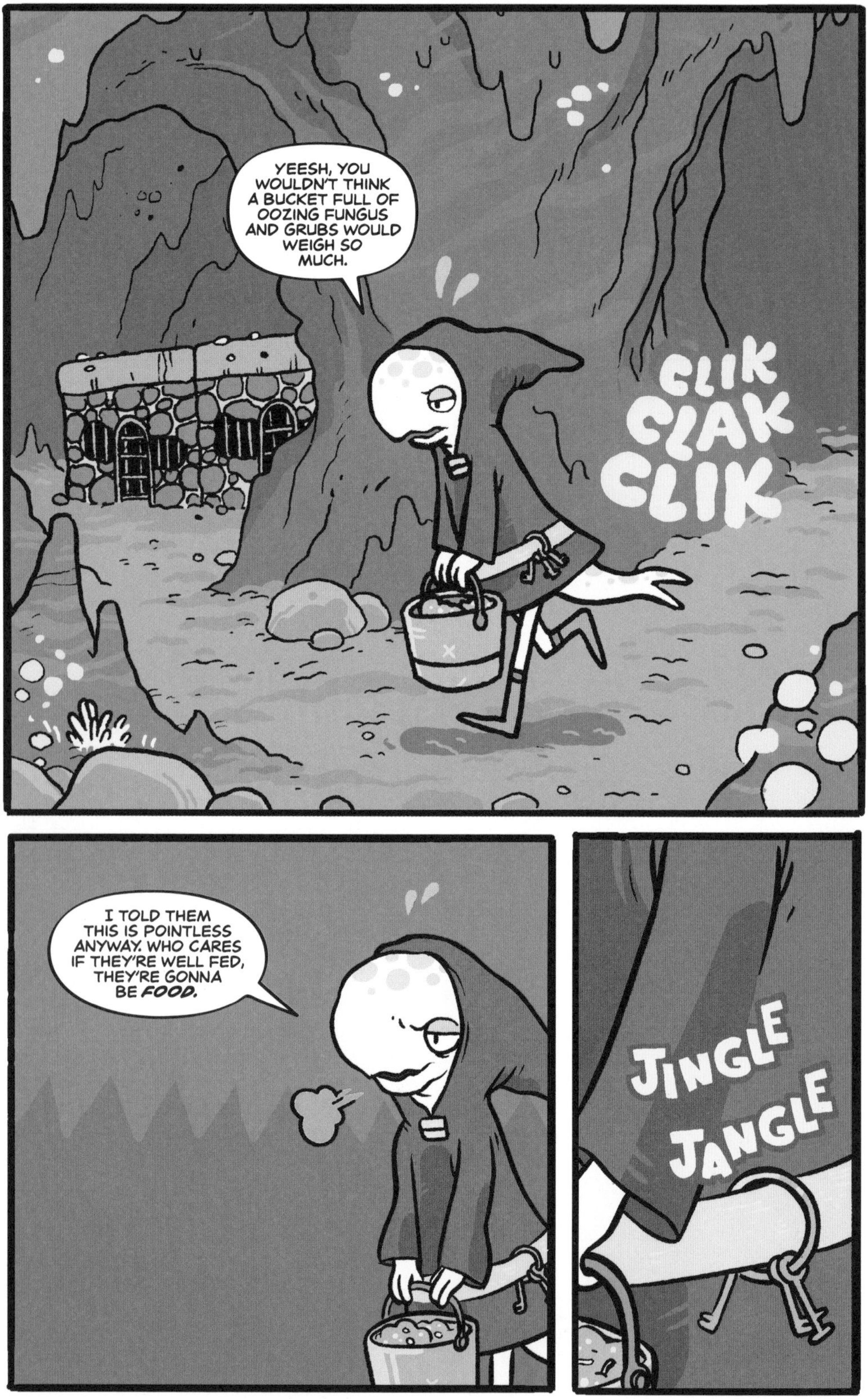
YEESH, YOU WOULDN'T THINK A BUCKET FULL OF OOZING FUNGUS AND GRUBS WOULD WEIGH SO MUCH.
CLIK CLAK CLIK
I TOLD THEM THIS IS POINTLESS ANYWAY. WHO CARES IF THEY'RE WELL FED, THEY'RE GONNA BE ***FOOD.***
JINGLE JANGLE

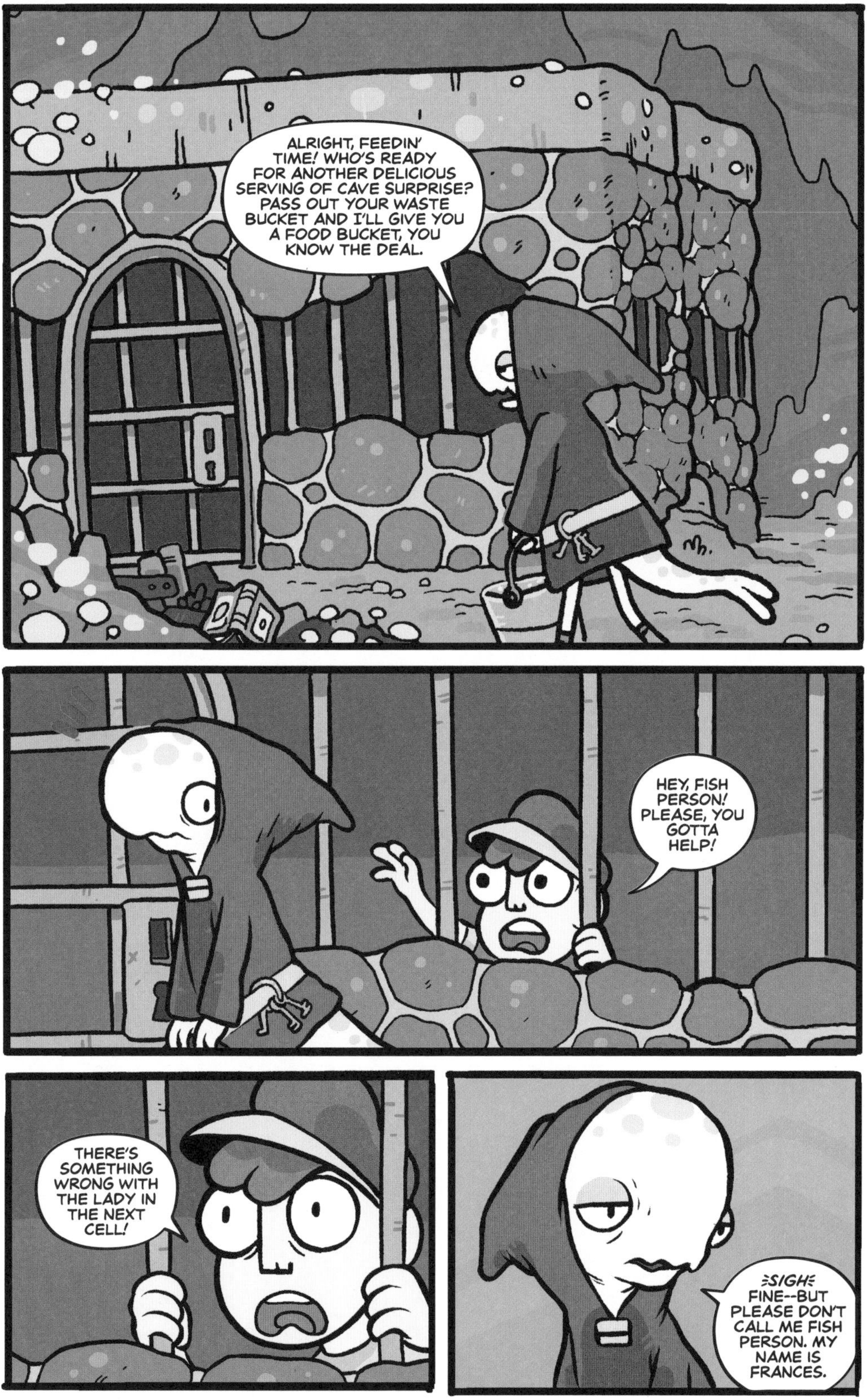
ALRIGHT, FEEDIN' TIME! WHO'S READY FOR ANOTHER DELICIOUS SERVING OF CAVE SURPRISE? PASS OUT YOUR WASTE BUCKET AND I'LL GIVE YOU A FOOD BUCKET, YOU KNOW THE DEAL.
HEY, FISH PERSON! PLEASE, YOU GOTTA HELP!
THERE'S SOMETHING WRONG WITH THE LADY IN THE NEXT CELL!
SIGH
FINE--BUT PLEASE DON'T CALL ME FISH PERSON. MY NAME IS FRANCES.

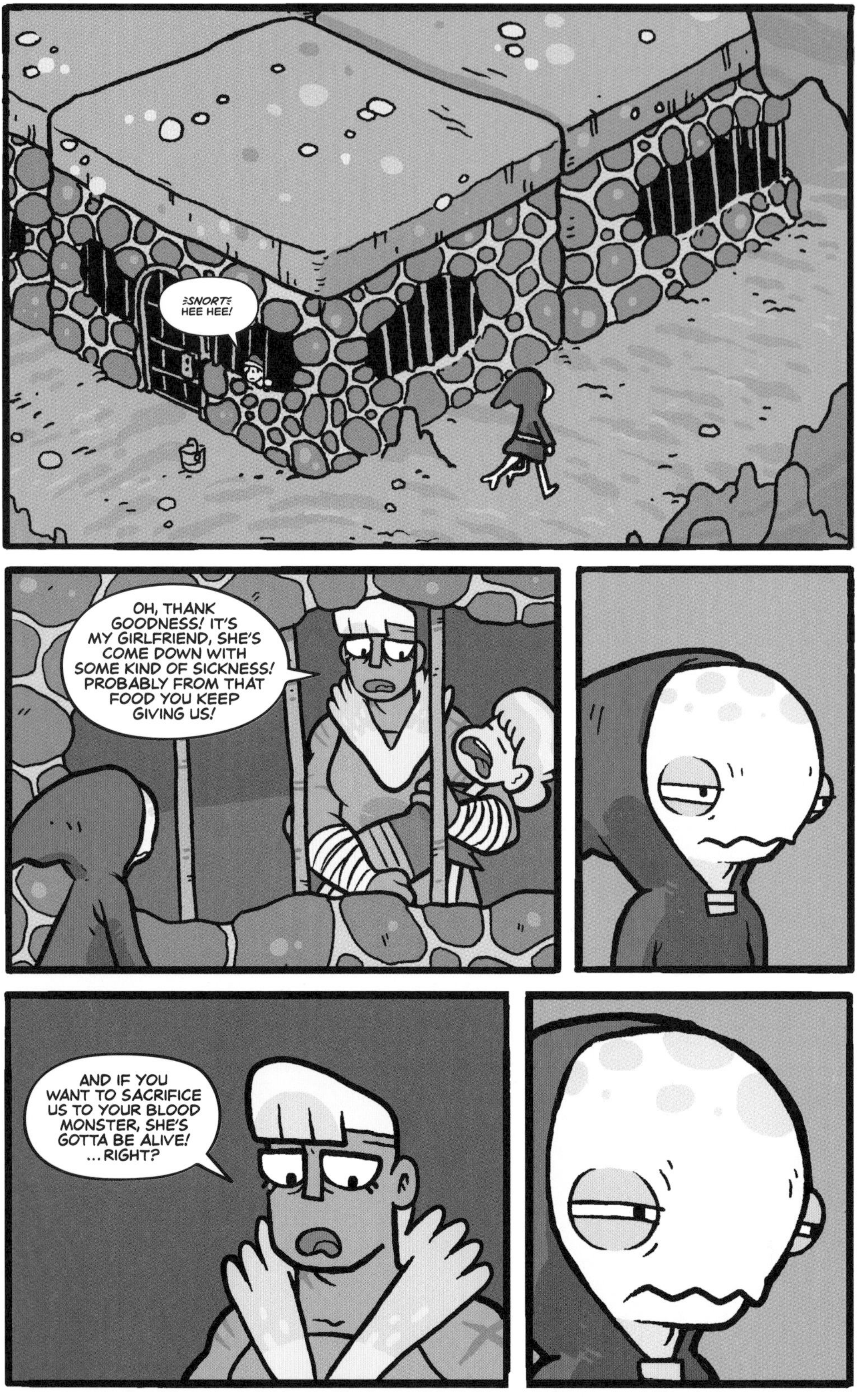
≡SNORT≡ HEE HEE!
OH, THANK GOODNESS! IT'S MY GIRLFRIEND, SHE'S COME DOWN WITH SOME KIND OF SICKNESS! PROBABLY FROM THAT FOOD YOU KEEP GIVING US!
AND IF YOU WANT TO SACRIFICE US TO YOUR BLOOD MONSTER, SHE'S GOTTA BE ALIVE! ...RIGHT?

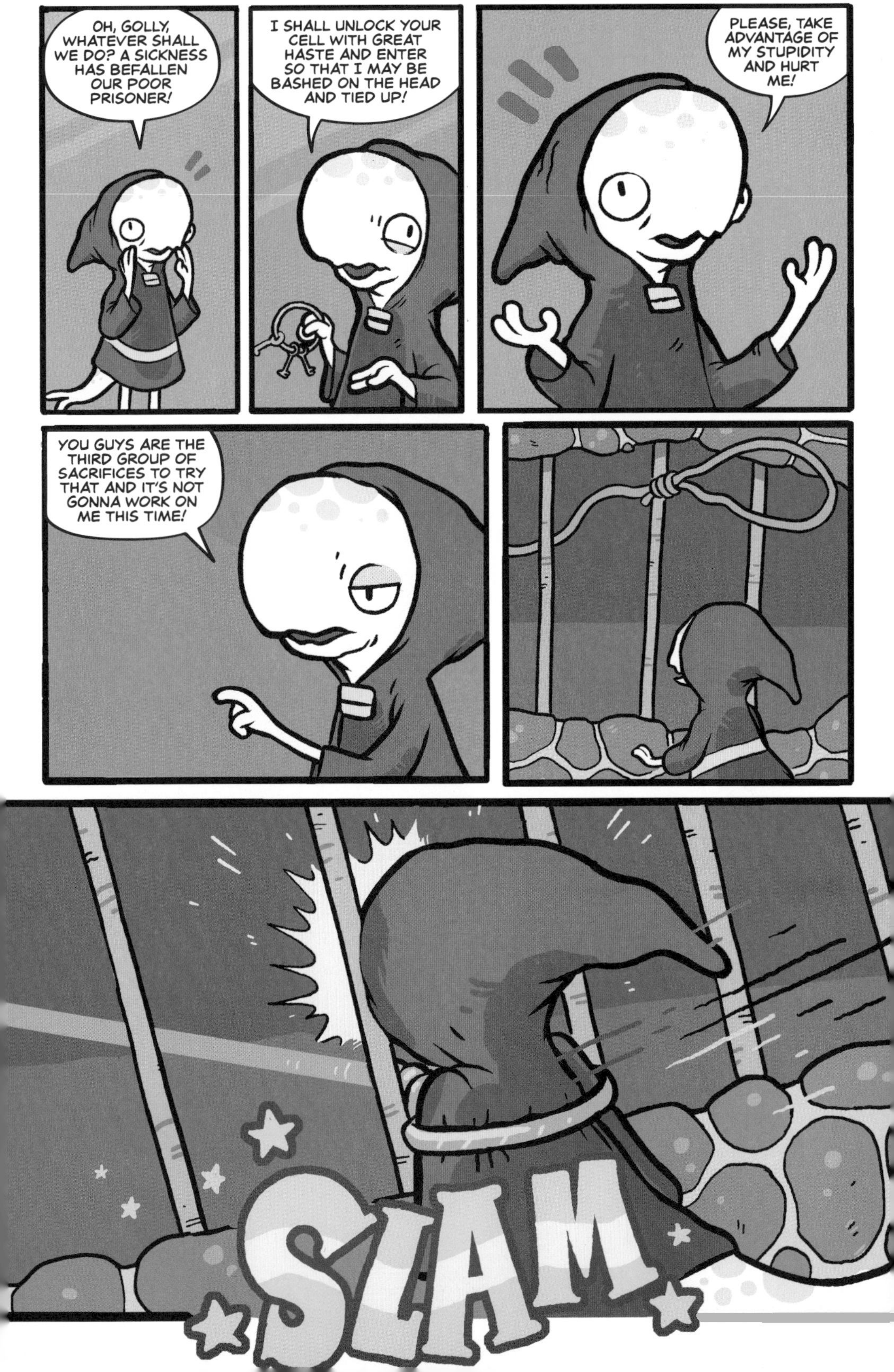
OH, GOLLY, WHATEVER SHALL WE DO? A SICKNESS HAS BEFALLEN OUR POOR PRISONER!
I SHALL UNLOCK YOUR CELL WITH GREAT HASTE AND ENTER SO THAT I MAY BE BASHED ON THE HEAD AND TIED UP!
PLEASE, TAKE ADVANTAGE OF MY STUPIDITY AND HURT ME!
YOU GUYS ARE THE THIRD GROUP OF SACRIFICES TO TRY THAT AND IT'S NOT GONNA WORK ON ME THIS TIME!
SLAM

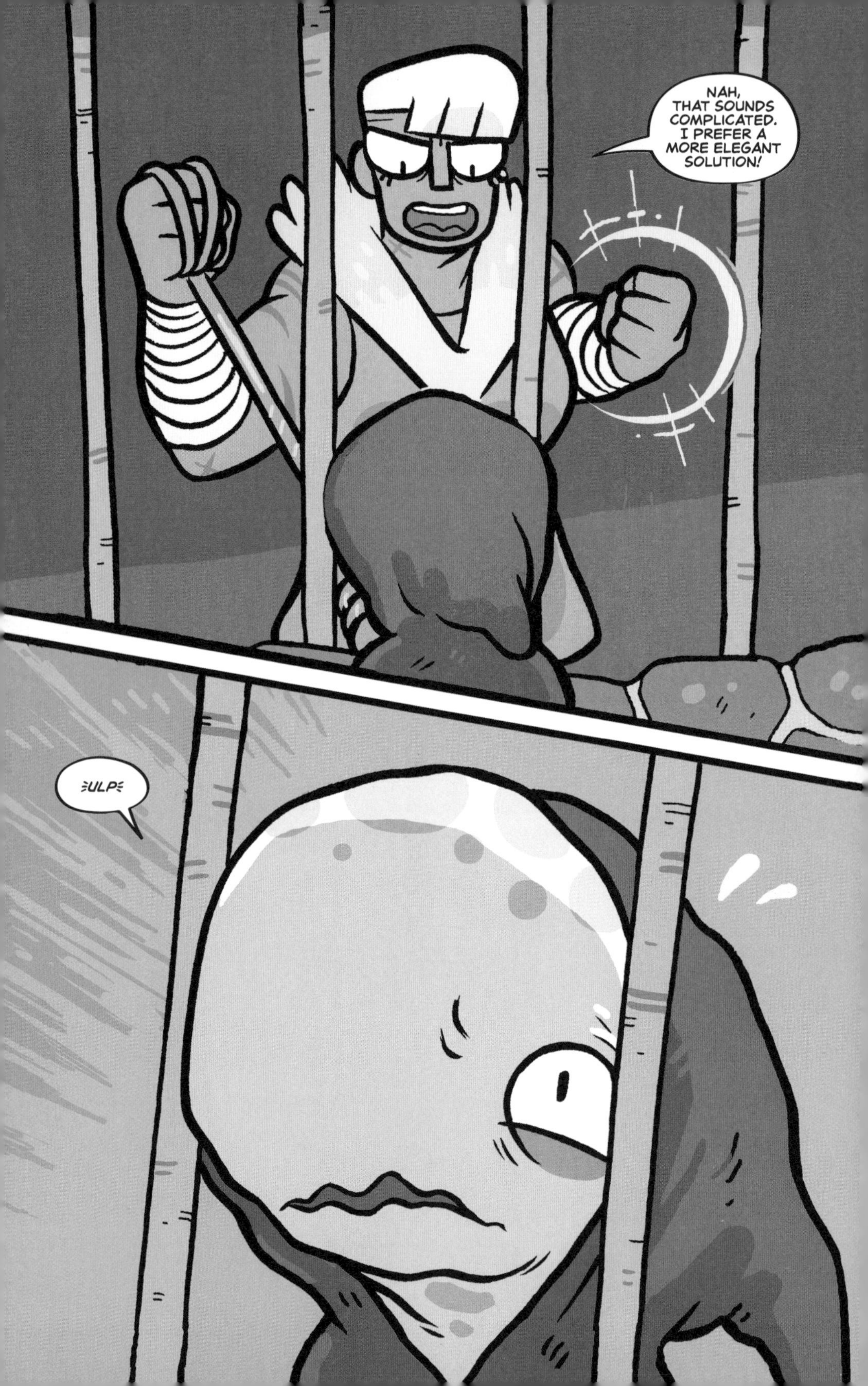
NAH, THAT SOUNDS COMPLICATED. I PREFER A MORE ELEGANT SOLUTION!
ULP

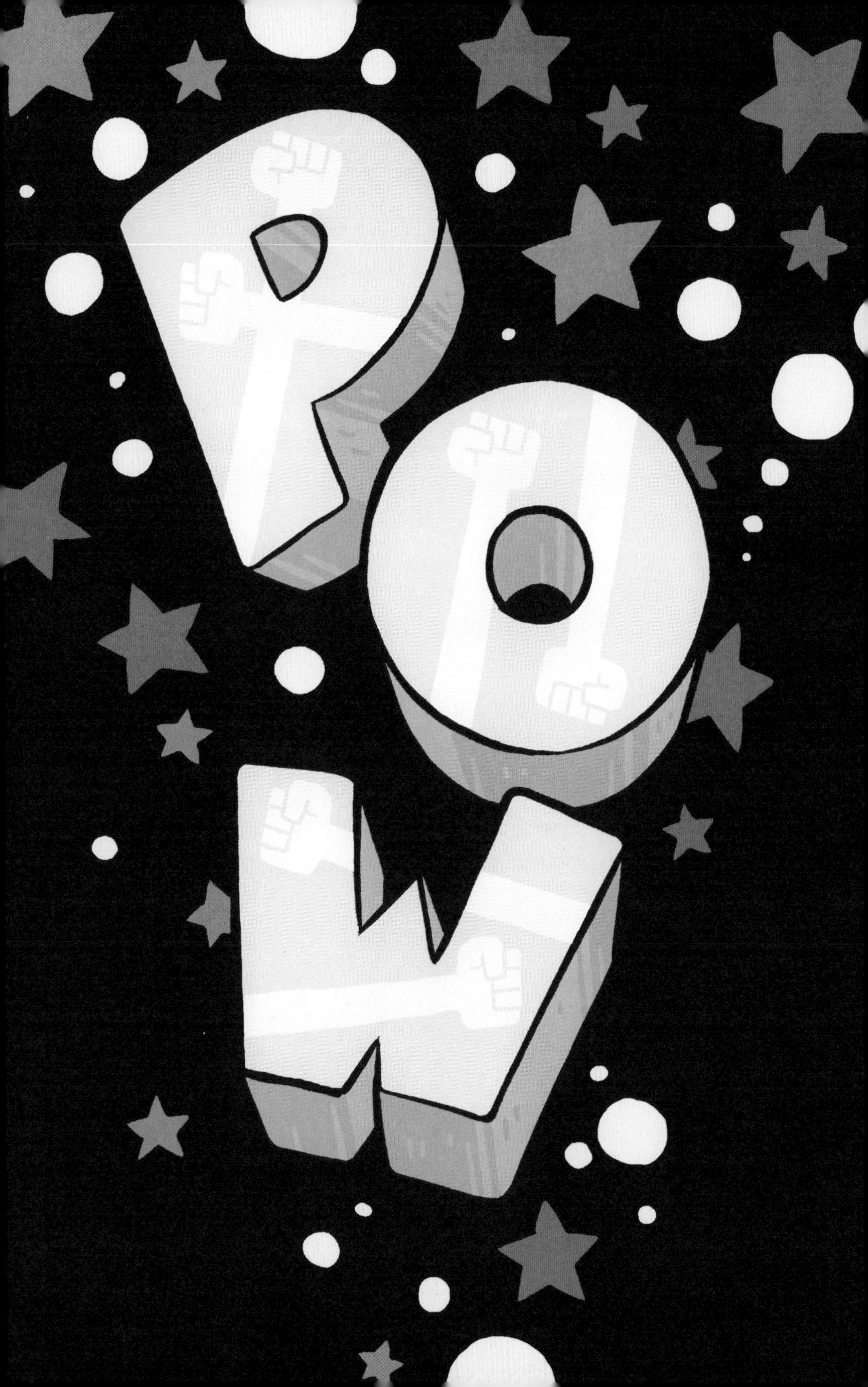
POW

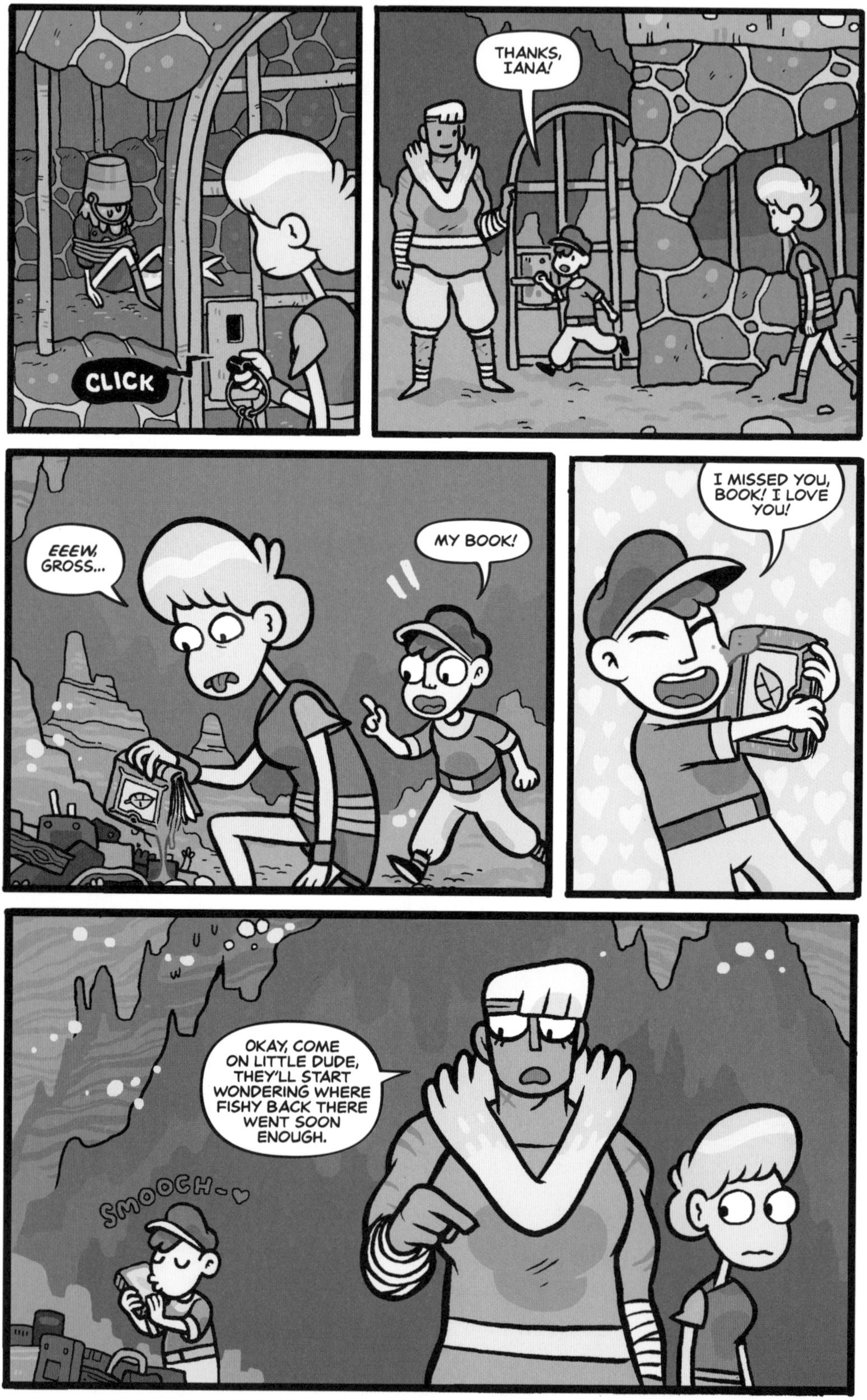
CLICK
THANKS, IANA!
EEEW, GROSS...
MY BOOK!
I MISSED YOU, BOOK! I LOVE YOU!
OKAY, COME ON LITTLE DUDE, THEY'LL START WONDERING WHERE FISHY BACK THERE WENT SOON ENOUGH.
SMOOCH-♡

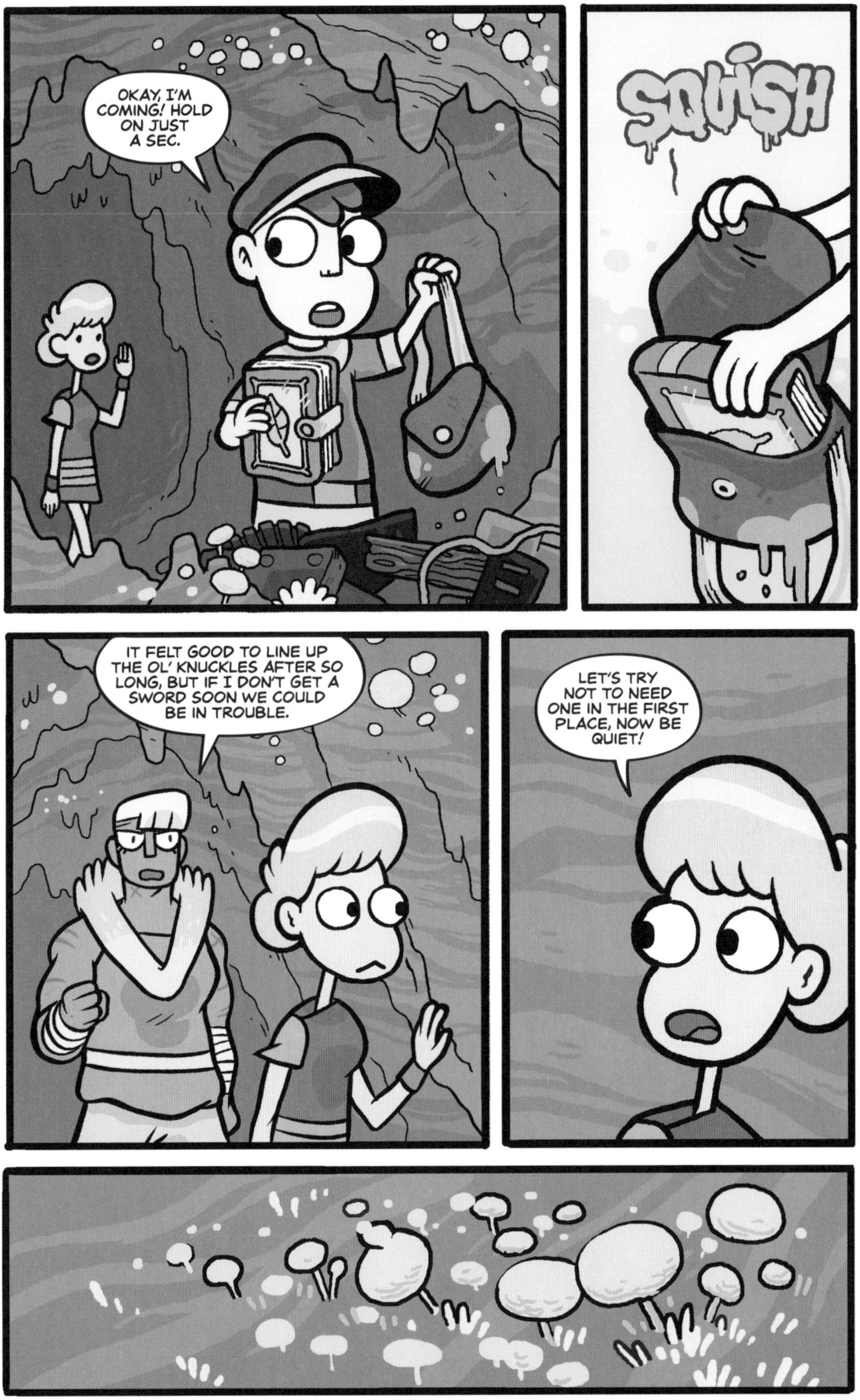
OKAY, I'M COMING! HOLD ON JUST A SEC.
SQUISH
IT FELT GOOD TO LINE UP THE OL' KNUCKLES AFTER SO LONG, BUT IF I DON'T GET A SWORD SOON WE COULD BE IN TROUBLE.
LET'S TRY NOT TO NEED ONE IN THE FIRST PLACE, NOW BE QUIET!

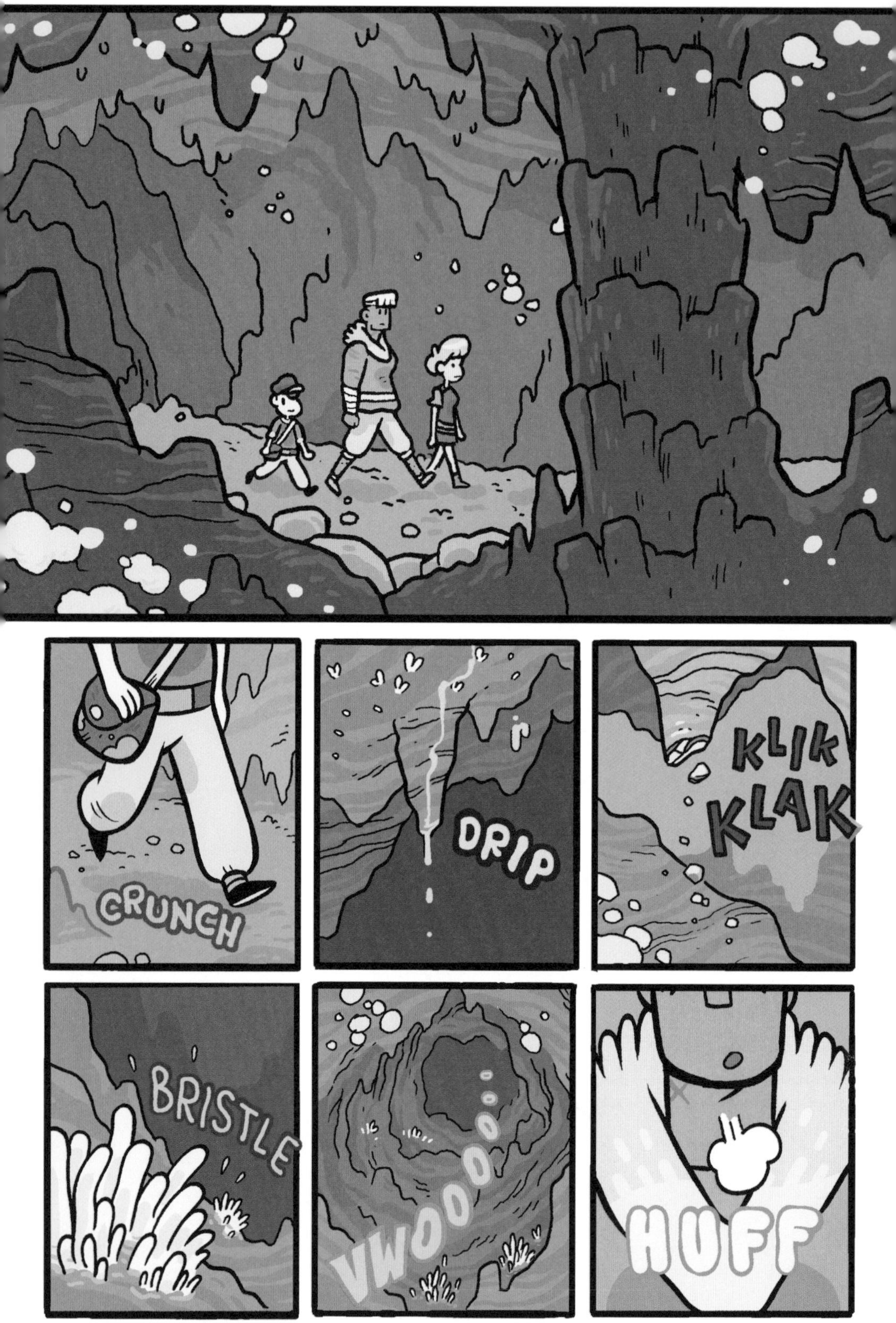
CRUNCH
DRIP
KLIK
KLAK
BRISTLE
VWOOOOOOO
HUFF

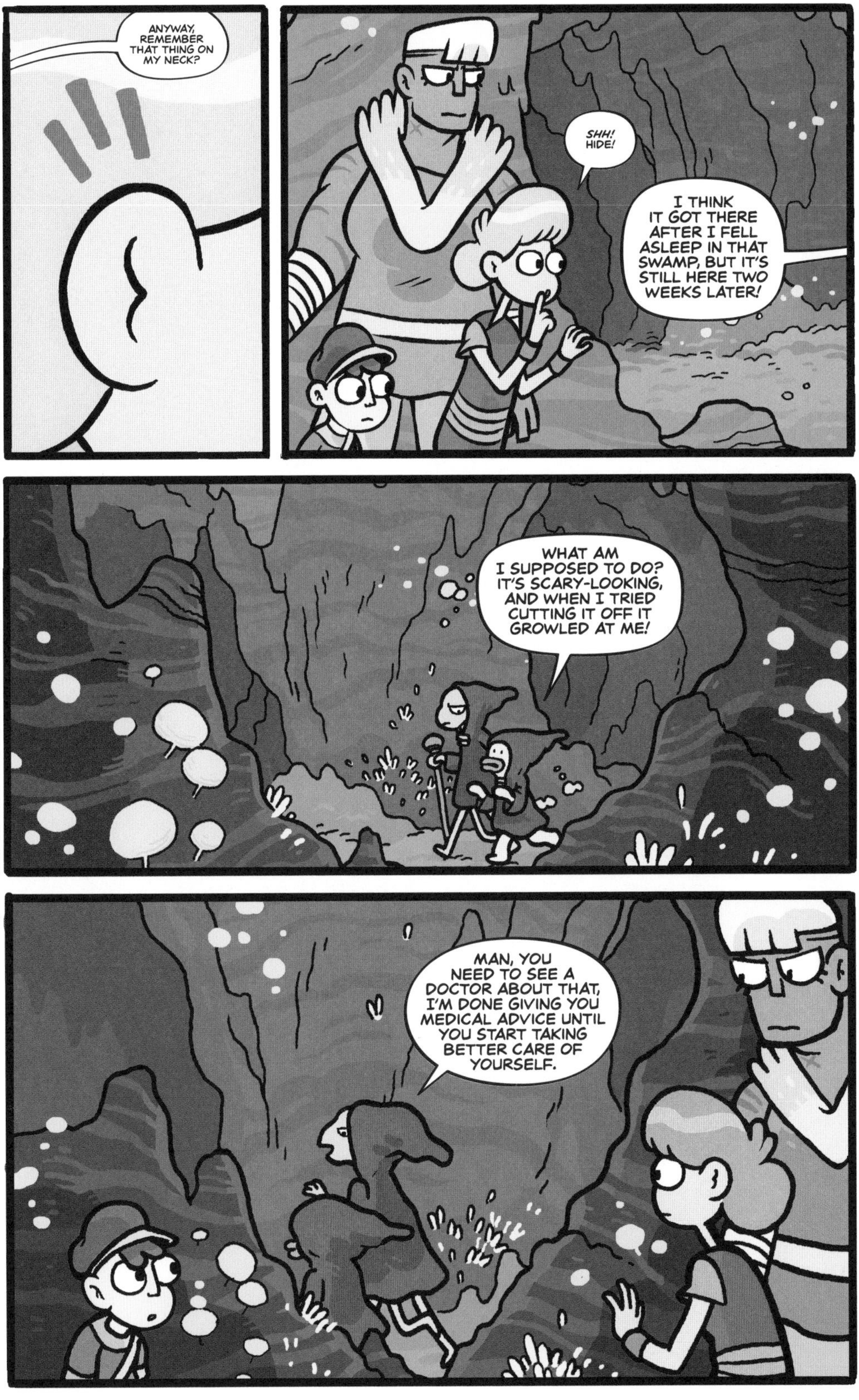
ANYWAY, REMEMBER THAT THING ON MY NECK?
SHH! HIDE!
I THINK IT GOT THERE AFTER I FELL ASLEEP IN THAT SWAMP, BUT IT'S STILL HERE TWO WEEKS LATER!
WHAT AM I SUPPOSED TO DO? IT'S SCARY-LOOKING, AND WHEN I TRIED CUTTING IT OFF IT GROWLED AT ME!
MAN, YOU NEED TO SEE A DOCTOR ABOUT THAT, I'M DONE GIVING YOU MEDICAL ADVICE UNTIL YOU START TAKING BETTER CARE OF YOURSELF.

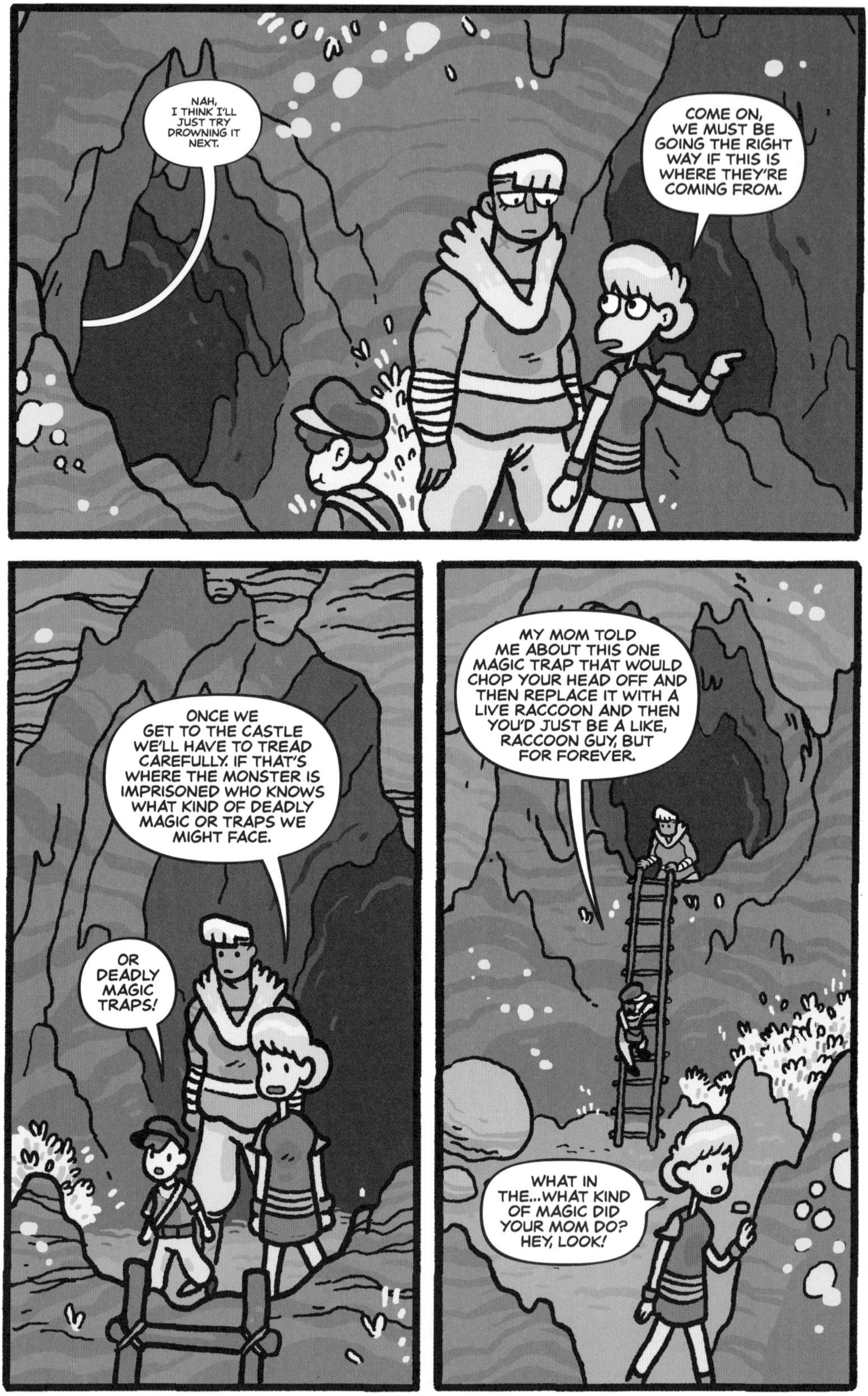
NAH, I THINK I'LL JUST TRY DROWNING IT NEXT.
COME ON, WE MUST BE GOING THE RIGHT WAY IF THIS IS WHERE THEY'RE COMING FROM.
ONCE WE GET TO THE CASTLE WE'LL HAVE TO TREAD CAREFULLY. IF THAT'S WHERE THE MONSTER IS IMPRISONED WHO KNOWS WHAT KIND OF DEADLY MAGIC OR TRAPS WE MIGHT FACE.
OR DEADLY MAGIC TRAPS!
MY MOM TOLD ME ABOUT THIS ONE MAGIC TRAP THAT WOULD CHOP YOUR HEAD OFF AND THEN REPLACE IT WITH A LIVE RACCOON AND THEN YOU'D JUST BE A LIKE, RACCOON GUY, BUT FOR FOREVER.
WHAT IN THE...WHAT KIND OF MAGIC DID YOUR MOM DO? HEY, LOOK!

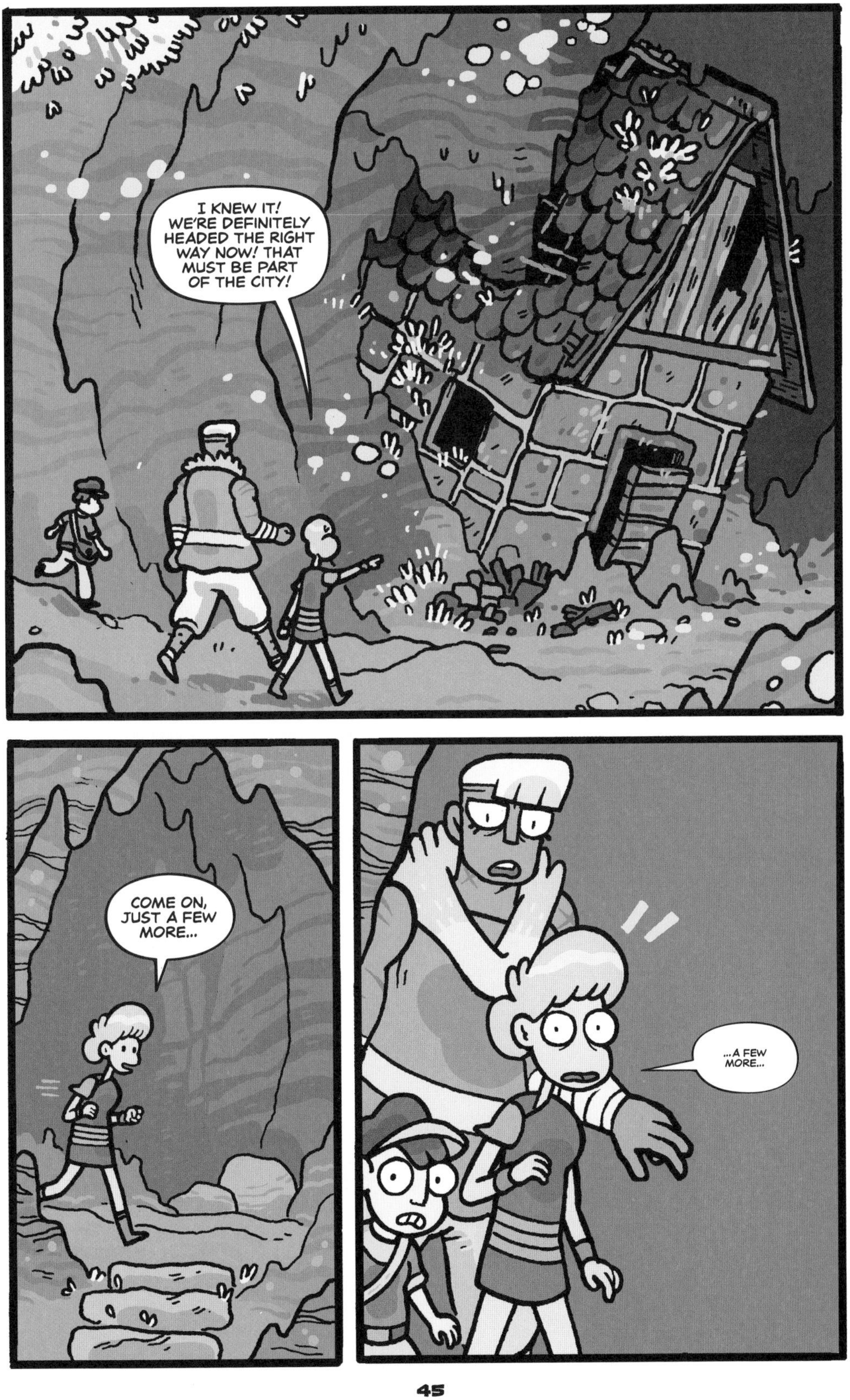
I KNEW IT! WE'RE DEFINITELY HEADED THE RIGHT WAY NOW! THAT MUST BE PART OF THE CITY!
COME ON, JUST A FEW MORE...
...A FEW MORE...

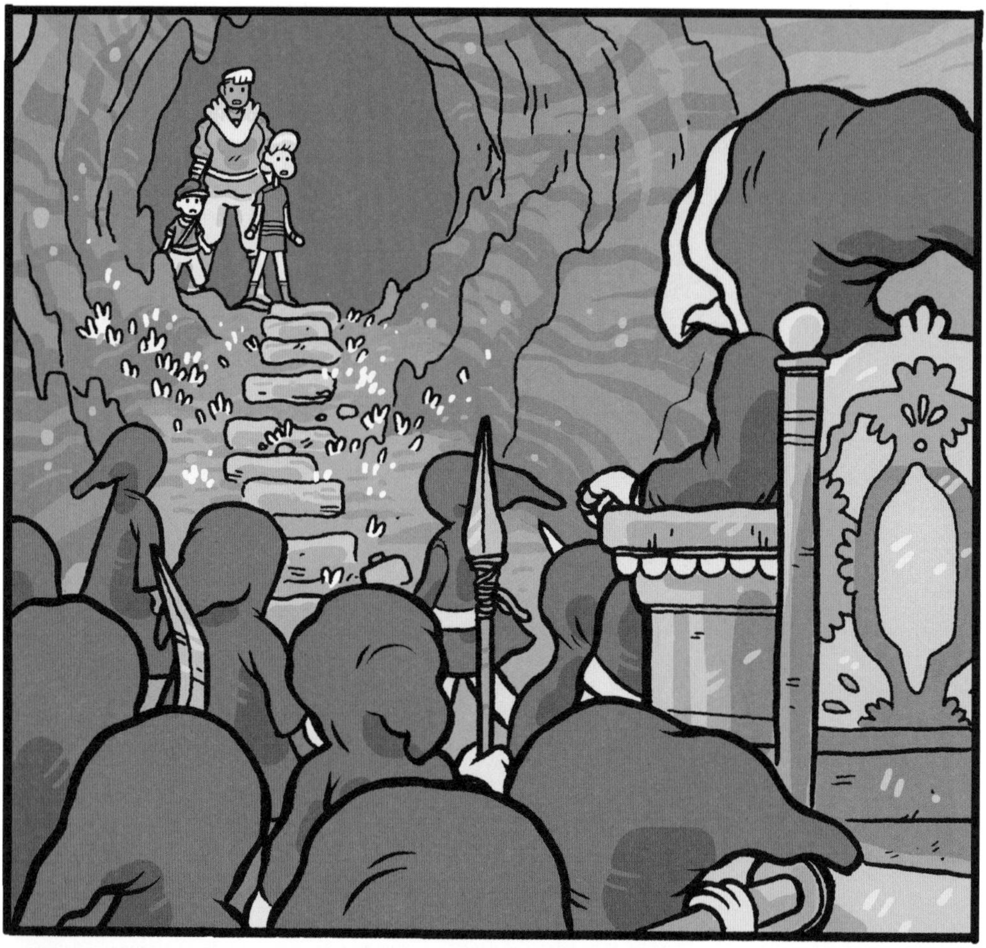

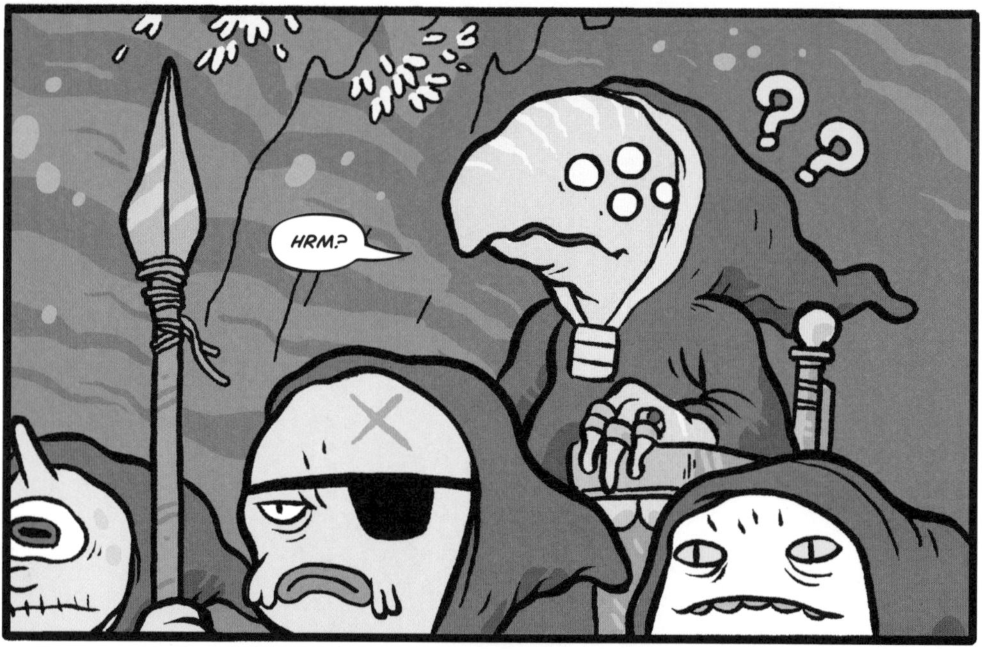
HRM?
??

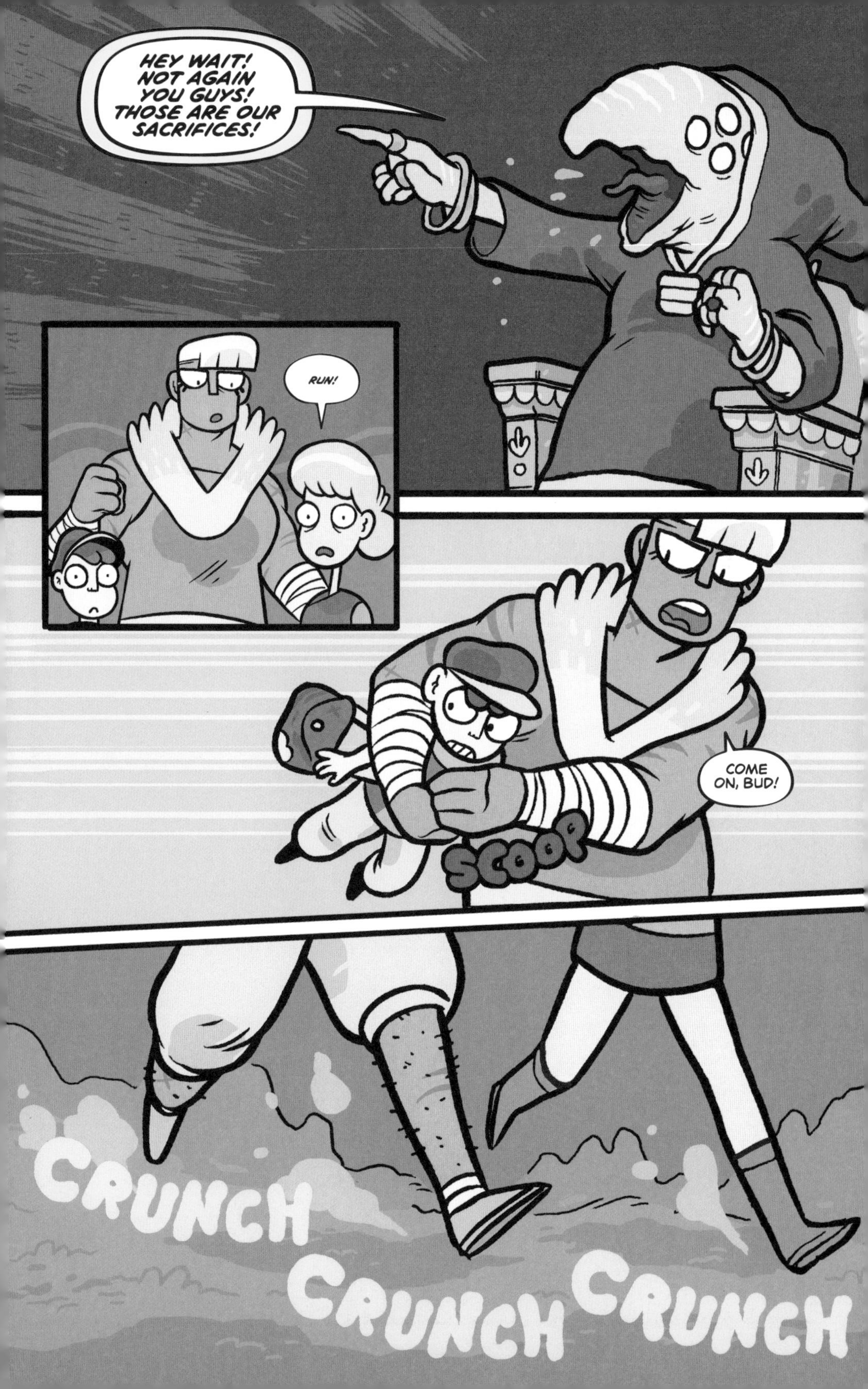
HEY WAIT! NOT AGAIN YOU GUYS! THOSE ARE OUR SACRIFICES!
RUN!
COME ON, BUD!
SCOOP
CRUNCH
CRUNCH
CRUNCH

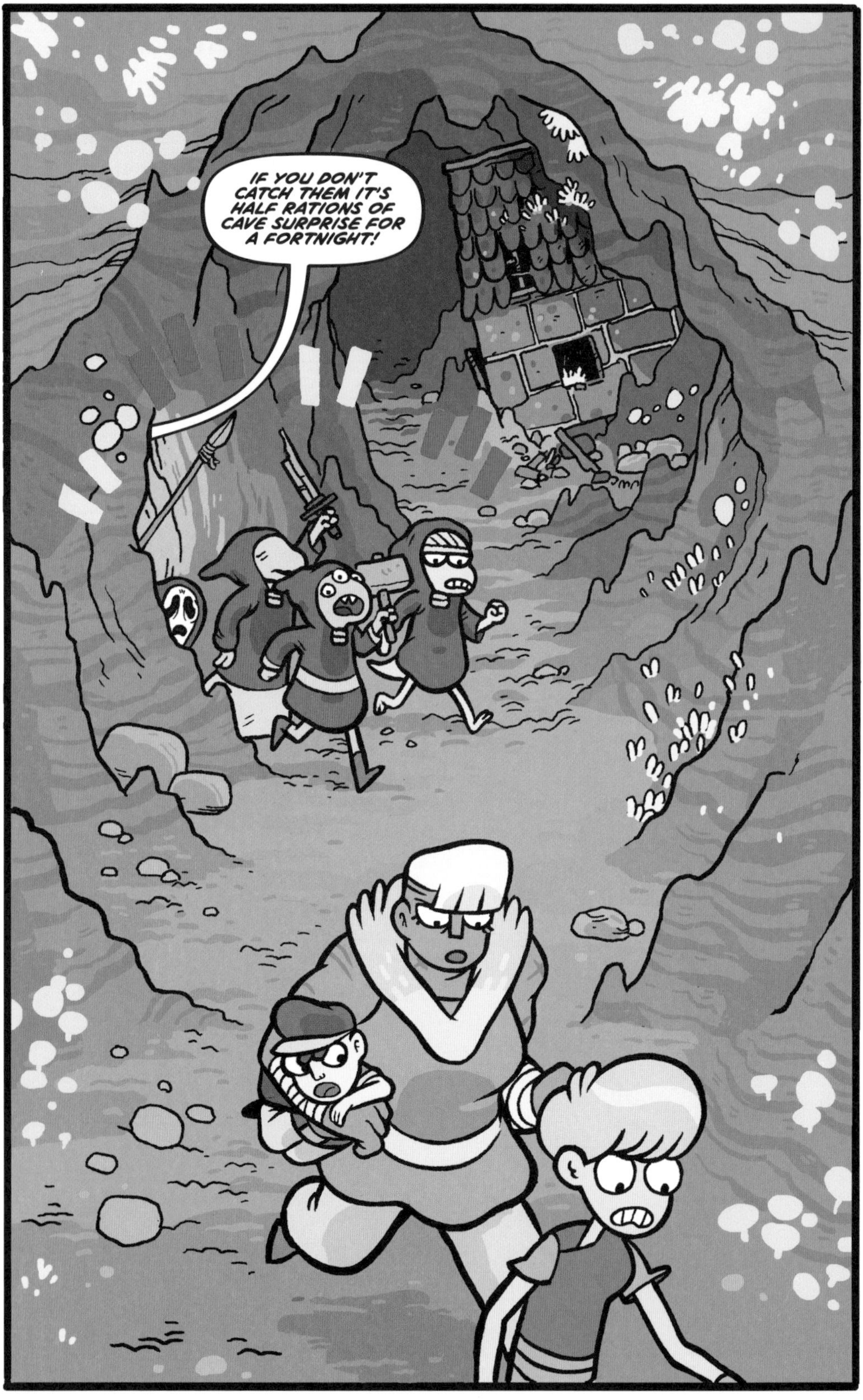
IF YOU DON'T CATCH THEM IT'S HALF RATIONS OF CAVE SURPRISE FOR A FORTNIGHT!

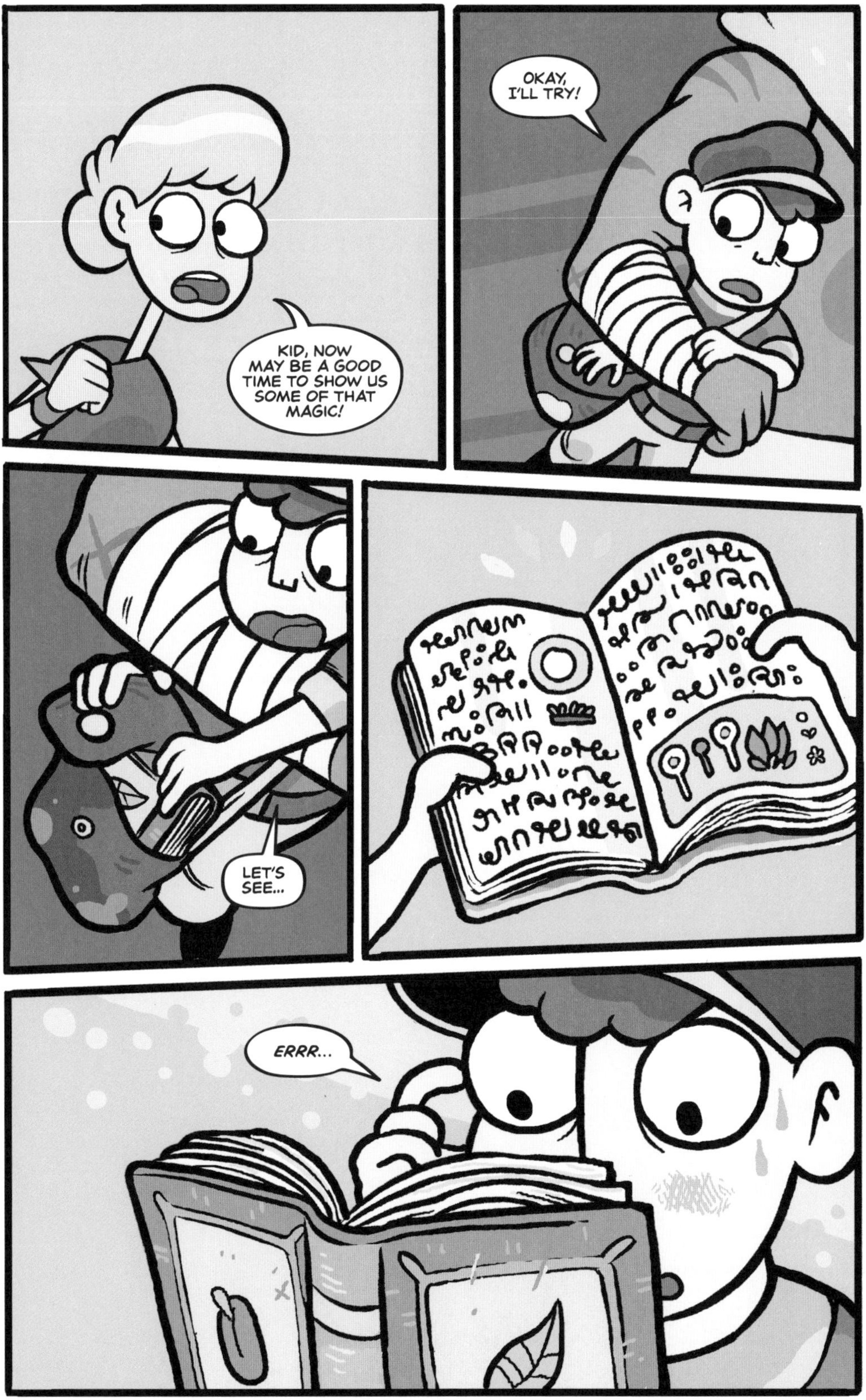
KID, NOW MAY BE A GOOD TIME TO SHOW US SOME OF THAT MAGIC!
OKAY, I'LL TRY!
LET'S SEE...
ERRR...

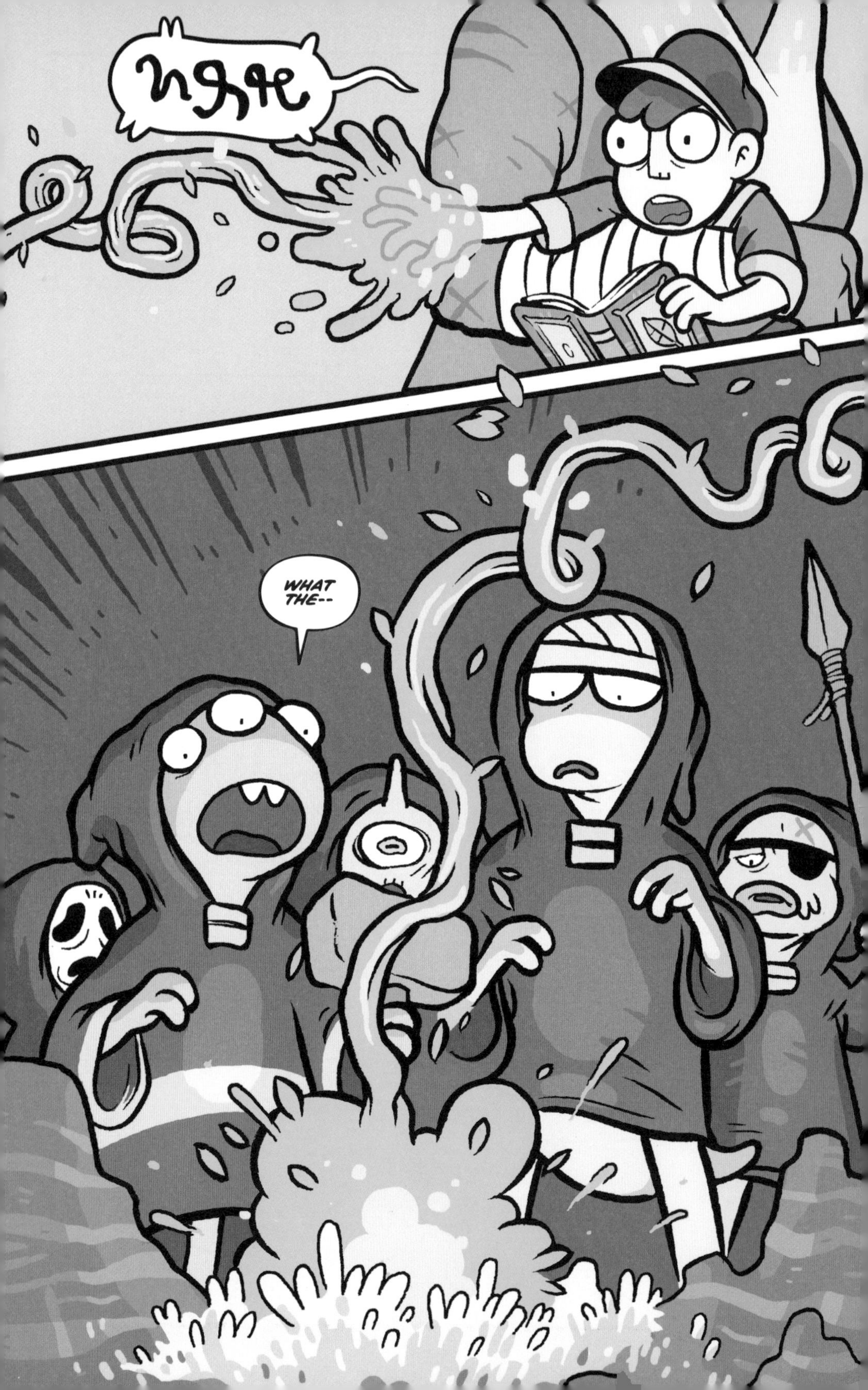
WHAT THE--

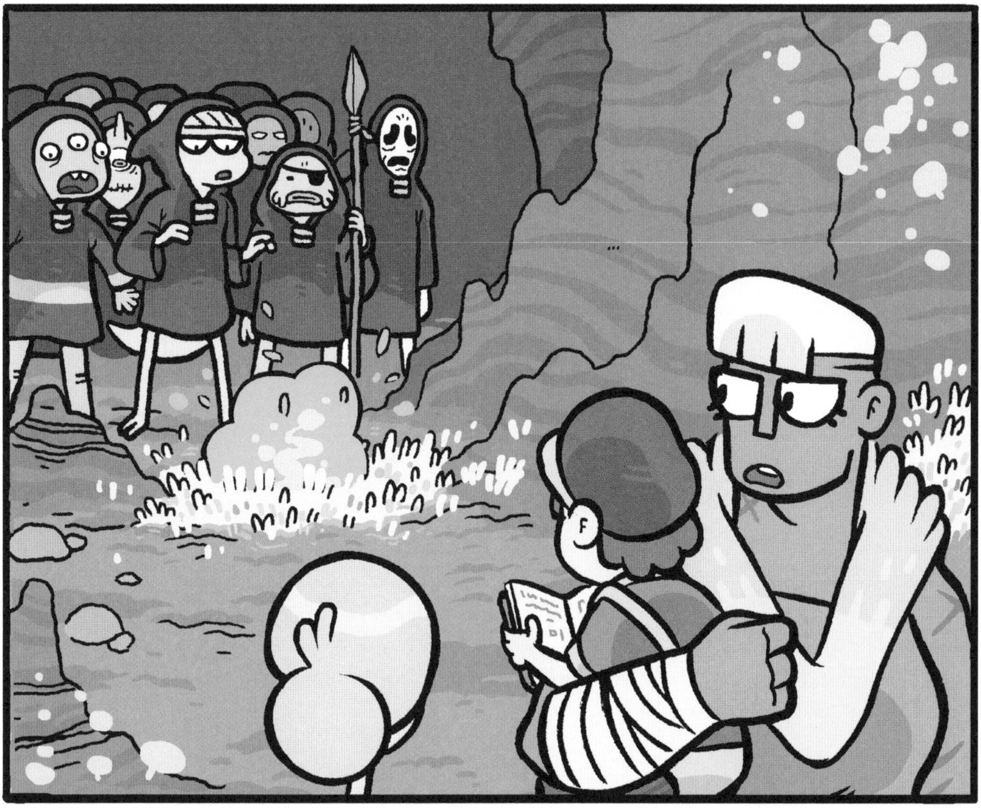

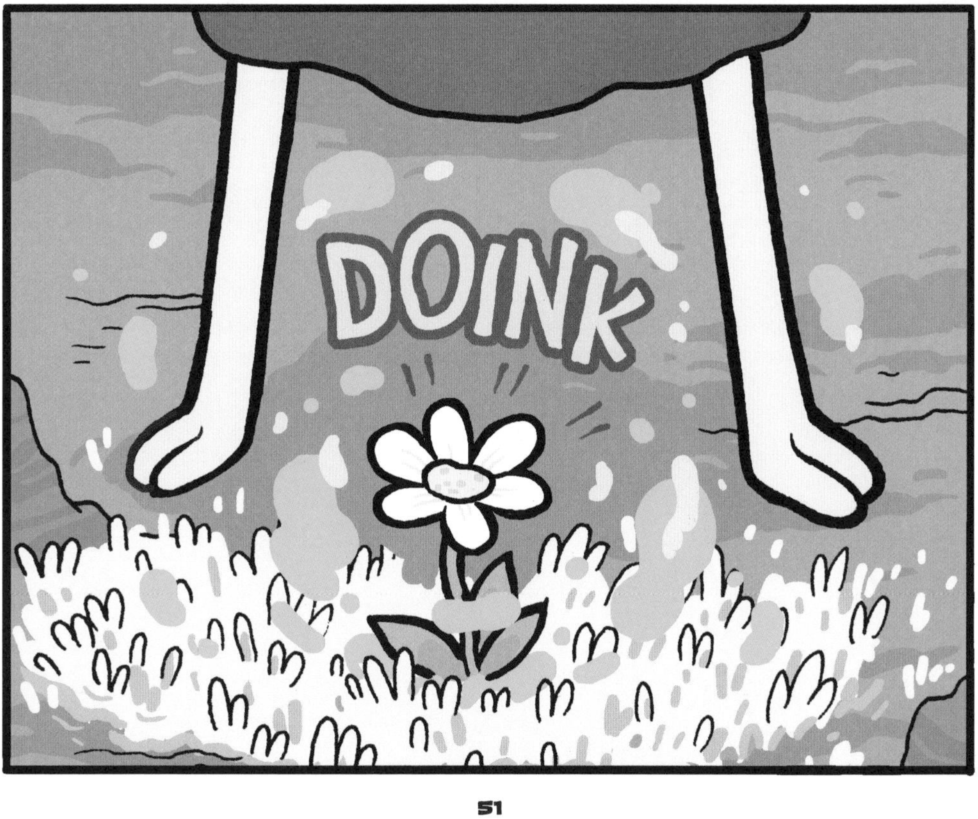
DOINK

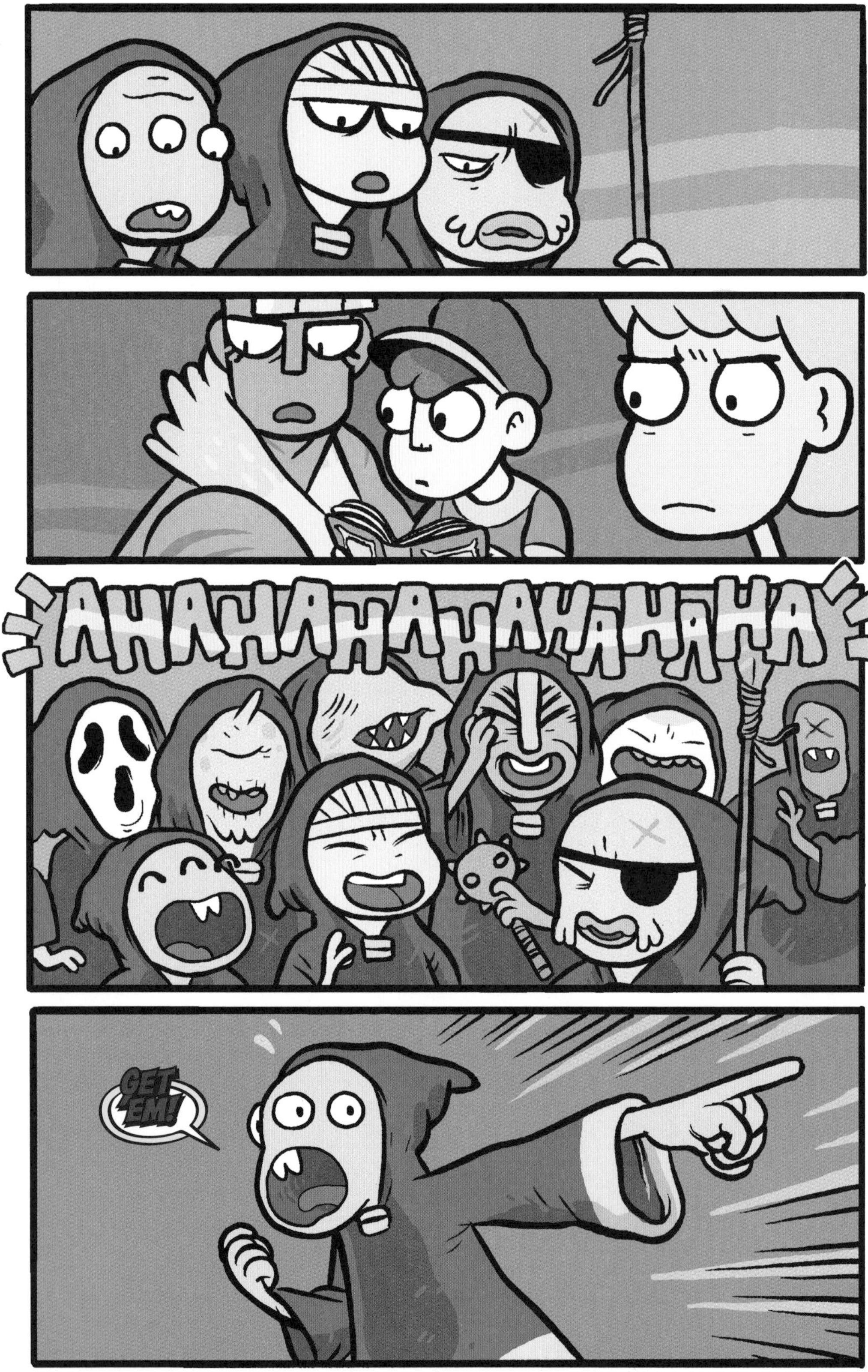
AHAHAHAHAHAHAHAHAHA
GET 'EM!

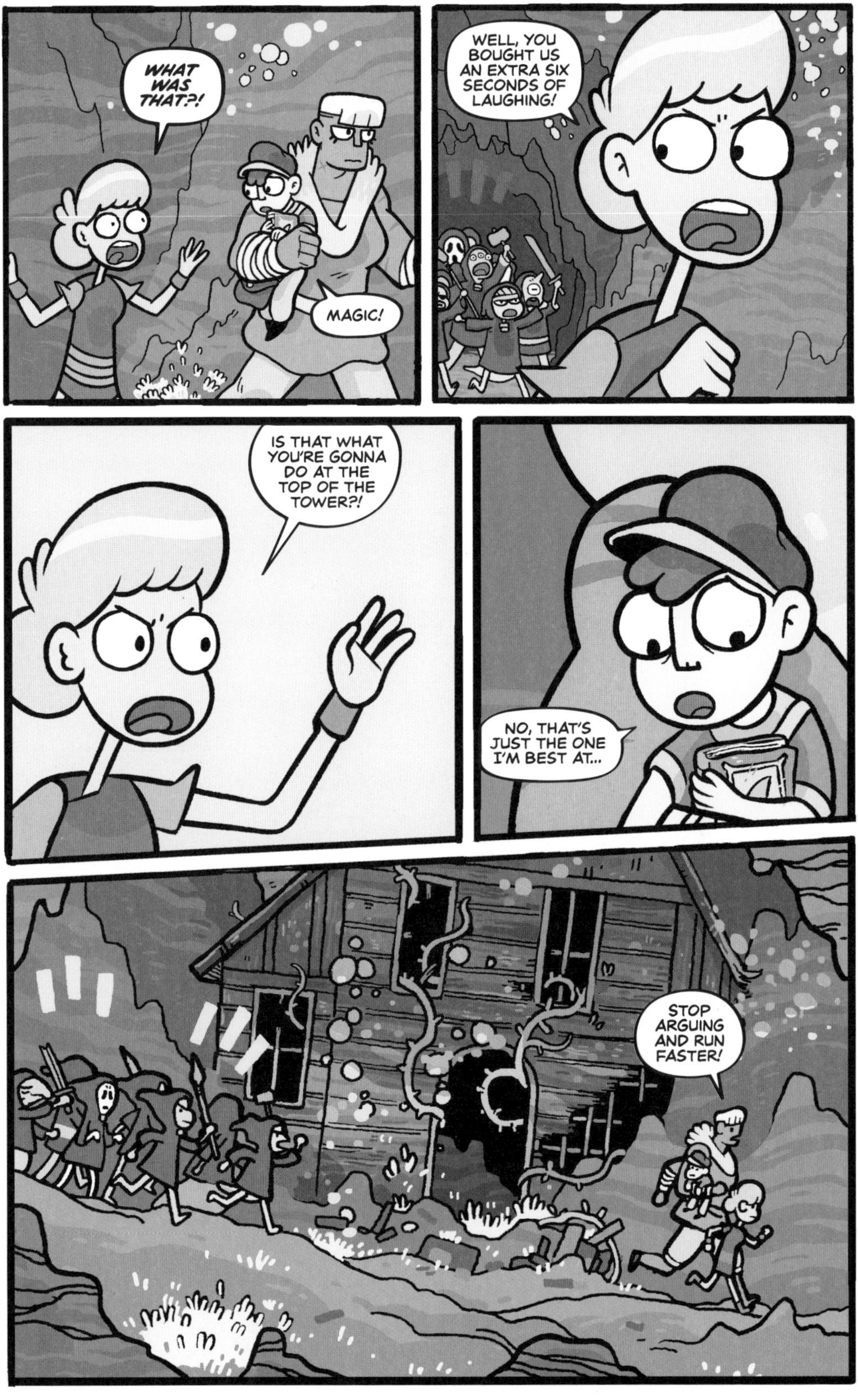
WHAT WAS THAT?!
MAGIC!
WELL, YOU BOUGHT US AN EXTRA SIX SECONDS OF LAUGHING!
IS THAT WHAT YOU'RE GONNA DO AT THE TOP OF THE TOWER?!
NO, THAT'S JUST THE ONE I'M BEST AT...
STOP ARGUING AND RUN FASTER!

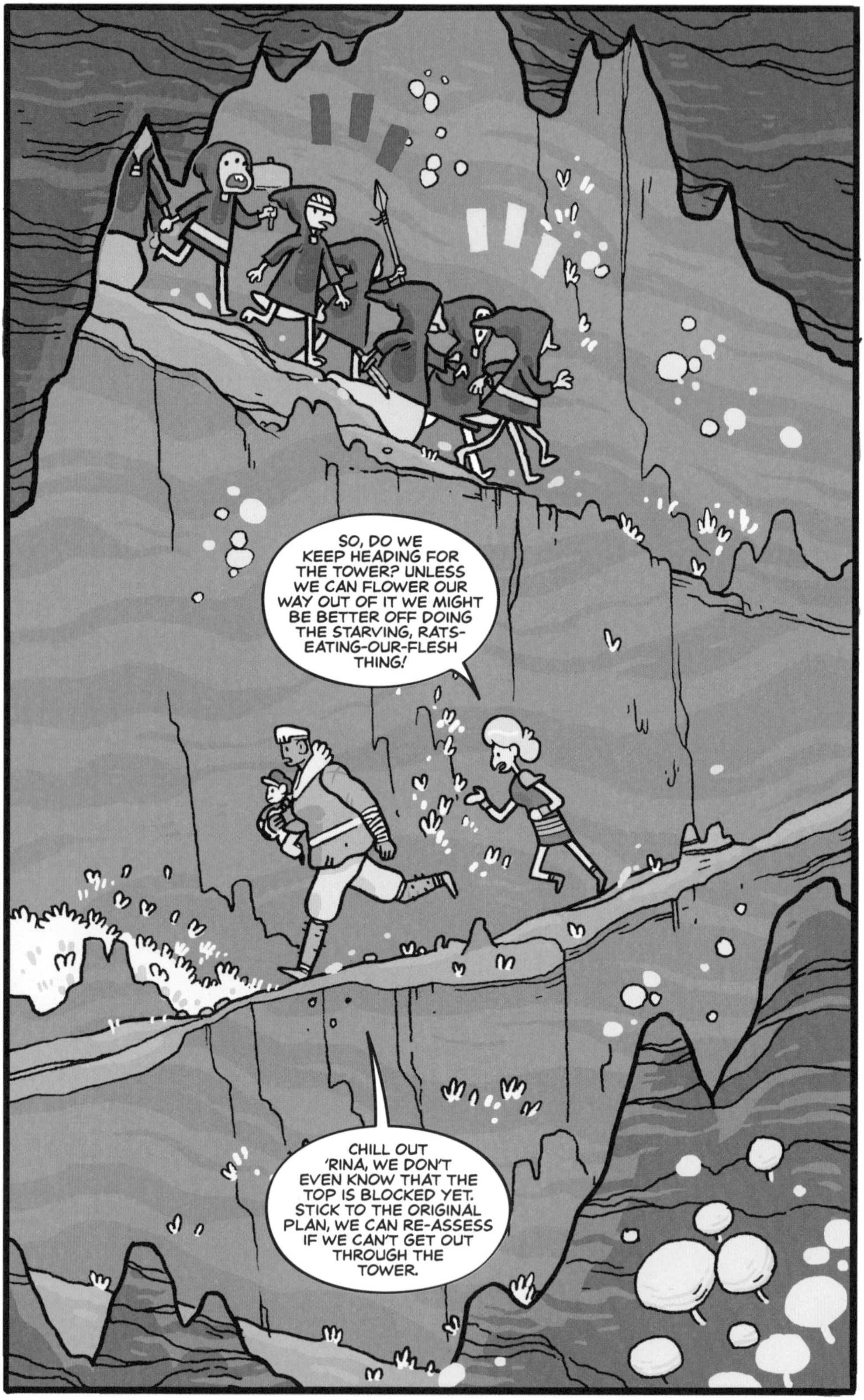
SO, DO WE KEEP HEADING FOR THE TOWER? UNLESS WE CAN FLOWER OUR WAY OUT OF IT WE MIGHT BE BETTER OFF DOING THE STARVING, RATS-EATING-OUR-FLESH THING!
CHILL OUT 'RINA, WE DON'T EVEN KNOW THAT THE TOP IS BLOCKED YET. STICK TO THE ORIGINAL PLAN, WE CAN RE-ASSESS IF WE CAN'T GET OUT THROUGH THE TOWER.

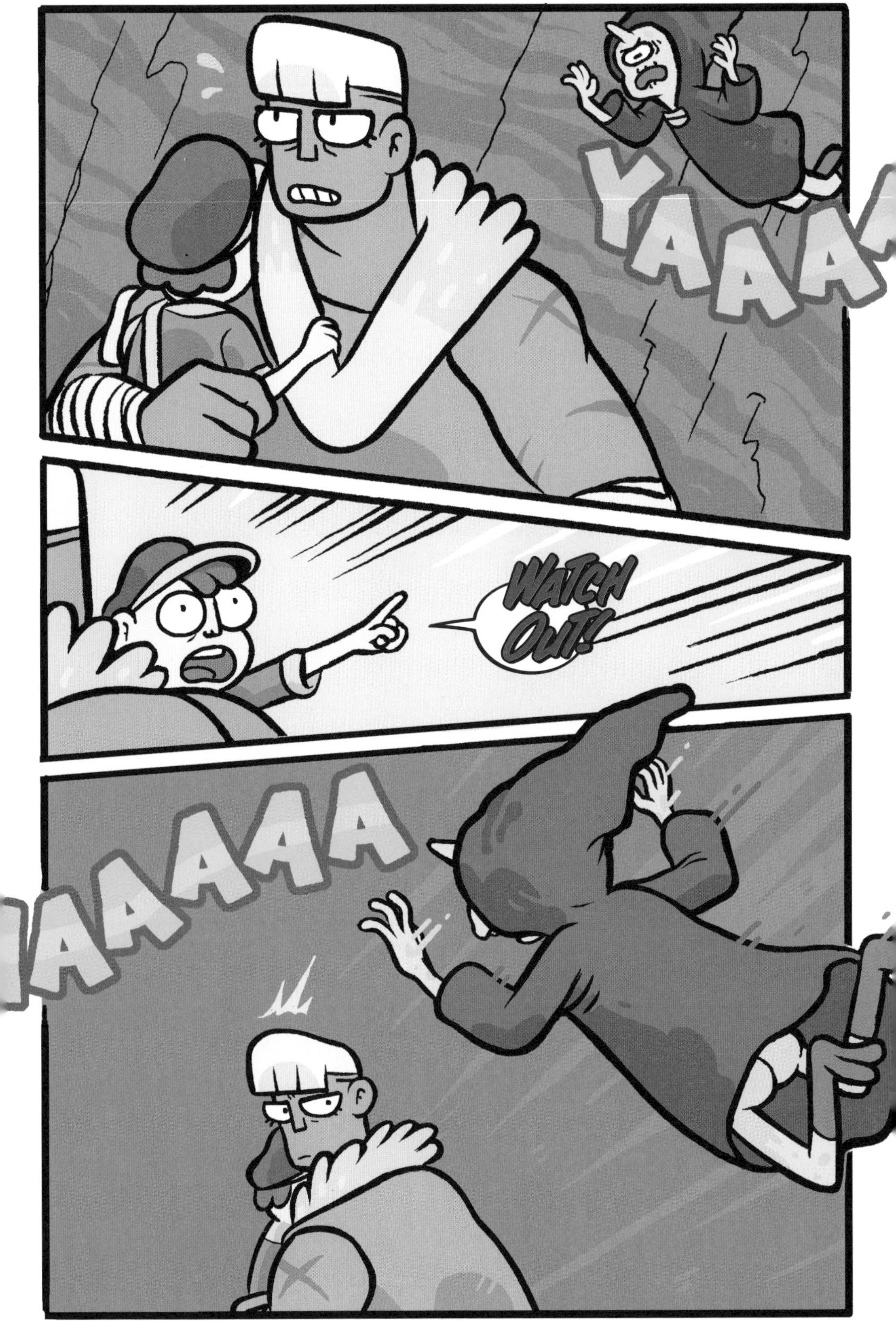
YAAAA
WATCH OUT!
AAAAAAA

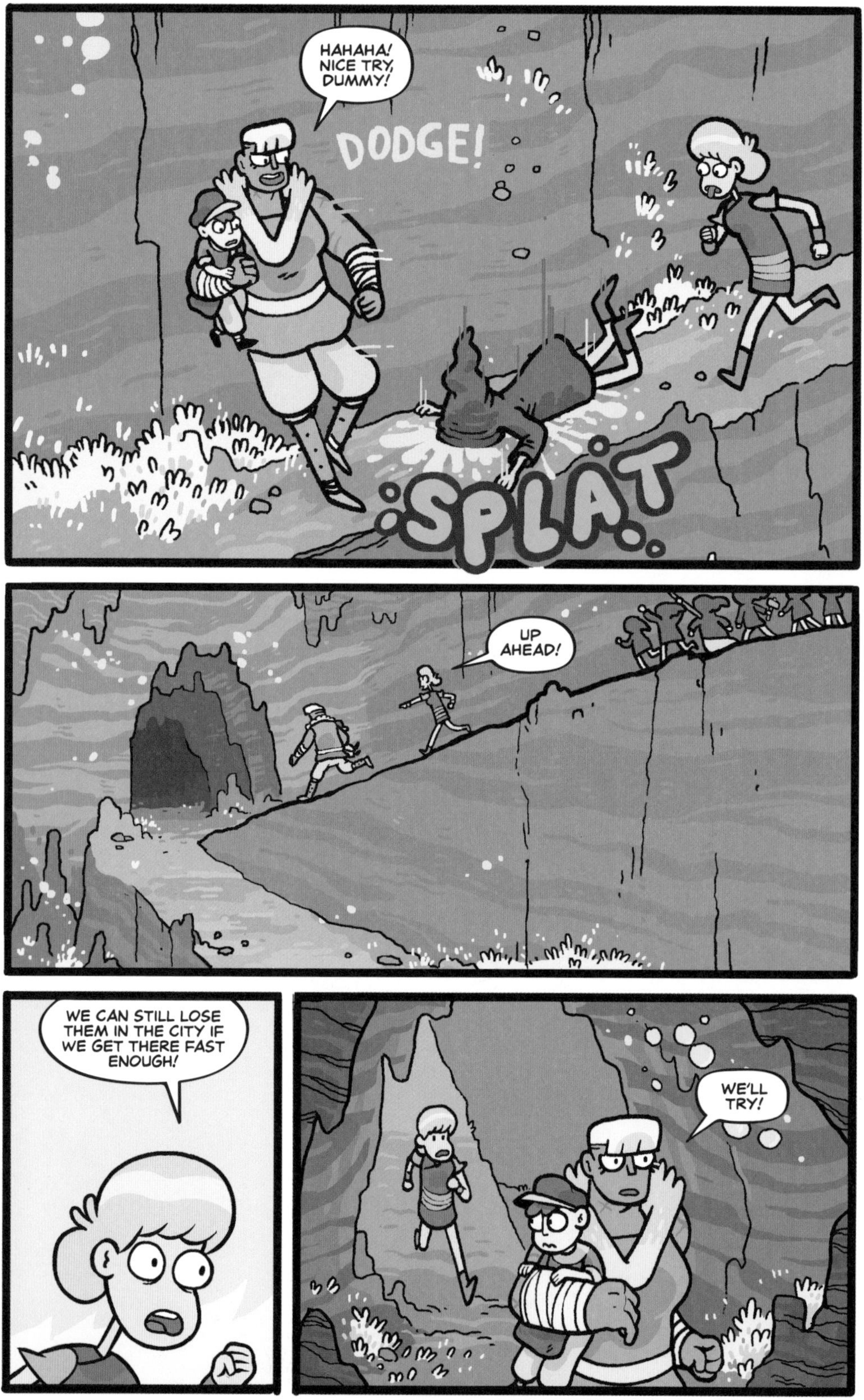
HAHAHA! NICE TRY, DUMMY!
DODGE!
SPLAT
UP AHEAD!
WE CAN STILL LOSE THEM IN THE CITY IF WE GET THERE FAST ENOUGH!
WE'LL TRY!

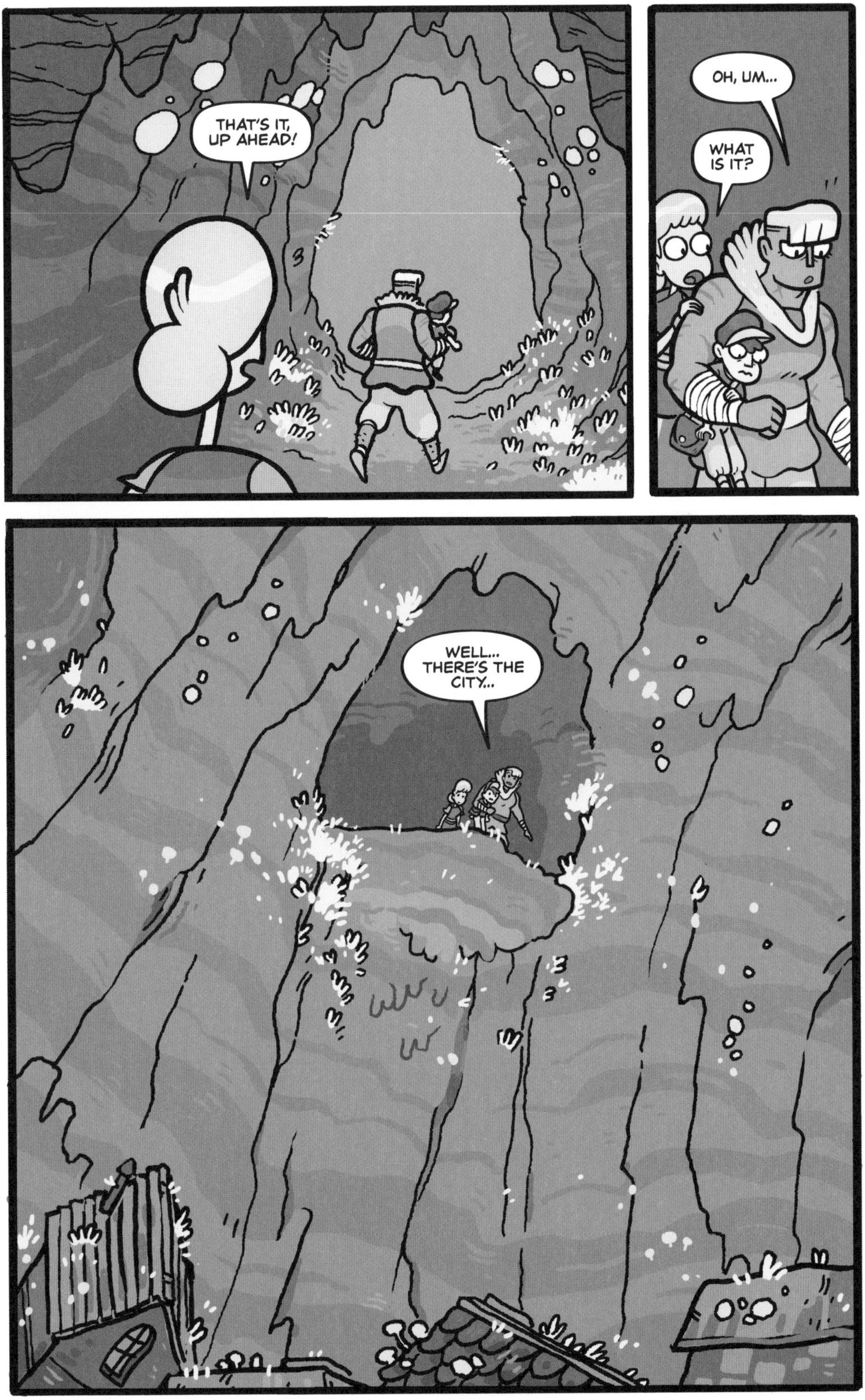
THAT'S IT, UP AHEAD!
OH, UM...
WHAT IS IT?
WELL... THERE'S THE CITY...

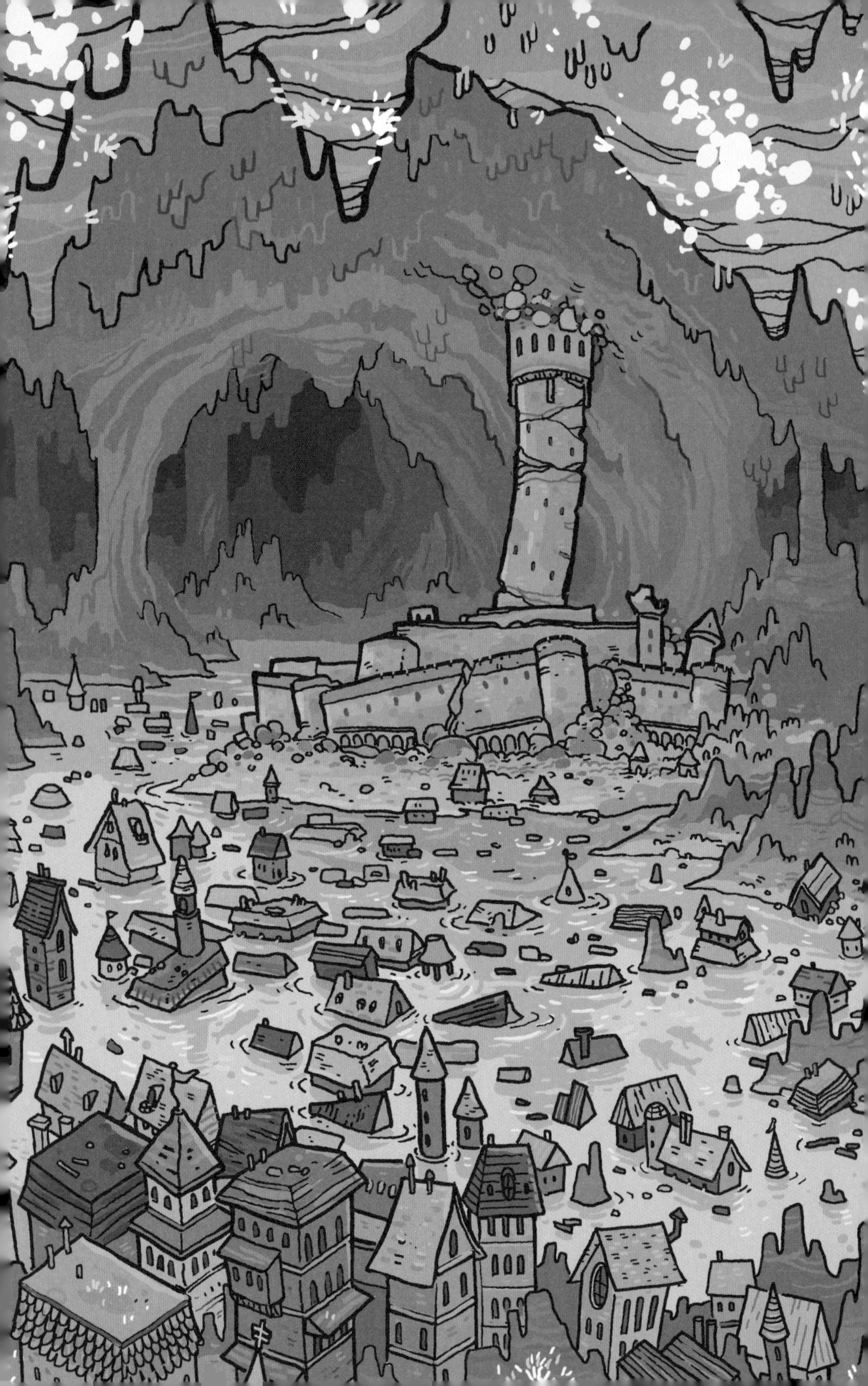

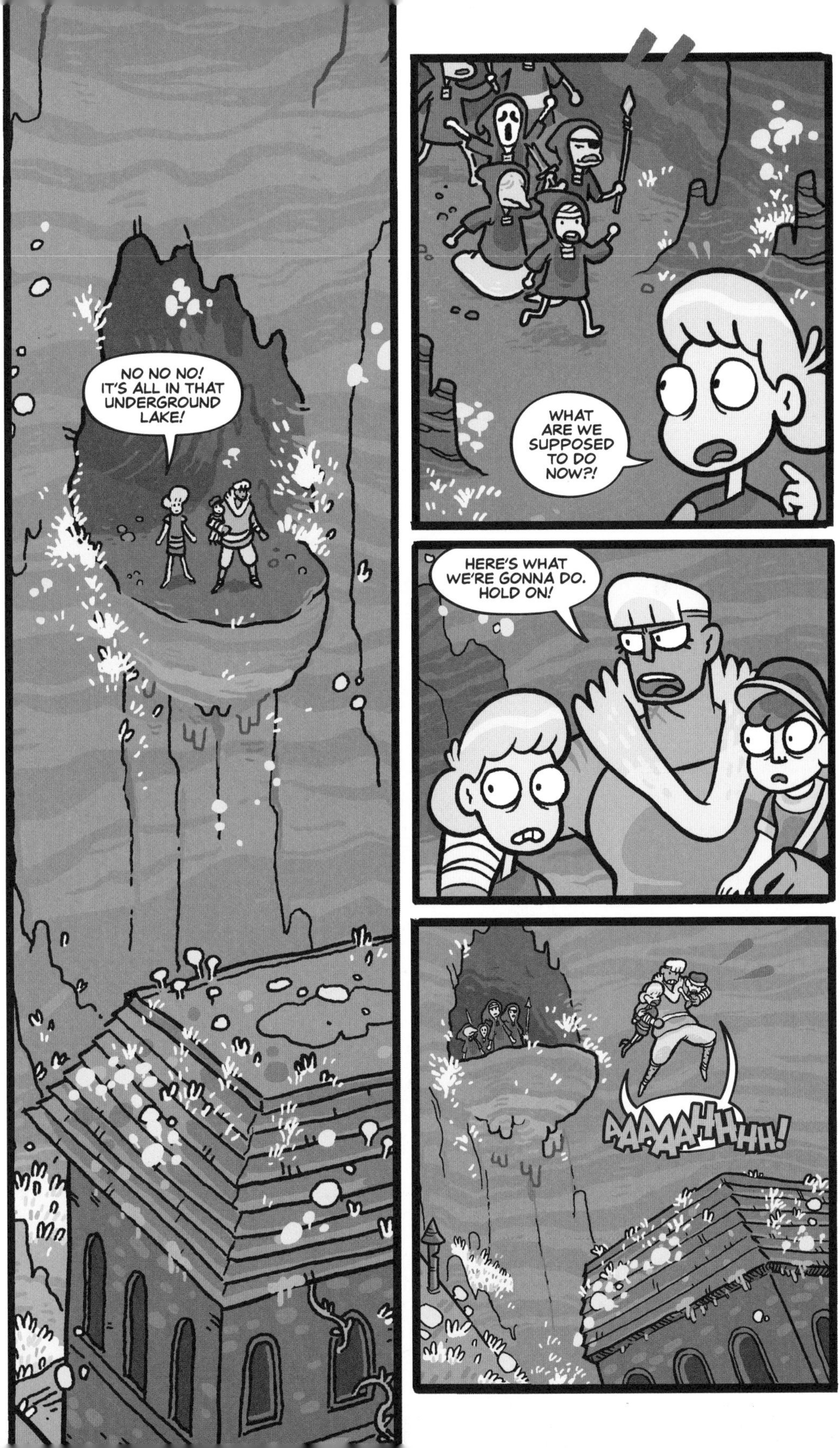
NO NO NO! IT'S ALL IN THAT UNDERGROUND LAKE!
WHAT ARE WE SUPPOSED TO DO NOW?!
HERE'S WHAT WE'RE GONNA DO. HOLD ON!
AAAAAHHHHH!

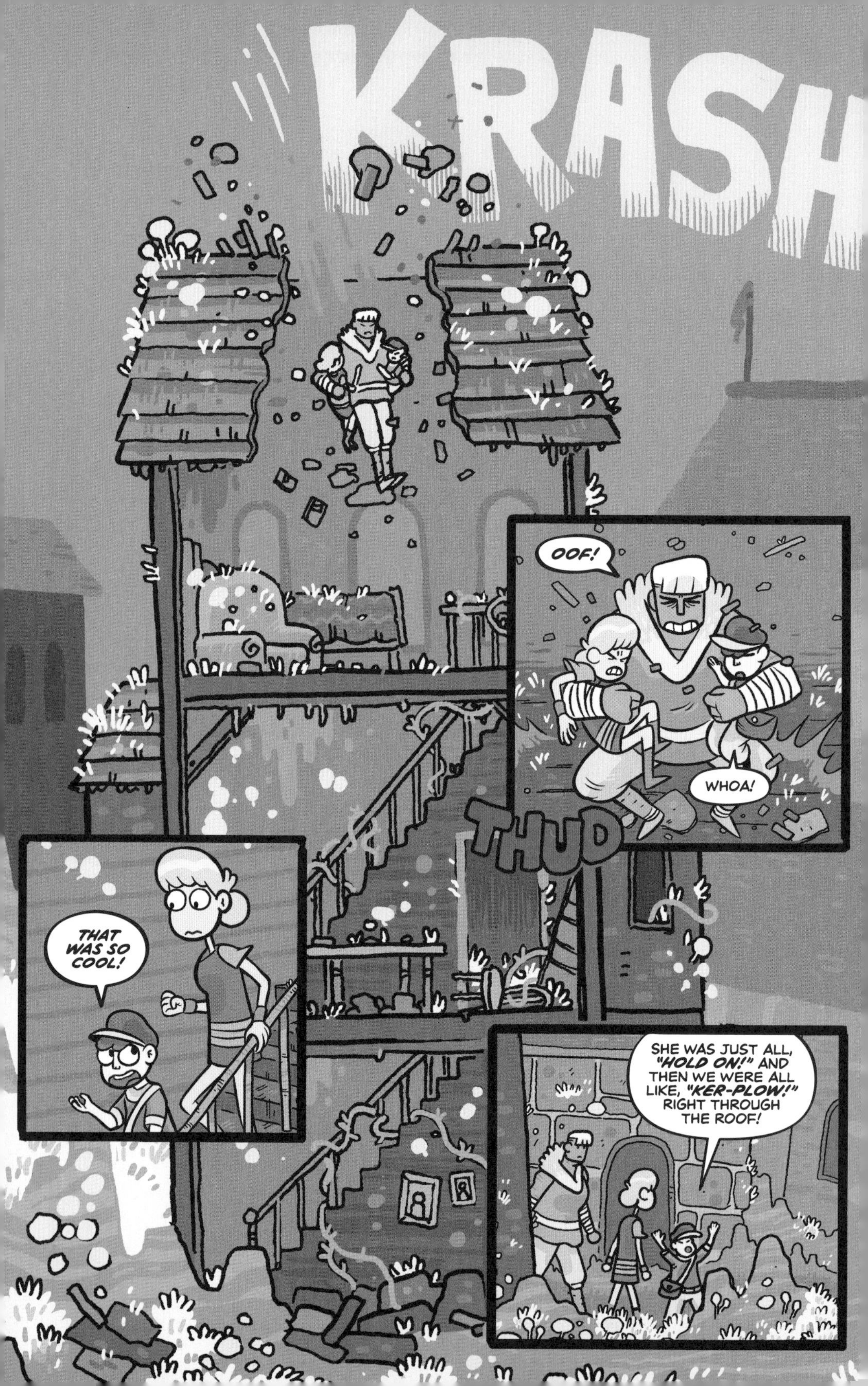
KRASH
OOF!
WHOA!
THUD
THAT WAS SO COOL!
SHE WAS JUST ALL, "HOLD ON!" AND THEN WE WERE ALL LIKE, "KER-PLOW!" RIGHT THROUGH THE ROOF!

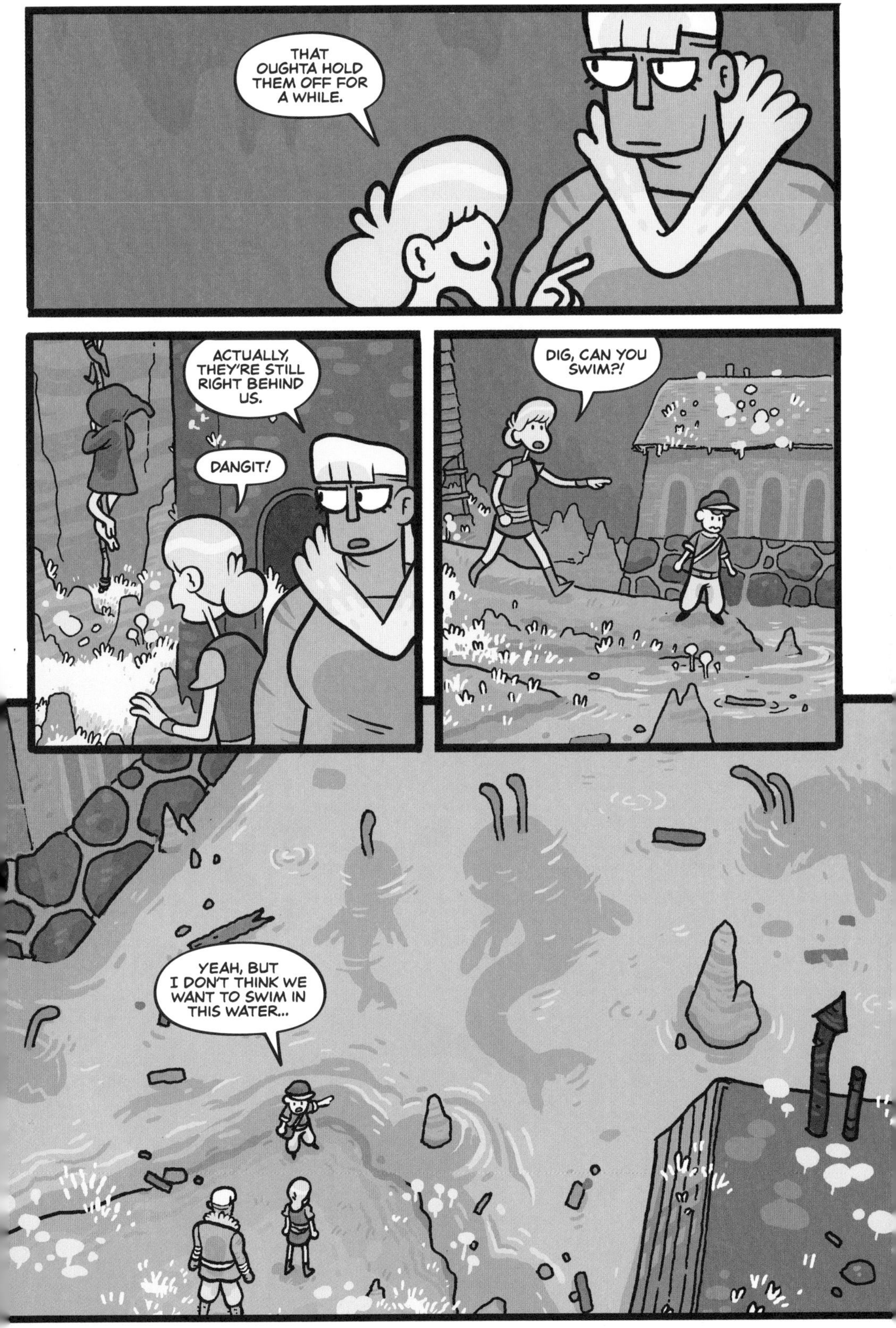
THAT OUGHTA HOLD THEM OFF FOR A WHILE.
ACTUALLY, THEY'RE STILL RIGHT BEHIND US.
DANGIT!
DIG, CAN YOU SWIM?!
YEAH, BUT I DON'T THINK WE WANT TO SWIM IN THIS WATER...

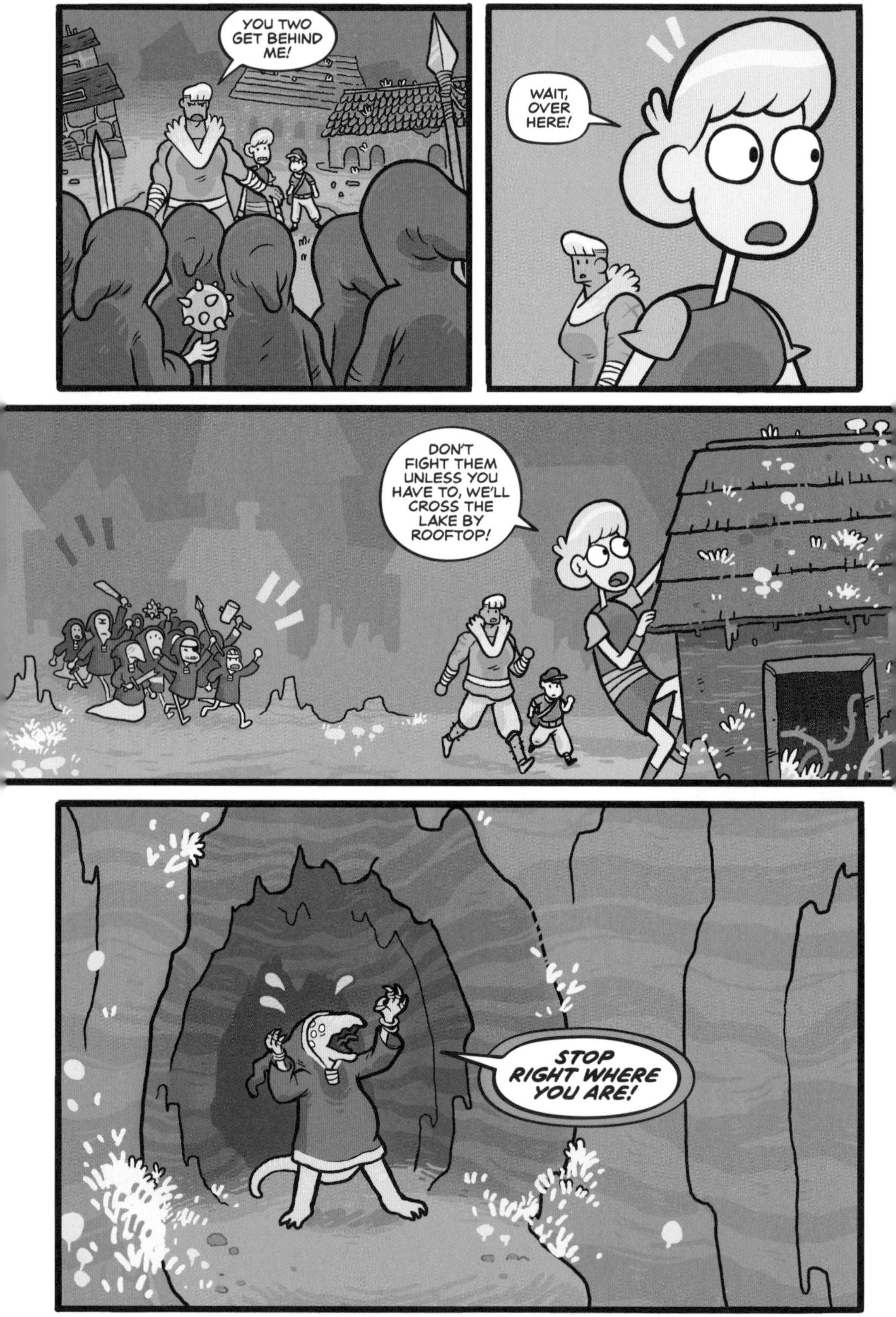
YOU TWO GET BEHIND ME!
WAIT, OVER HERE!
DON'T FIGHT THEM UNLESS YOU HAVE TO, WE'LL CROSS THE LAKE BY ROOFTOP!
STOP RIGHT WHERE YOU ARE!

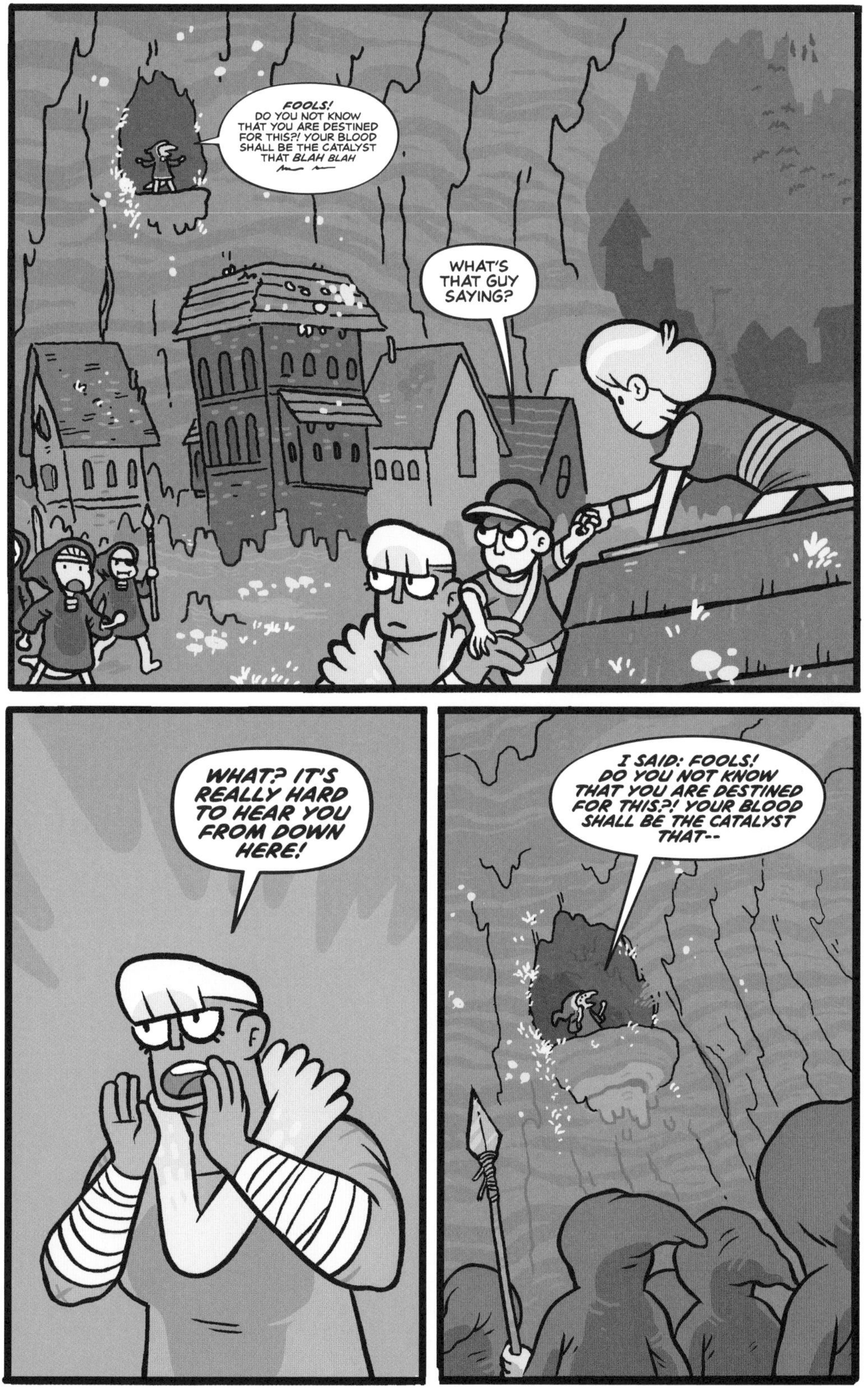
FOOLS! DO YOU NOT KNOW THAT YOU ARE DESTINED FOR THIS?! YOUR BLOOD SHALL BE THE CATALYST THAT BLAH BLAH
WHAT'S THAT GUY SAYING?
WHAT? IT'S REALLY HARD TO HEAR YOU FROM DOWN HERE!
I SAID: FOOLS! DO YOU NOT KNOW THAT YOU ARE DESTINED FOR THIS?! YOUR BLOOD SHALL BE THE CATALYST THAT--

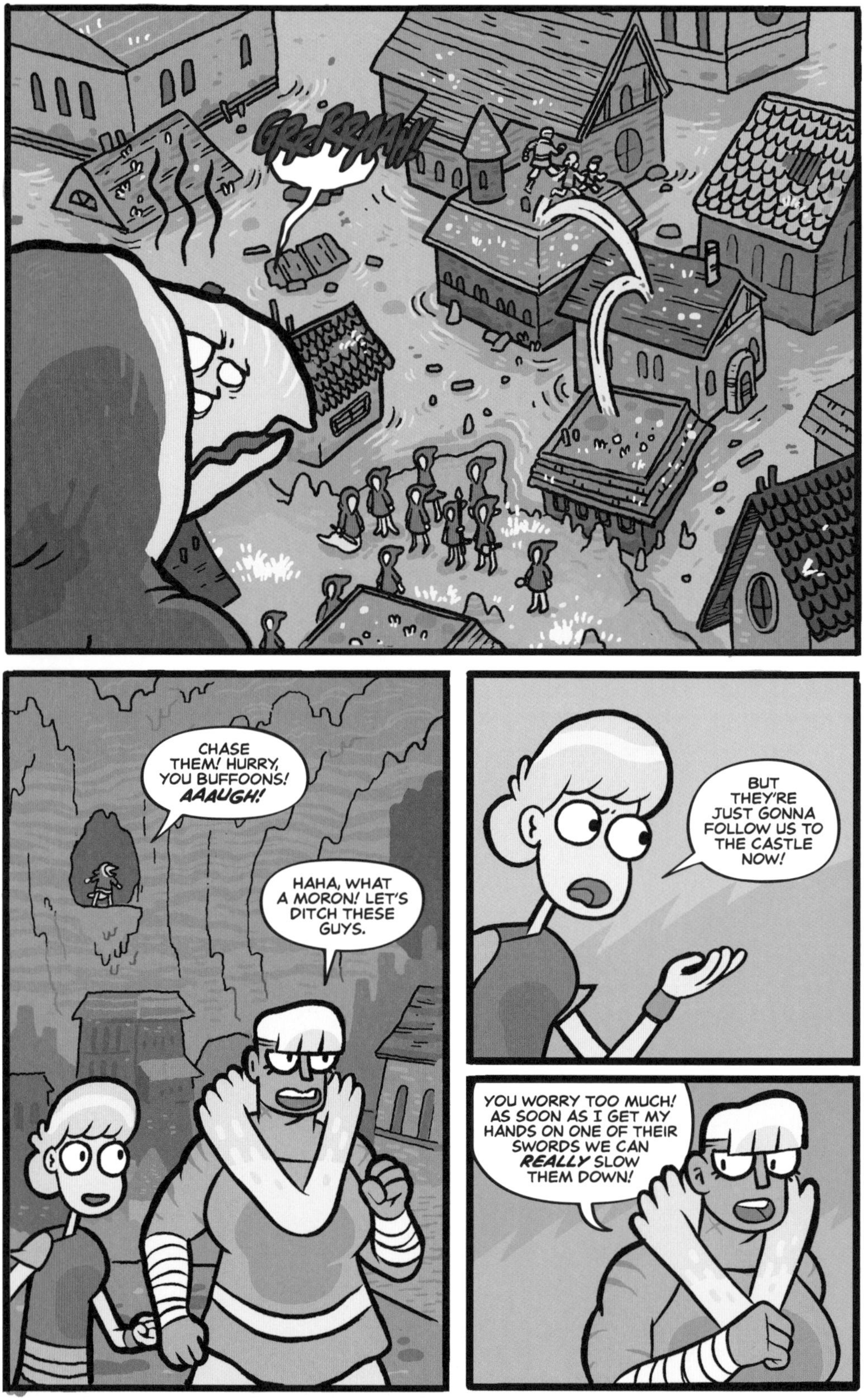
GRRRAAH!
CHASE THEM! HURRY, YOU BUFFOONS! ***AAAUGH!***
HAHA, WHAT A MORON! LET'S DITCH THESE GUYS.
BUT THEY'RE JUST GONNA FOLLOW US TO THE CASTLE NOW!
YOU WORRY TOO MUCH! AS SOON AS I GET MY HANDS ON ONE OF THEIR SWORDS WE CAN ***REALLY*** SLOW THEM DOWN!

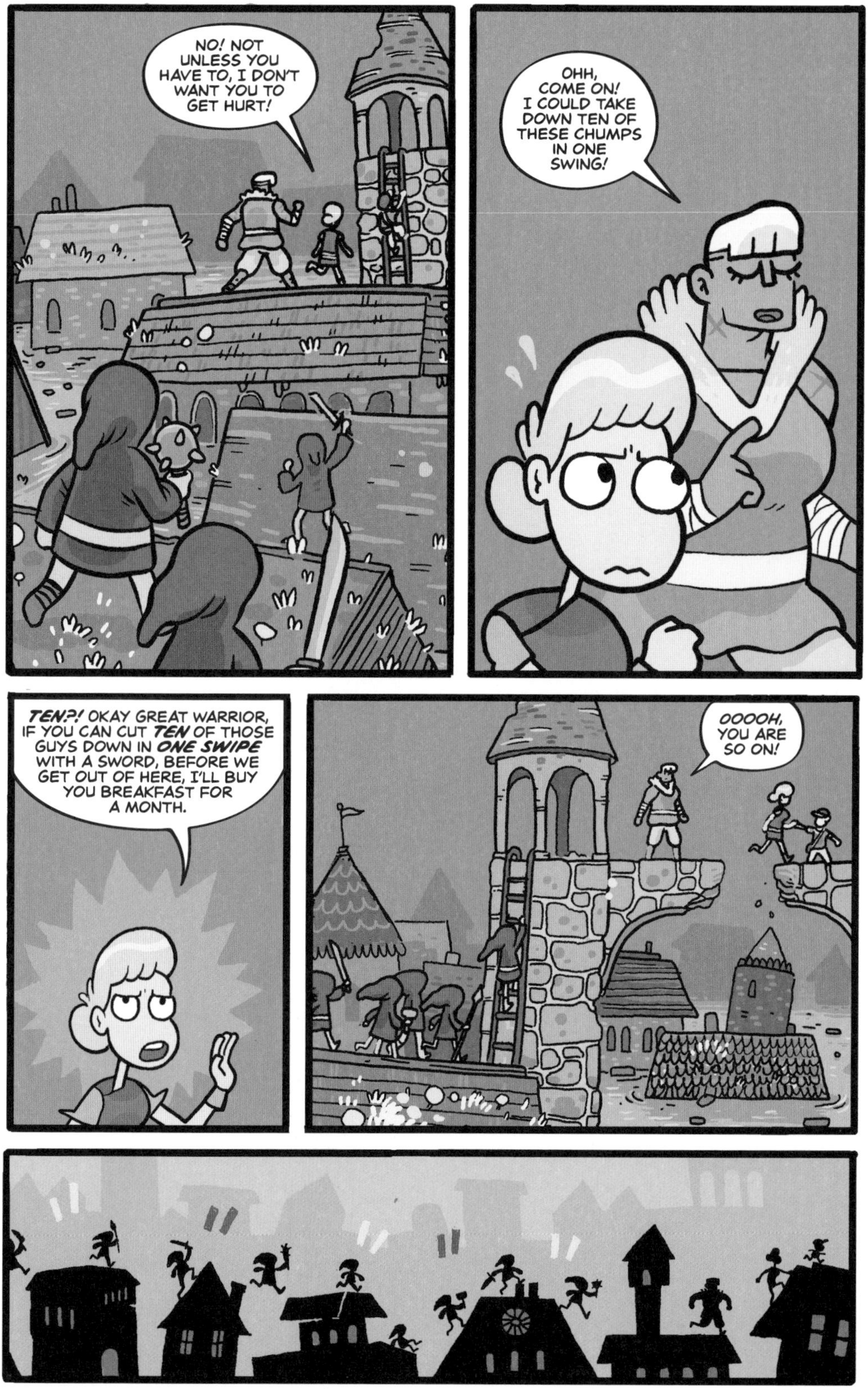
NO! NOT UNLESS YOU HAVE TO, I DON'T WANT YOU TO GET HURT!
OHH, COME ON! I COULD TAKE DOWN TEN OF THESE CHUMPS IN ONE SWING!
TEN?! OKAY GREAT WARRIOR, IF YOU CAN CUT TEN OF THOSE GUYS DOWN IN ONE SWIPE WITH A SWORD, BEFORE WE GET OUT OF HERE, I'LL BUY YOU BREAKFAST FOR A MONTH.
OOOOH, YOU ARE SO ON!

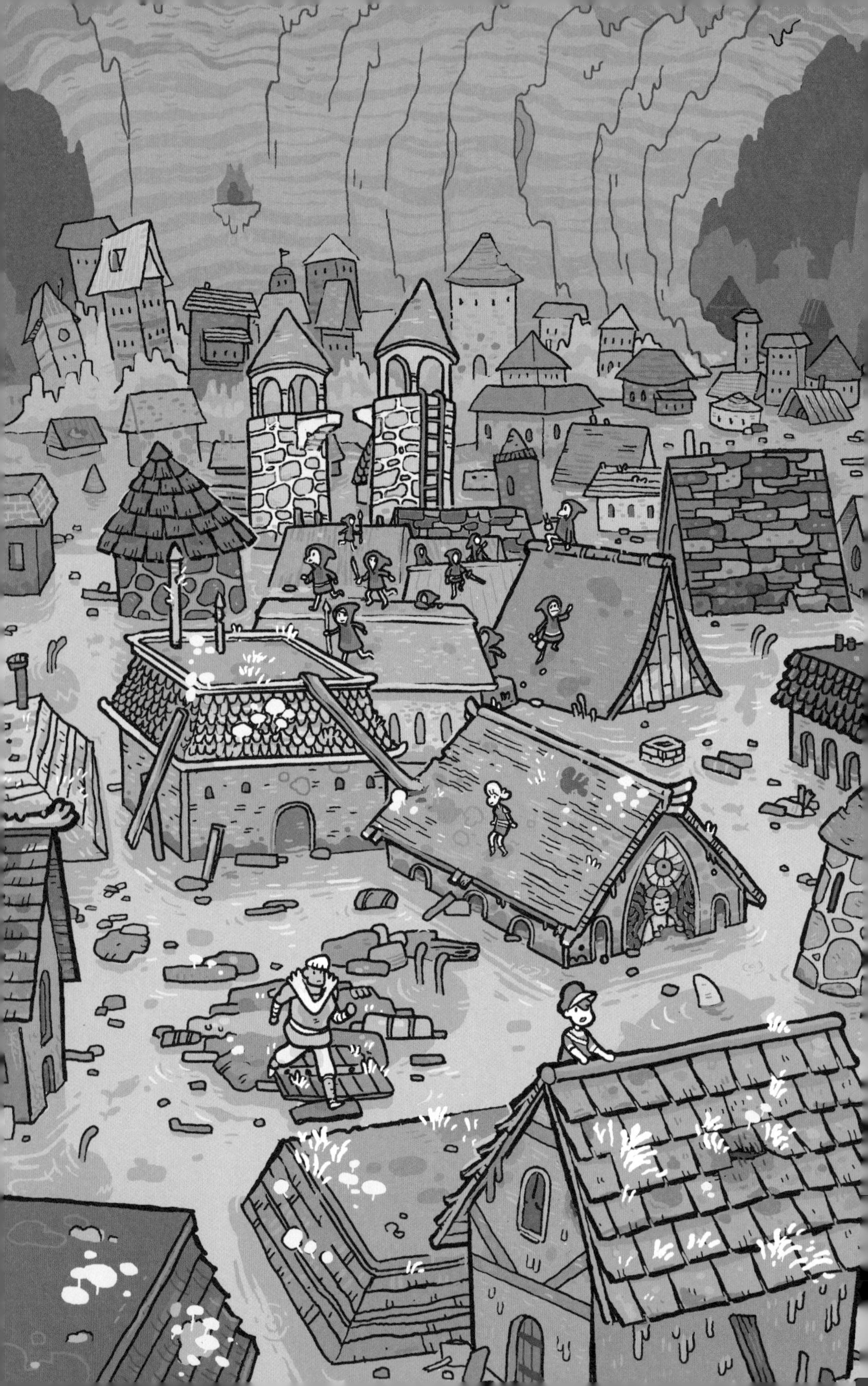

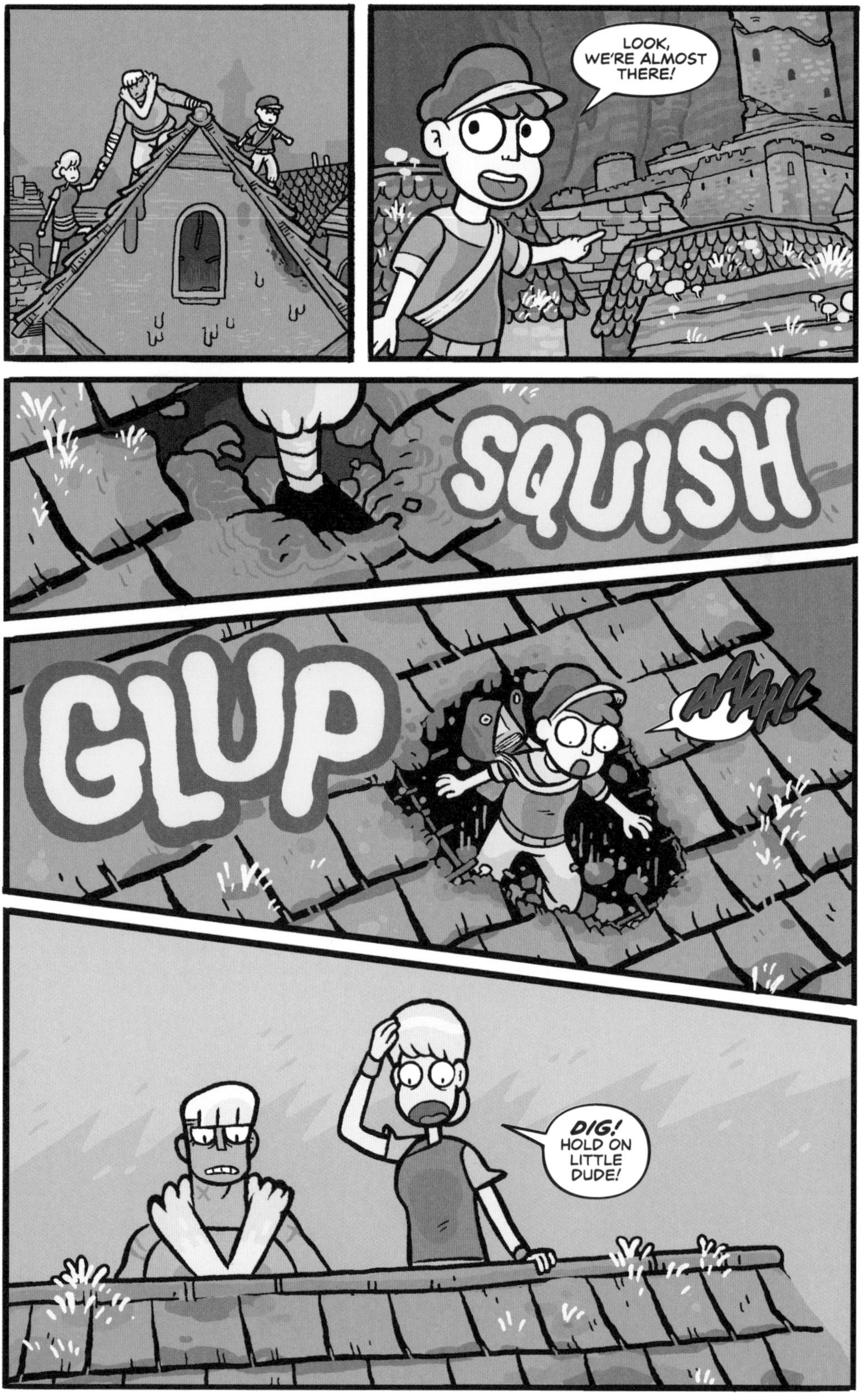
LOOK, WE'RE ALMOST THERE!
SQUISH
GLUP
AAAAH!
DIG! HOLD ON LITTLE DUDE!

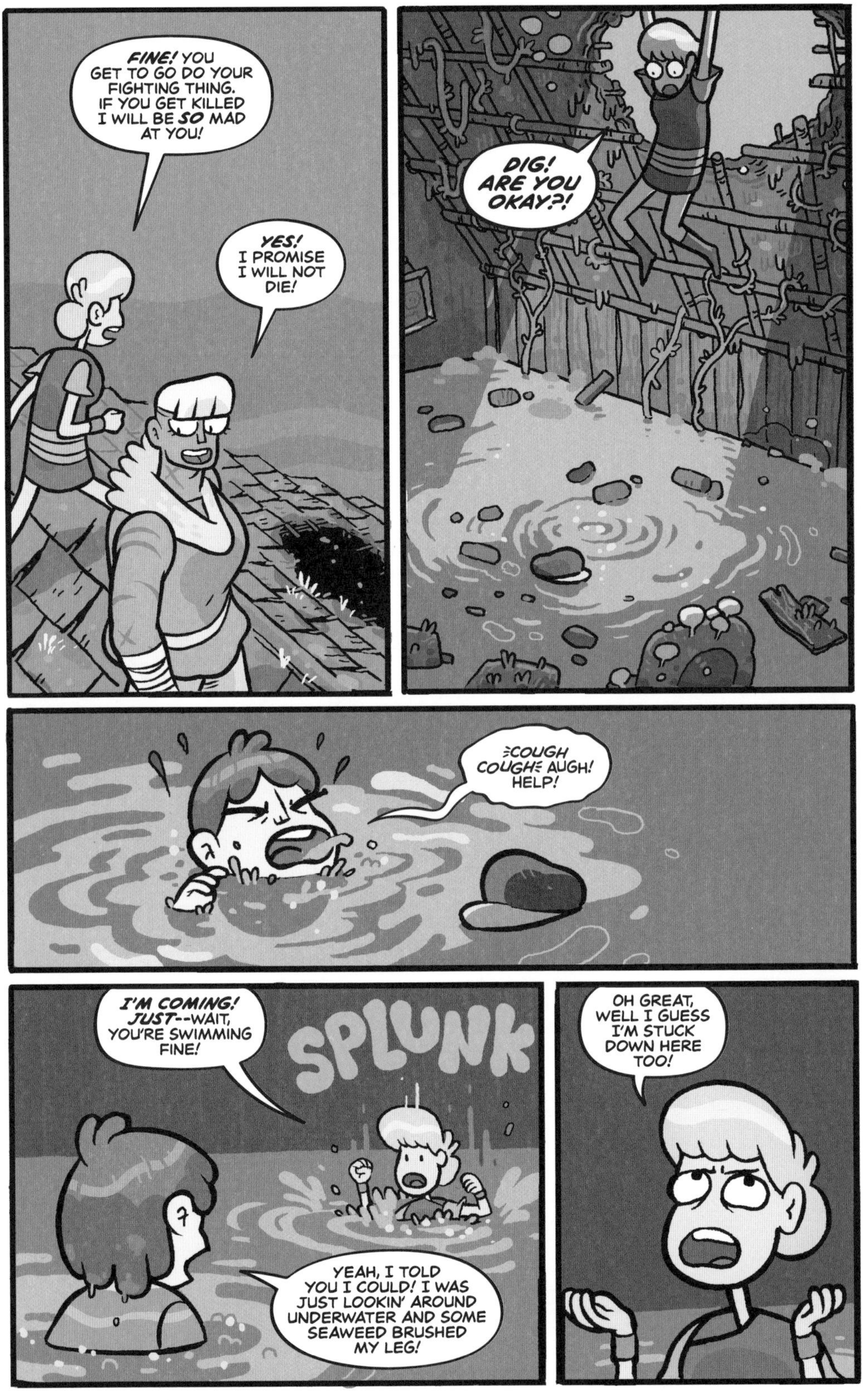

FINE! YOU GET TO GO DO YOUR FIGHTING THING. IF YOU GET KILLED I WILL BE SO MAD AT YOU!
YES! I PROMISE I WILL NOT DIE!
DIG! ARE YOU OKAY?!
COUGH COUGH AUGH! HELP!
I'M COMING! JUST--WAIT, YOU'RE SWIMMING FINE!
SPLUNK
YEAH, I TOLD YOU I COULD! I WAS JUST LOOKIN' AROUND UNDERWATER AND SOME SEAWEED BRUSHED MY LEG!
OH GREAT, WELL I GUESS I'M STUCK DOWN HERE TOO!

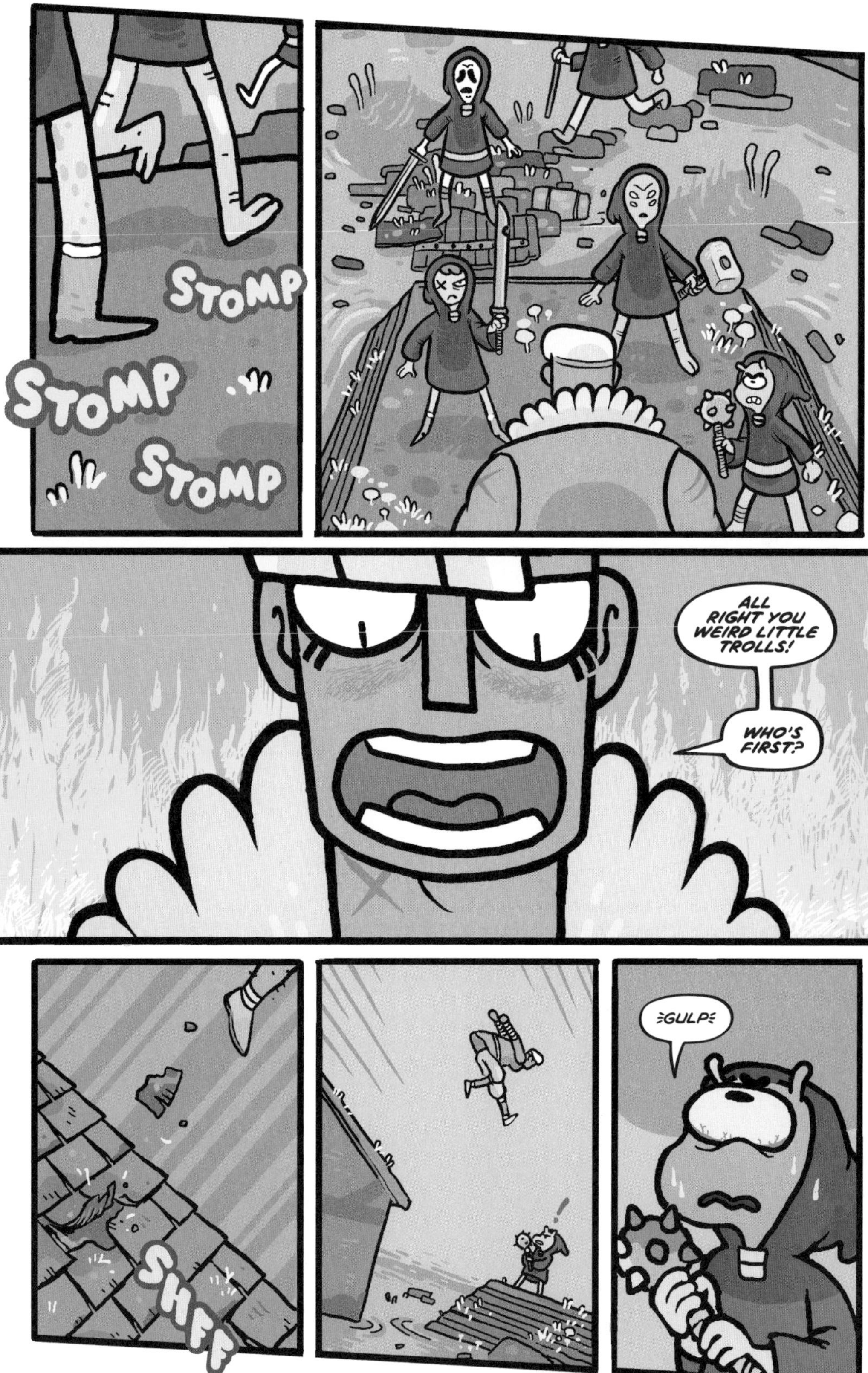
STOMP
STOMP
STOMP
ALL RIGHT YOU WEIRD LITTLE TROLLS!
WHO'S FIRST?
SHFF
GULP

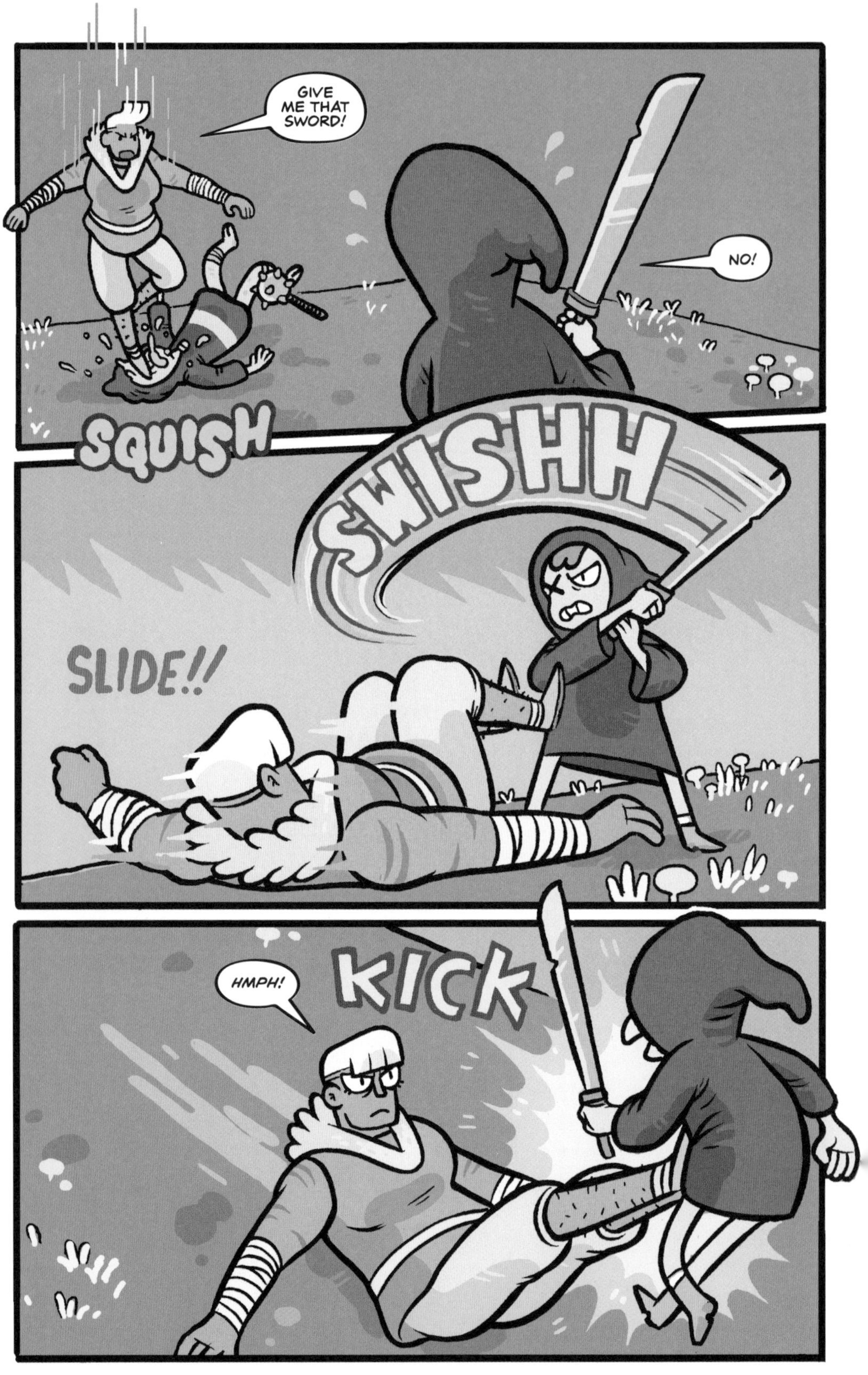
GIVE ME THAT SWORD!
NO!
SQUISH
SWISHH
SLIDE!!
HMPH!
KICK

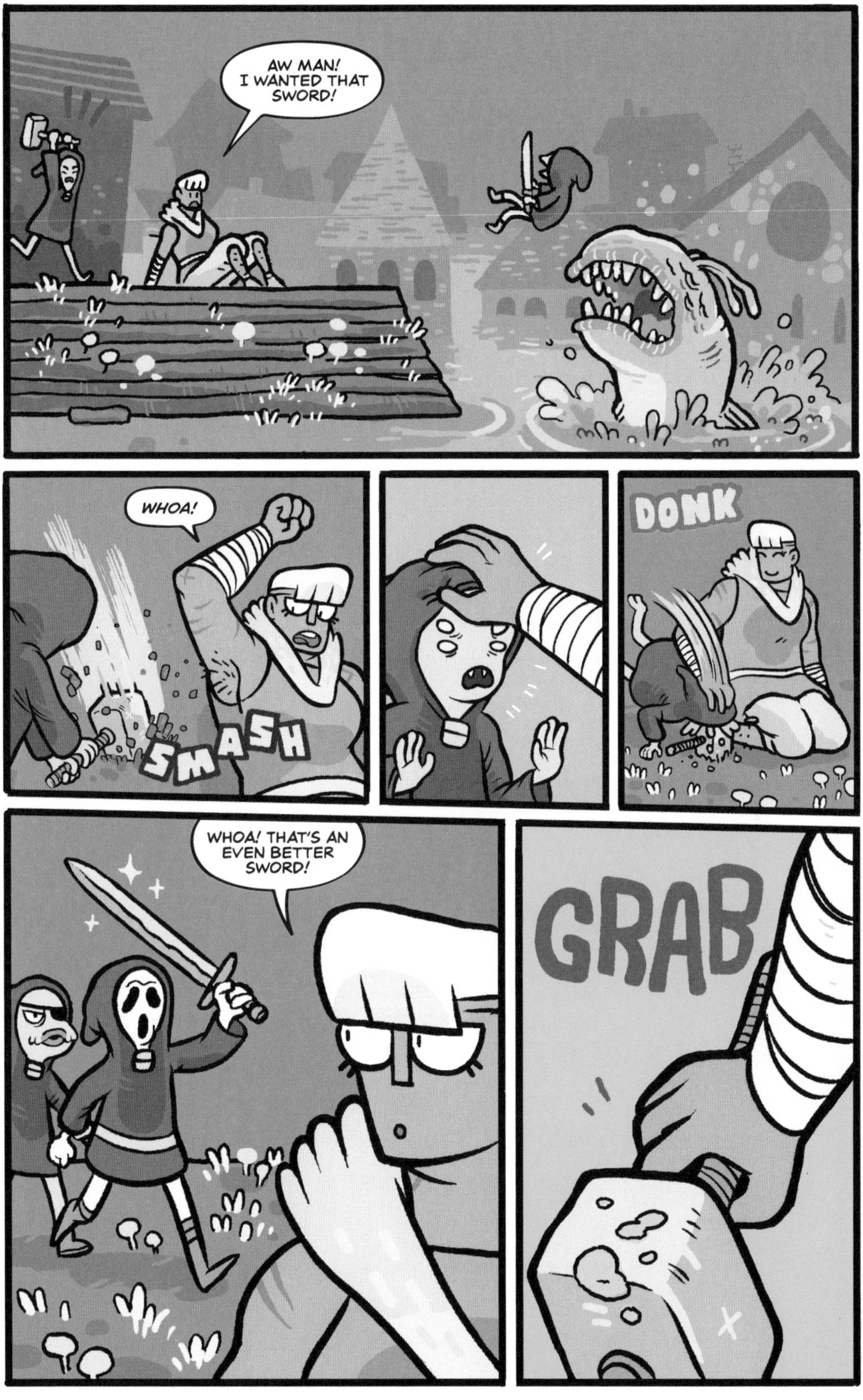
AW MAN! I WANTED THAT SWORD!
WHOA!
SMASH
DONK
WHOA! THAT'S AN EVEN BETTER SWORD!
GRAB

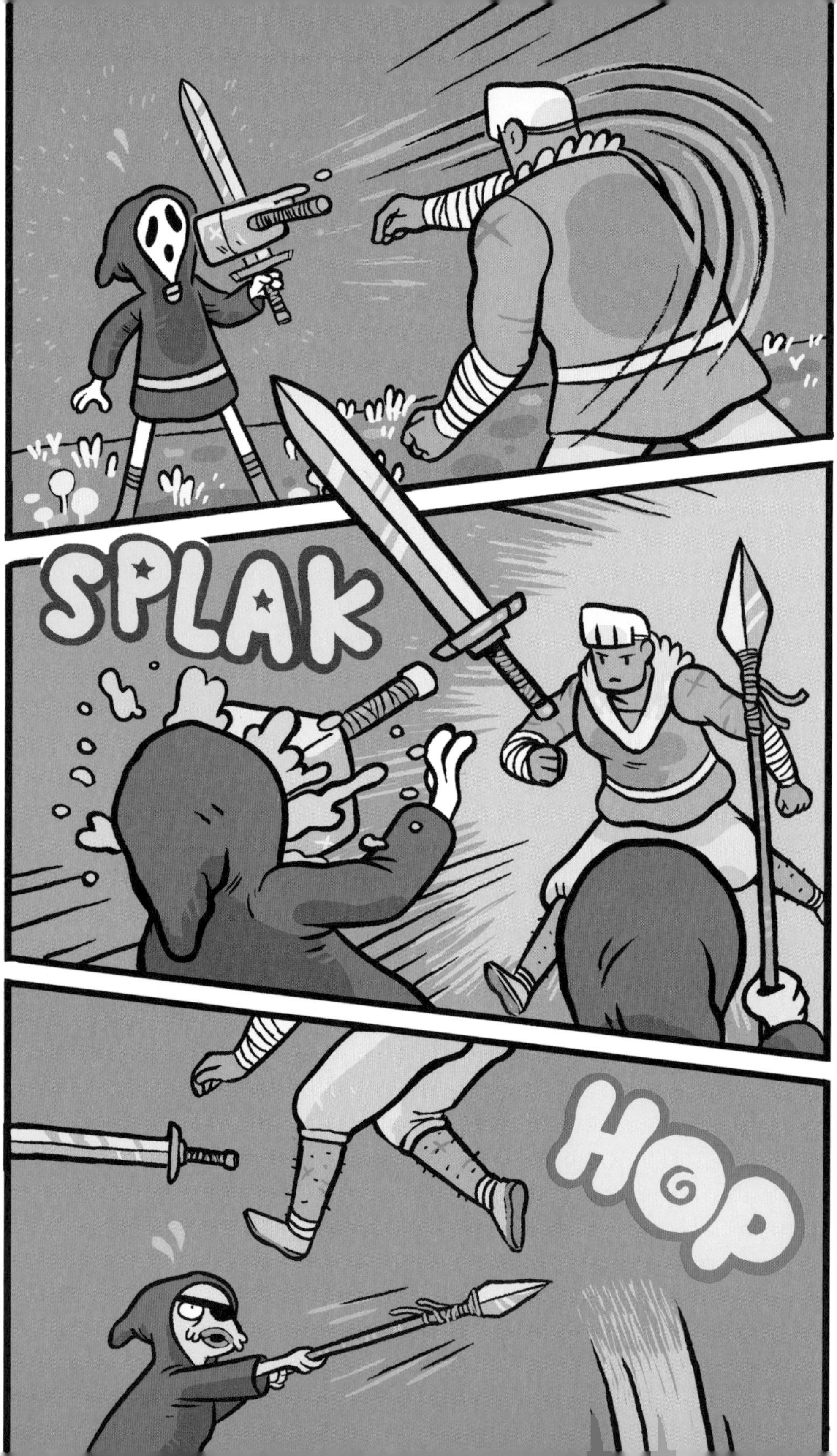
SPLAK
HOP

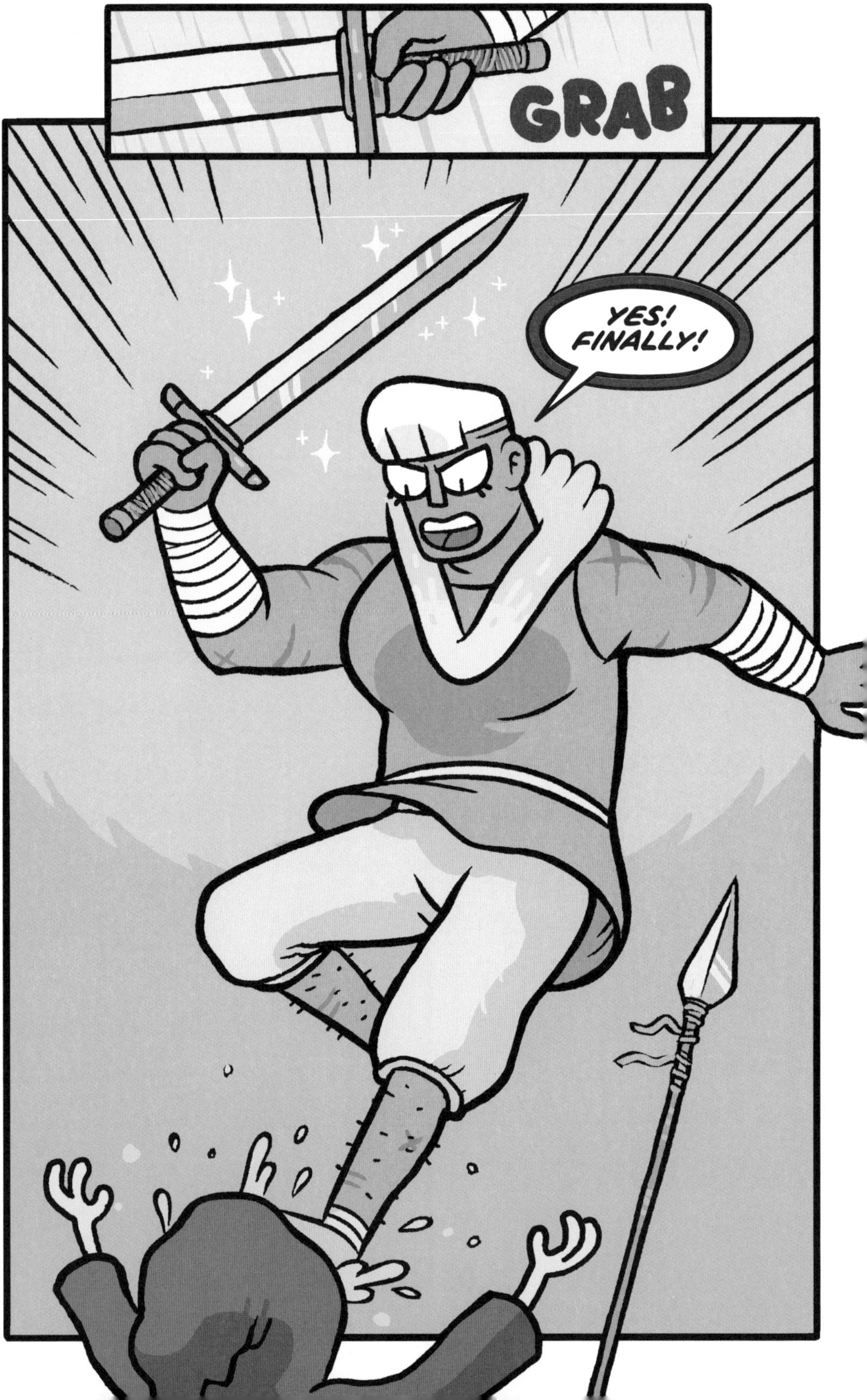
GRAB
YES! FINALLY!

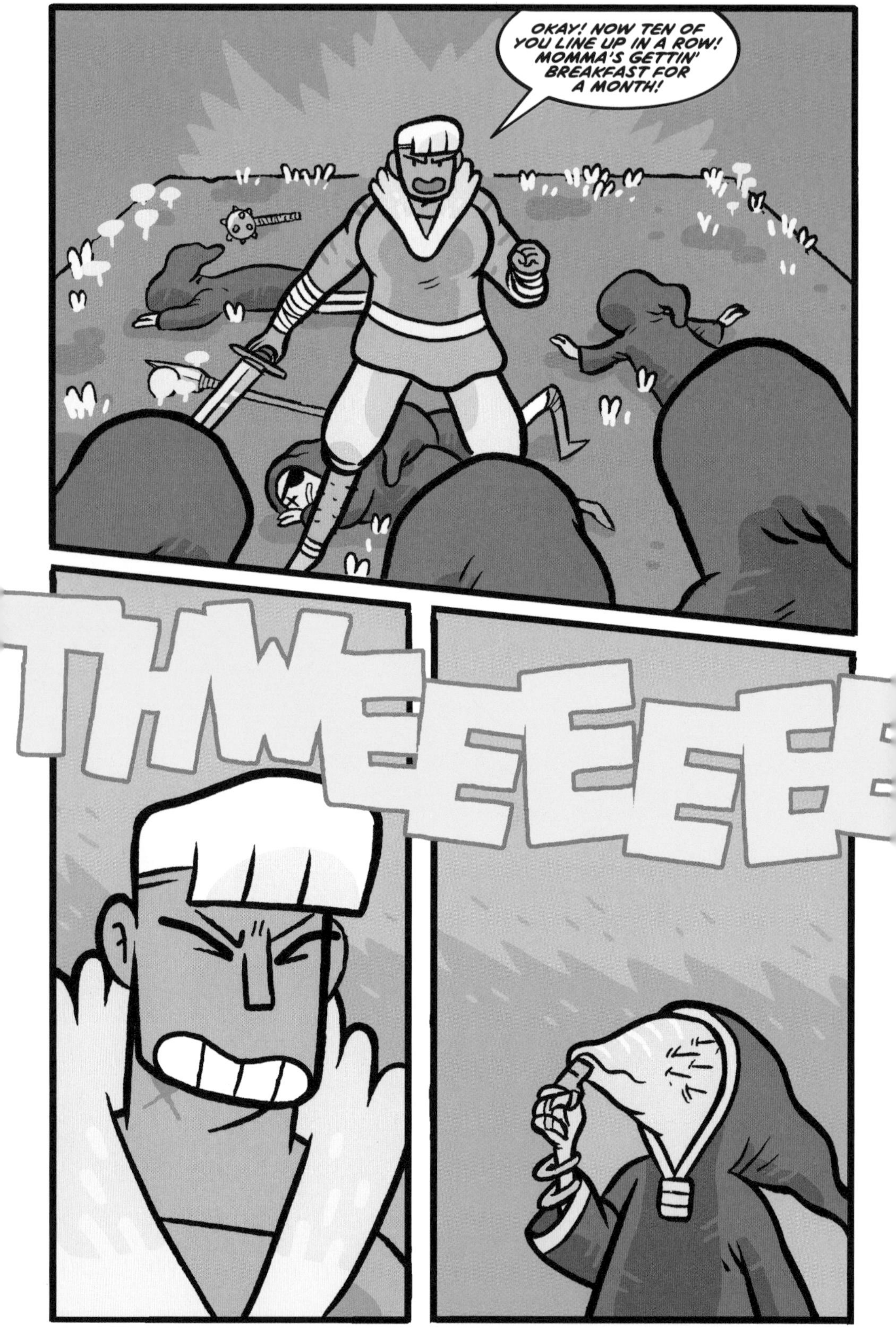
OKAY! NOW TEN OF YOU LINE UP IN A ROW! MOMMA'S GETTIN' BREAKFAST FOR A MONTH!
THWEEEEE

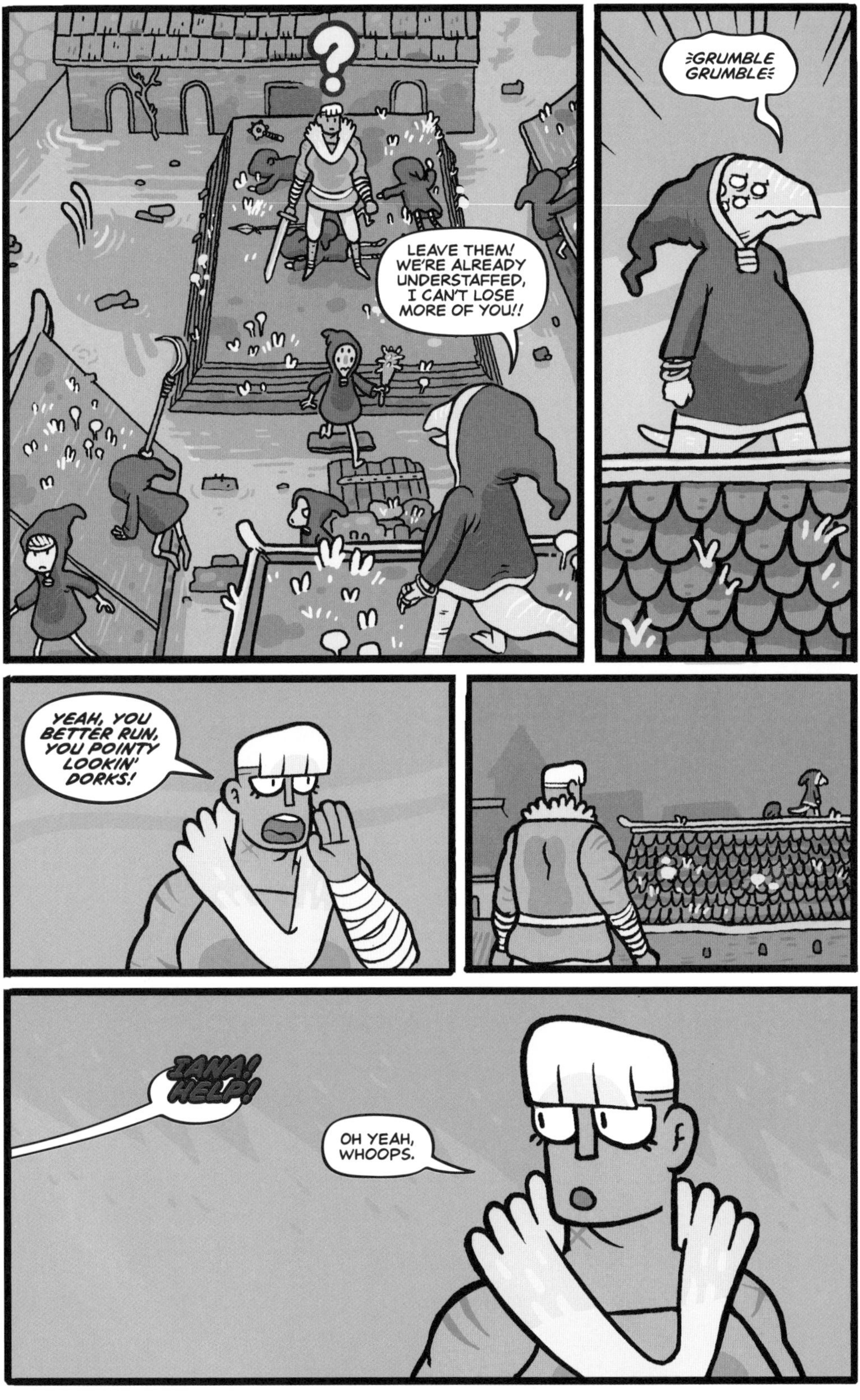
?
LEAVE THEM! WE'RE ALREADY UNDERSTAFFED, I CAN'T LOSE MORE OF YOU!!
GRUMBLE GRUMBLE
YEAH, YOU BETTER RUN, YOU POINTY LOOKIN' DORKS!
IANA! HELP!
OH YEAH, WHOOPS.

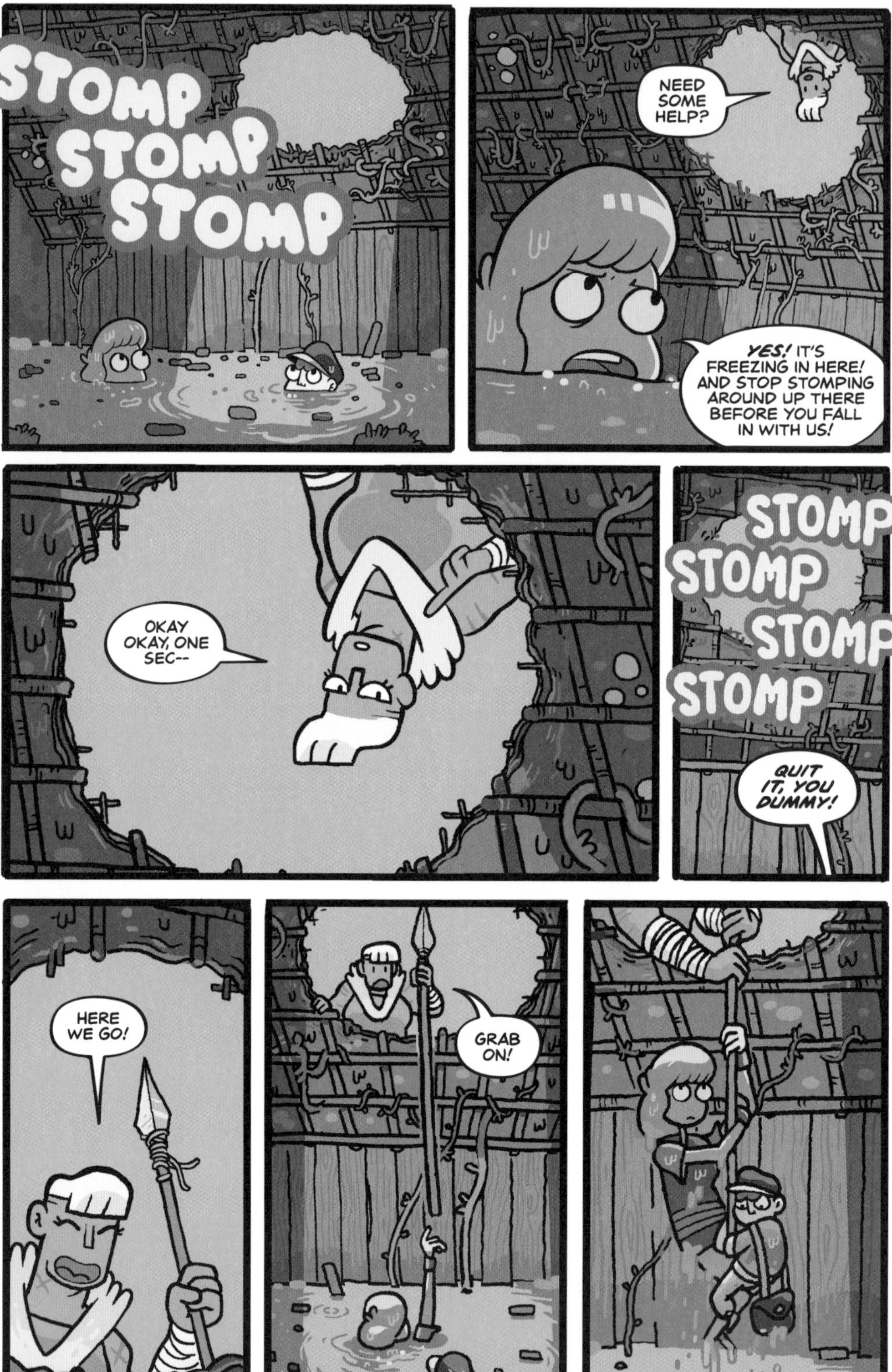
STOMP
STOMP
STOMP
NEED SOME HELP?
YES! IT'S FREEZING IN HERE! AND STOP STOMPING AROUND UP THERE BEFORE YOU FALL IN WITH US!
OKAY OKAY, ONE SEC--
STOMP
STOMP
STOMP
STOMP
QUIT IT, YOU DUMMY!
HERE WE GO!
GRAB ON!

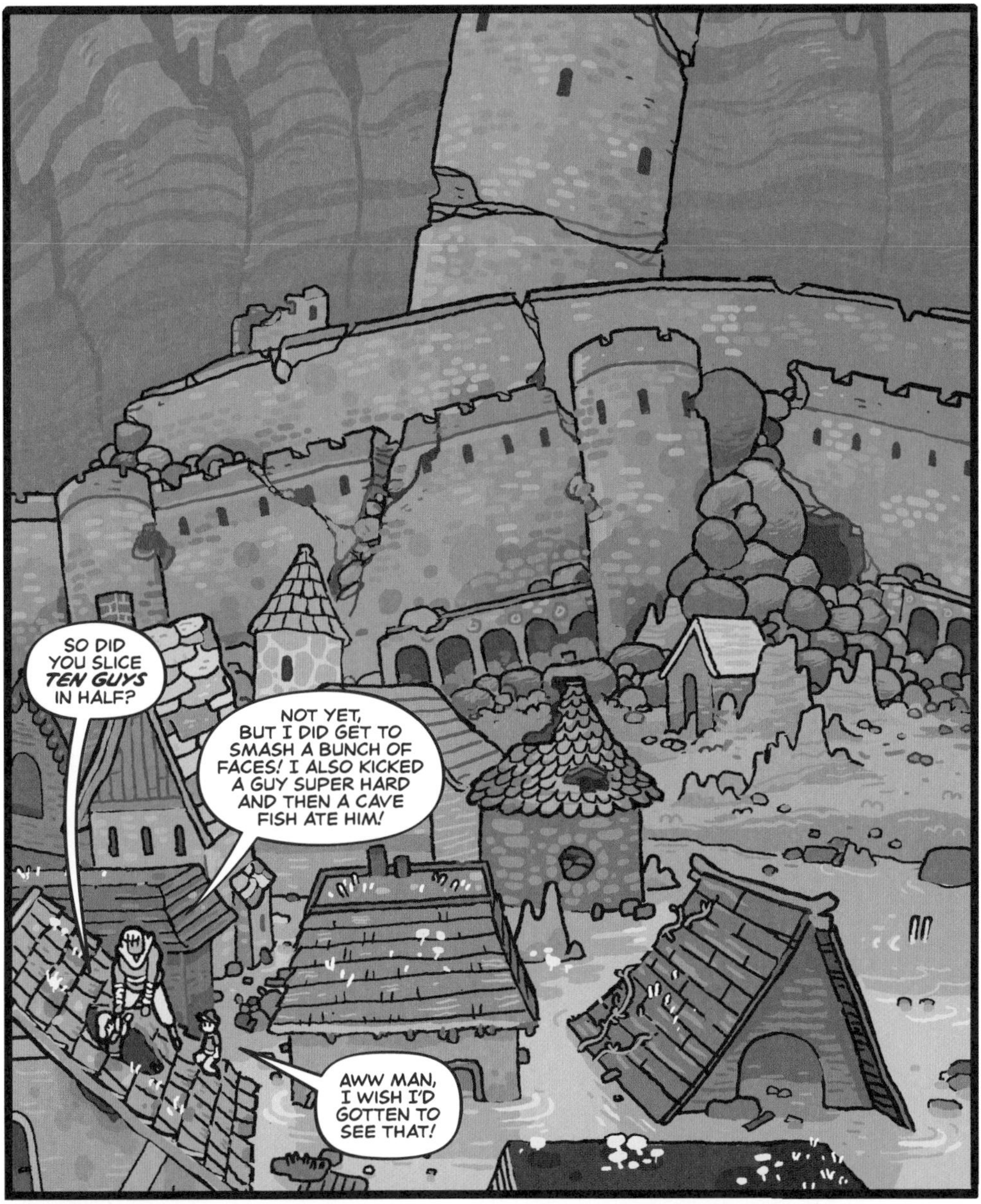
SO DID YOU SLICE ***TEN GUYS*** IN HALF?
NOT YET, BUT I DID GET TO SMASH A BUNCH OF FACES! I ALSO KICKED A GUY SUPER HARD AND THEN A CAVE FISH ATE HIM!
AWW MAN, I WISH I'D GOTTEN TO SEE THAT!

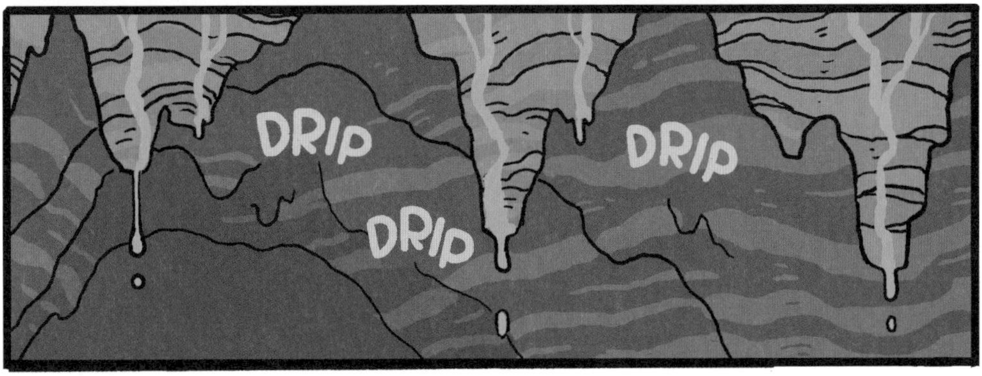
DRIP
DRIP
DRIP

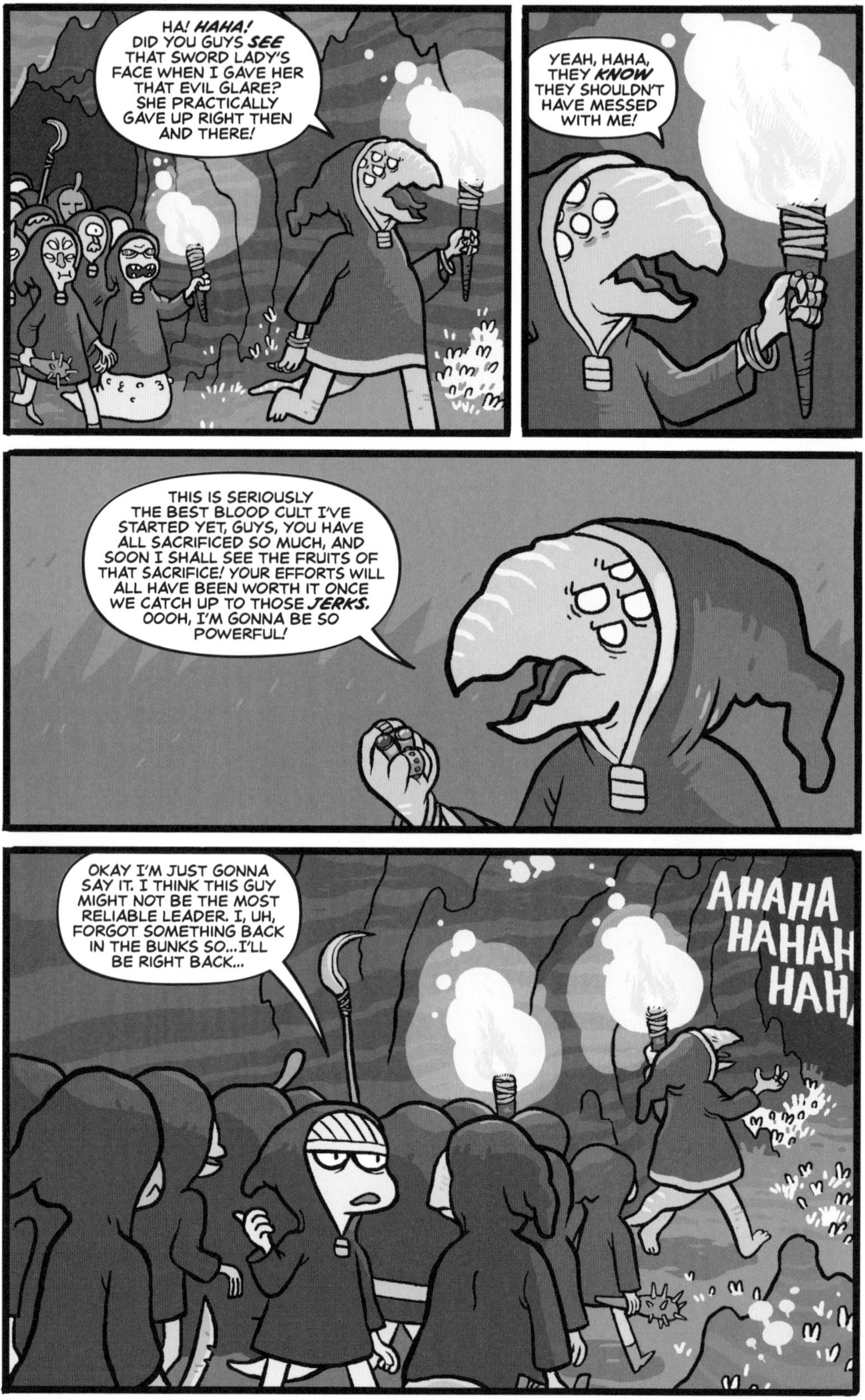
HA! HAHA! DID YOU GUYS SEE THAT SWORD LADY'S FACE WHEN I GAVE HER THAT EVIL GLARE? SHE PRACTICALLY GAVE UP RIGHT THEN AND THERE!
YEAH, HAHA, THEY KNOW THEY SHOULDN'T HAVE MESSED WITH ME!
THIS IS SERIOUSLY THE BEST BLOOD CULT I'VE STARTED YET, GUYS, YOU HAVE ALL SACRIFICED SO MUCH, AND SOON I SHALL SEE THE FRUITS OF THAT SACRIFICE! YOUR EFFORTS WILL ALL HAVE BEEN WORTH IT ONCE WE CATCH UP TO THOSE JERKS. OOOH, I'M GONNA BE SO POWERFUL!
OKAY I'M JUST GONNA SAY IT. I THINK THIS GUY MIGHT NOT BE THE MOST RELIABLE LEADER. I, UH, FORGOT SOMETHING BACK IN THE BUNKS SO...I'LL BE RIGHT BACK...
AHAHA HAHAH HAH

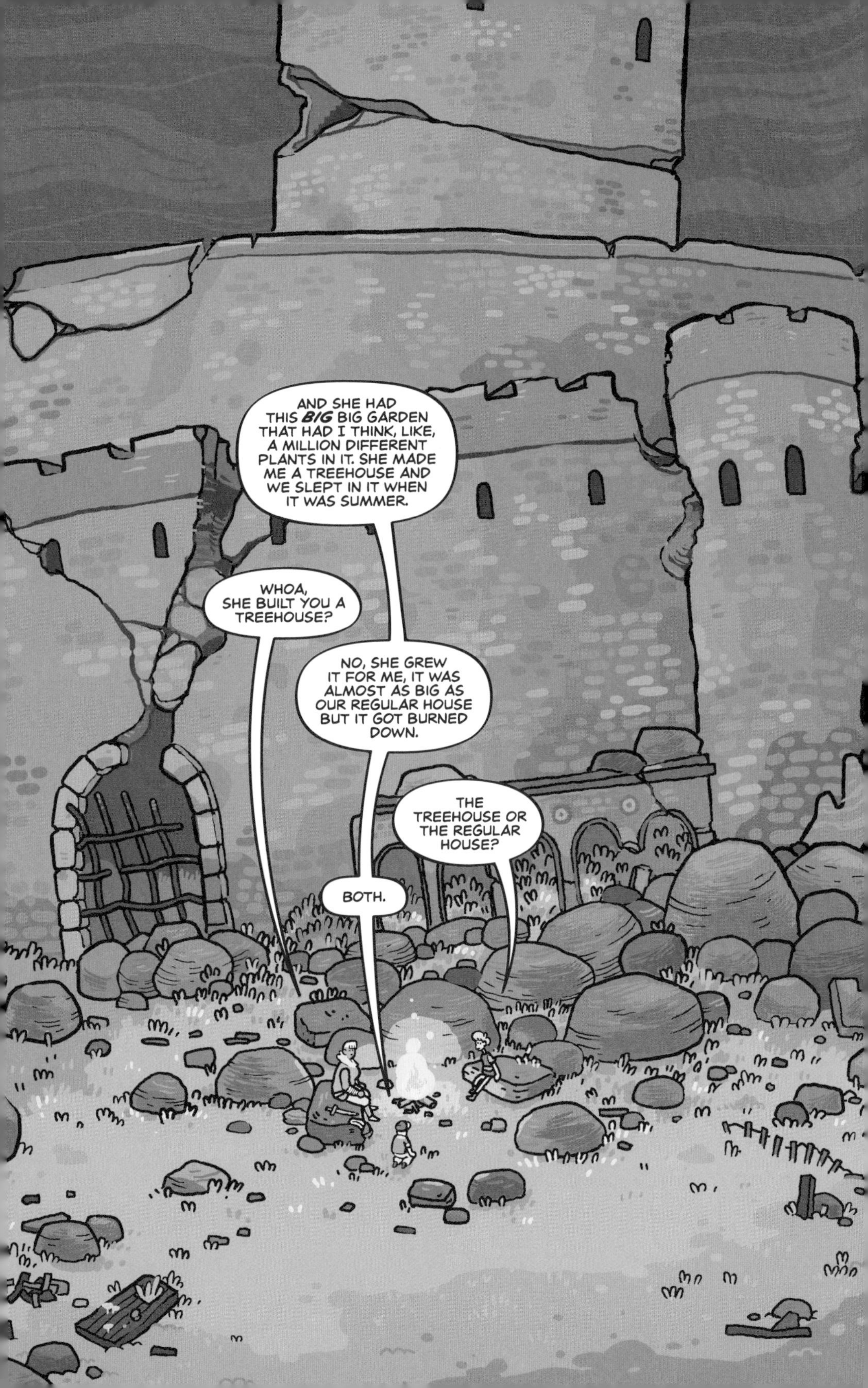
AND SHE HAD THIS *BIG* BIG GARDEN THAT HAD I THINK, LIKE, A MILLION DIFFERENT PLANTS IN IT. SHE MADE ME A TREEHOUSE AND WE SLEPT IN IT WHEN IT WAS SUMMER.
WHOA, SHE BUILT YOU A TREEHOUSE?
NO, SHE GREW IT FOR ME, IT WAS ALMOST AS BIG AS OUR REGULAR HOUSE BUT IT GOT BURNED DOWN.
THE TREEHOUSE OR THE REGULAR HOUSE?
BOTH.

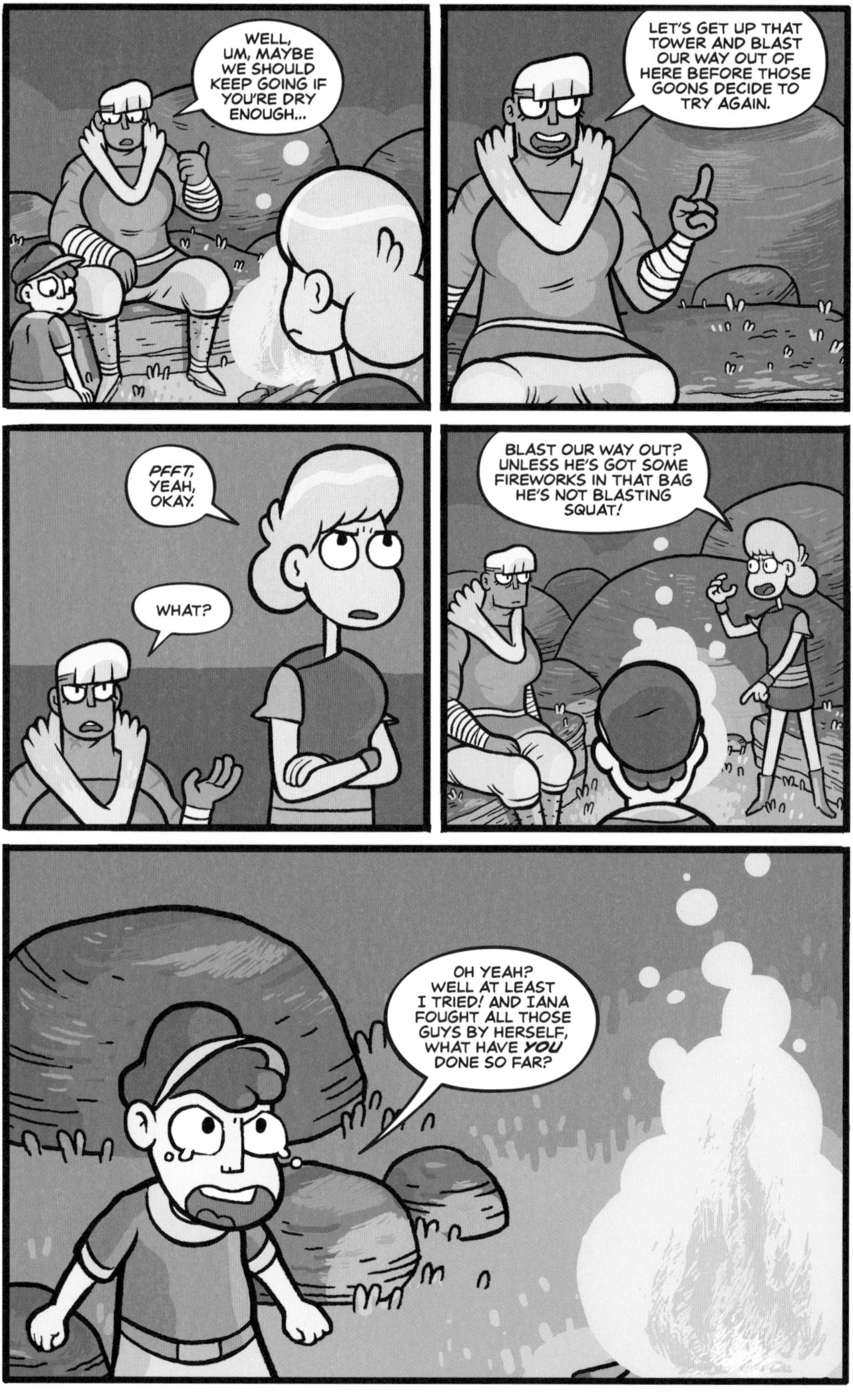
WELL, UM, MAYBE WE SHOULD KEEP GOING IF YOU'RE DRY ENOUGH...
LET'S GET UP THAT TOWER AND BLAST OUR WAY OUT OF HERE BEFORE THOSE GOONS DECIDE TO TRY AGAIN.
PFFT, YEAH, OKAY.
WHAT?
BLAST OUR WAY OUT? UNLESS HE'S GOT SOME FIREWORKS IN THAT BAG HE'S NOT BLASTING SQUAT!
OH YEAH? WELL AT LEAST I TRIED! AND IANA FOUGHT ALL THOSE GUYS BY HERSELF, WHAT HAVE ***YOU*** DONE SO FAR?

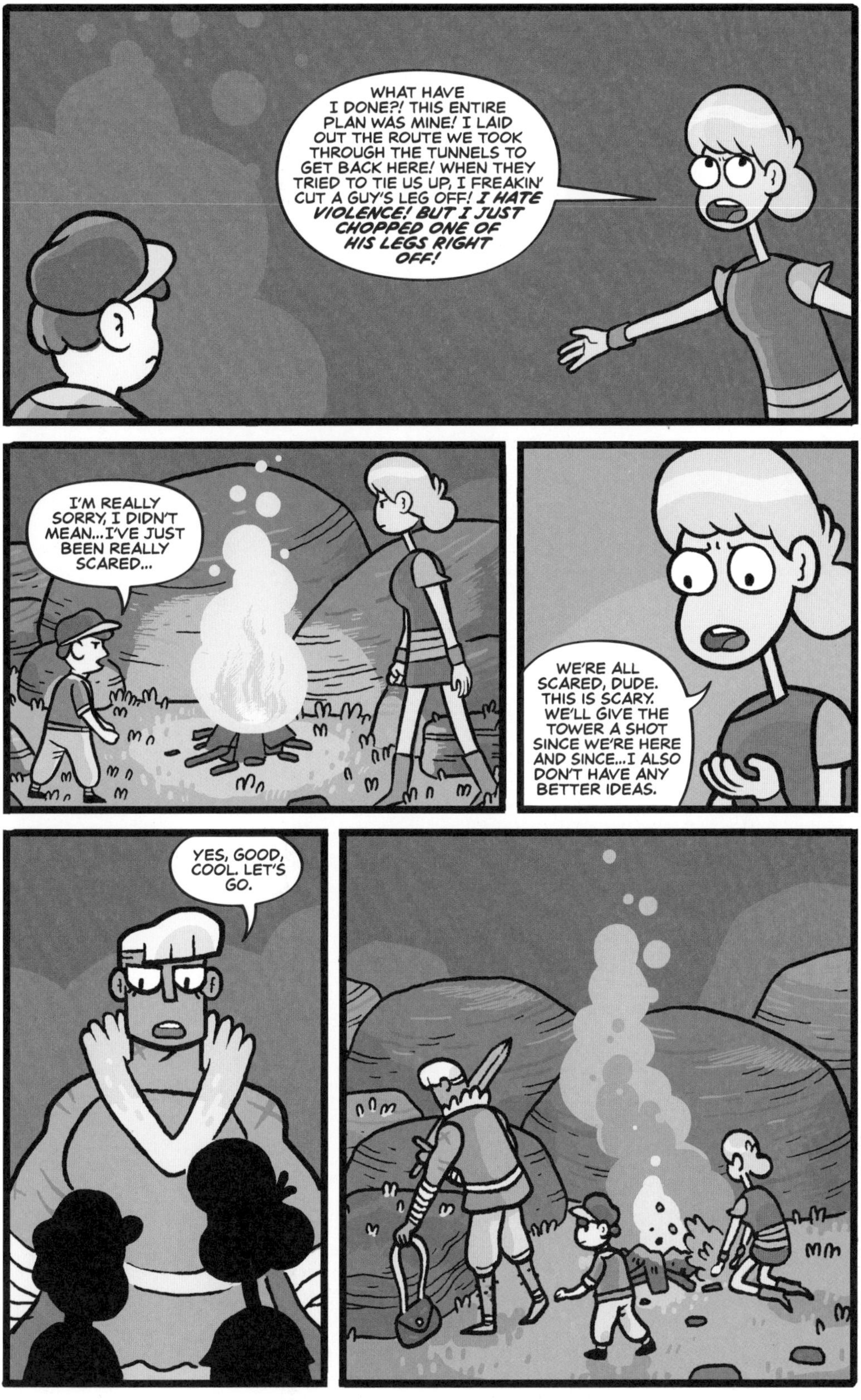
WHAT HAVE I DONE?! THIS ENTIRE PLAN WAS MINE! I LAID OUT THE ROUTE WE TOOK THROUGH THE TUNNELS TO GET BACK HERE! WHEN THEY TRIED TO TIE US UP, I FREAKIN' CUT A GUY'S LEG OFF! I HATE VIOLENCE! BUT I JUST CHOPPED ONE OF HIS LEGS RIGHT OFF!
I'M REALLY SORRY, I DIDN'T MEAN...I'VE JUST BEEN REALLY SCARED...
WE'RE ALL SCARED, DUDE. THIS IS SCARY. WE'LL GIVE THE TOWER A SHOT SINCE WE'RE HERE AND SINCE...I ALSO DON'T HAVE ANY BETTER IDEAS.
YES, GOOD, COOL. LET'S GO.

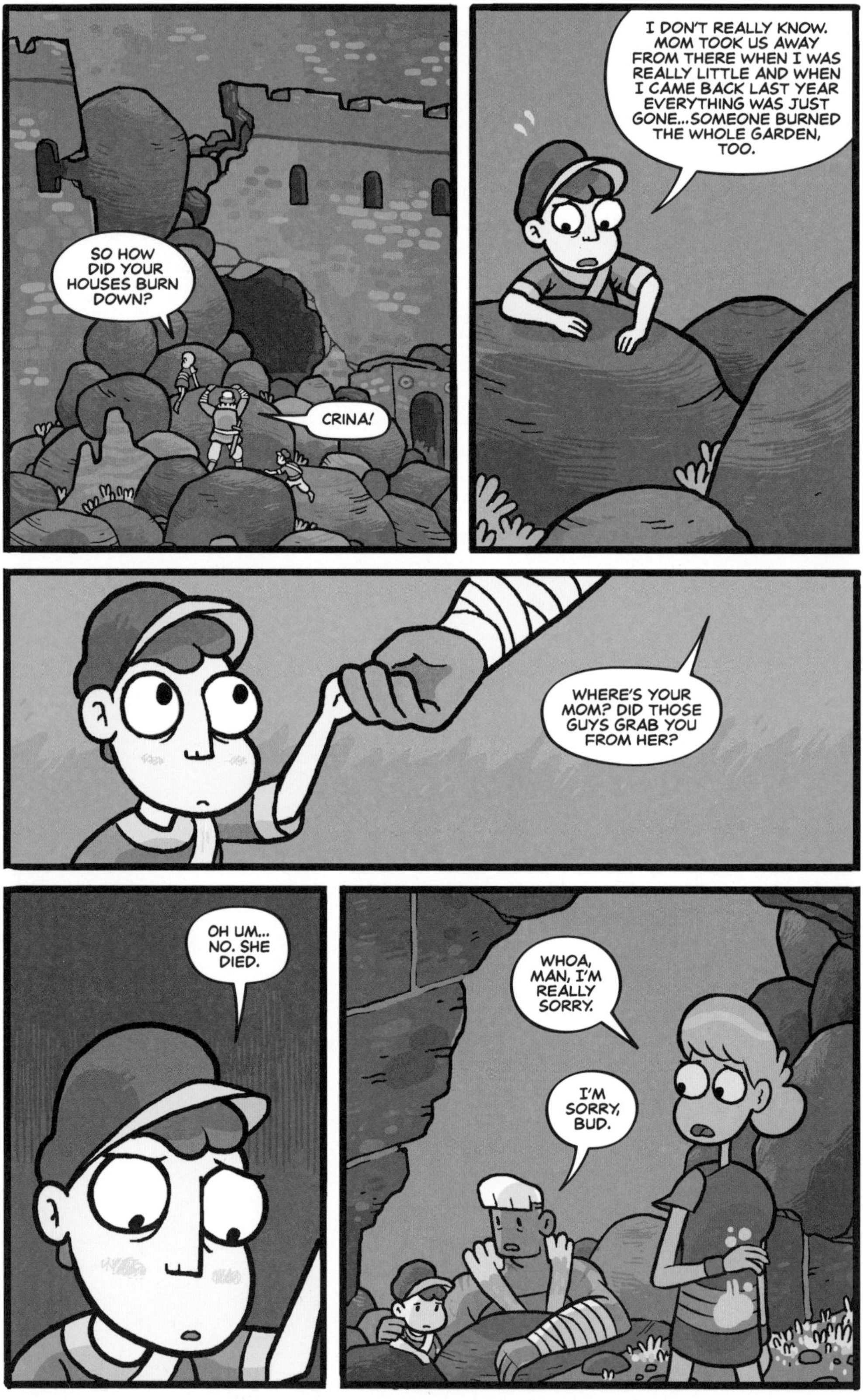
SO HOW DID YOUR HOUSES BURN DOWN?
CRINA!
I DON'T REALLY KNOW. MOM TOOK US AWAY FROM THERE WHEN I WAS REALLY LITTLE AND WHEN I CAME BACK LAST YEAR EVERYTHING WAS JUST GONE...SOMEONE BURNED THE WHOLE GARDEN, TOO.
WHERE'S YOUR MOM? DID THOSE GUYS GRAB YOU FROM HER?
OH UM... NO. SHE DIED.
WHOA, MAN, I'M REALLY SORRY.
I'M SORRY, BUD.

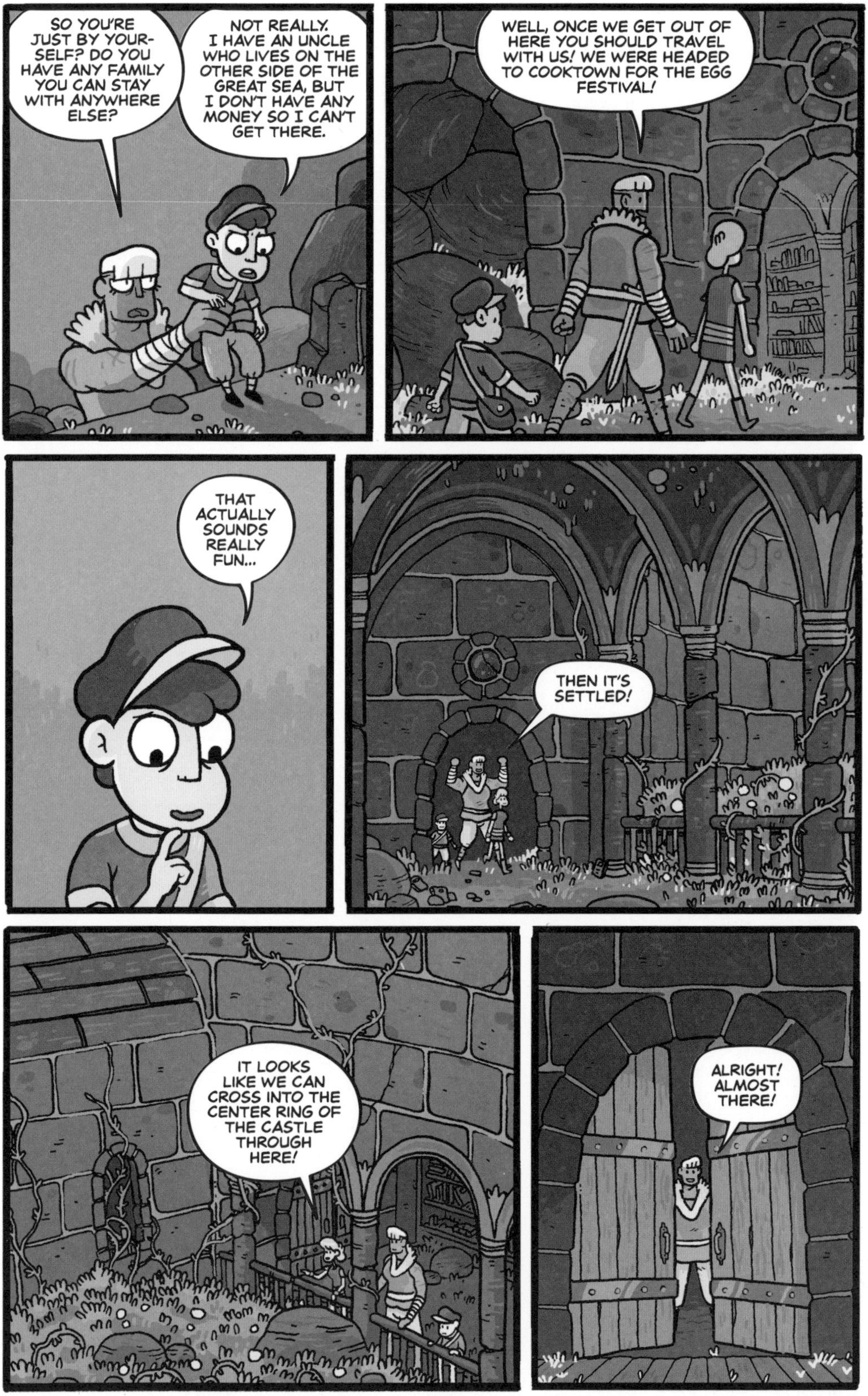
SO YOU'RE JUST BY YOURSELF? DO YOU HAVE ANY FAMILY YOU CAN STAY WITH ANYWHERE ELSE?
NOT REALLY. I HAVE AN UNCLE WHO LIVES ON THE OTHER SIDE OF THE GREAT SEA, BUT I DON'T HAVE ANY MONEY SO I CAN'T GET THERE.
WELL, ONCE WE GET OUT OF HERE YOU SHOULD TRAVEL WITH US! WE WERE HEADED TO COOKTOWN FOR THE EGG FESTIVAL!
THAT ACTUALLY SOUNDS REALLY FUN...
THEN IT'S SETTLED!
IT LOOKS LIKE WE CAN CROSS INTO THE CENTER RING OF THE CASTLE THROUGH HERE!
ALRIGHT! ALMOST THERE!

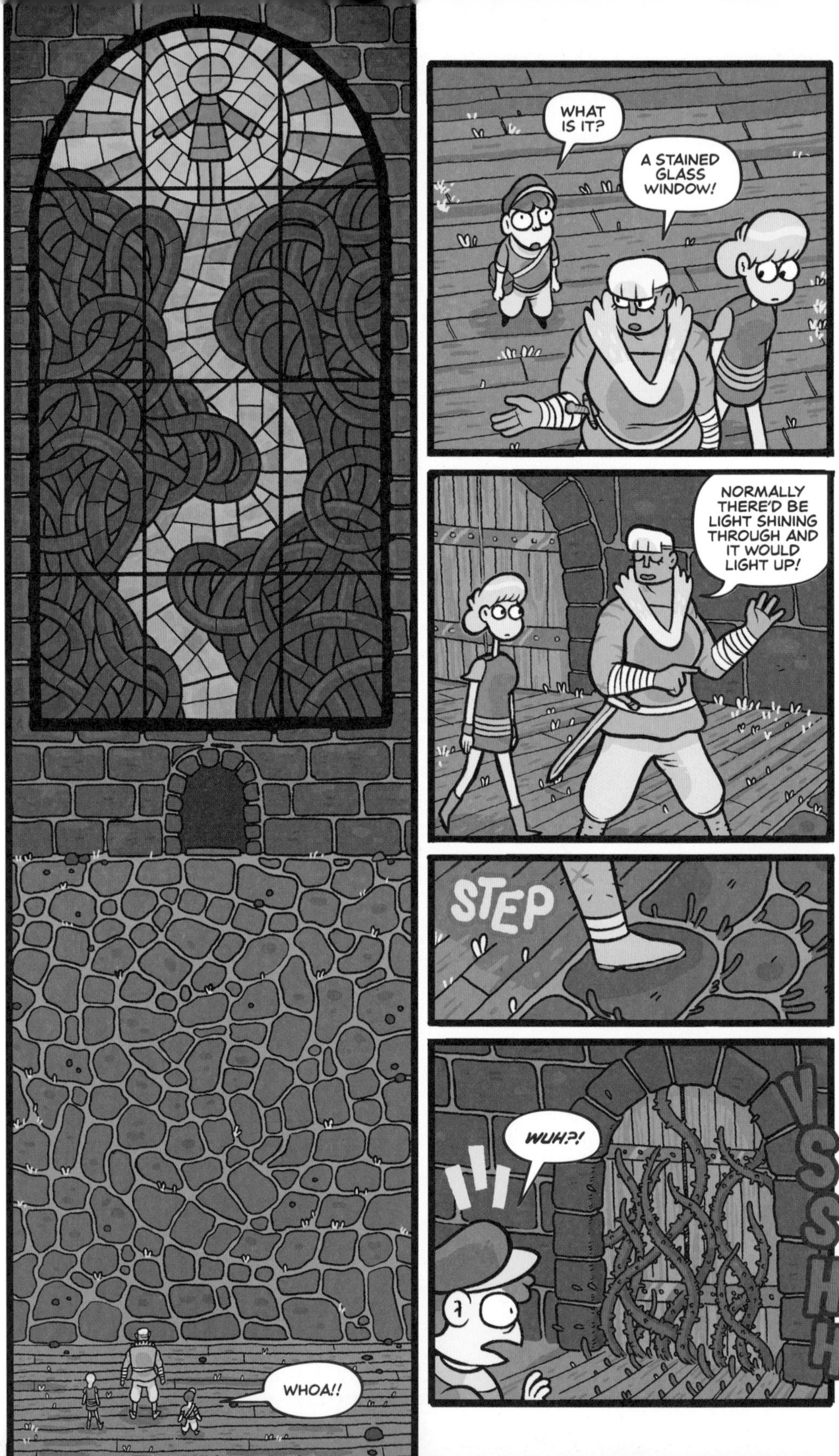
WHOA!!
WHAT IS IT?
A STAINED GLASS WINDOW!
NORMALLY THERE'D BE LIGHT SHINING THROUGH AND IT WOULD LIGHT UP!
STEP
WUH?!
VSSHH

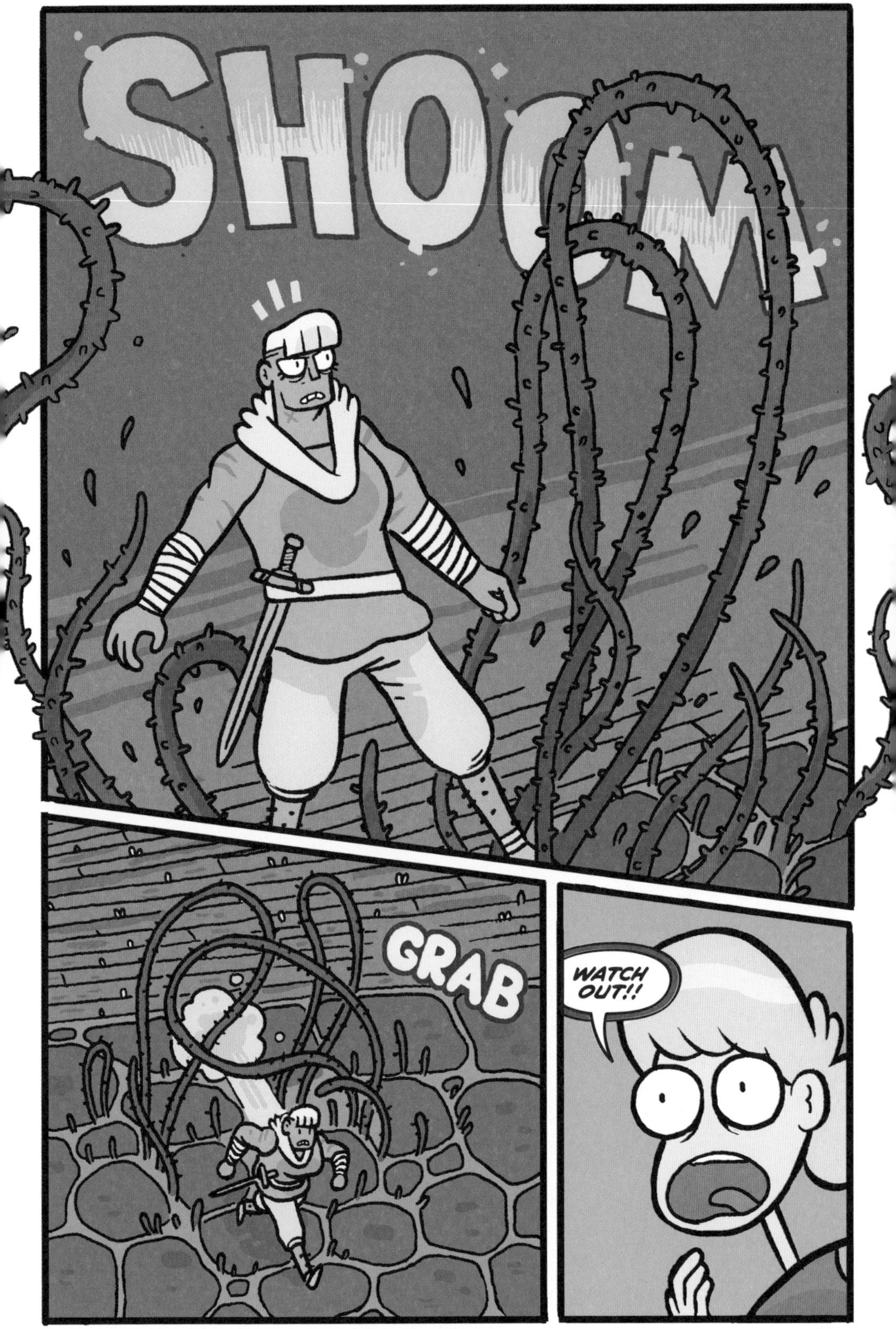
SHOOM
GRAB
WATCH OUT!!

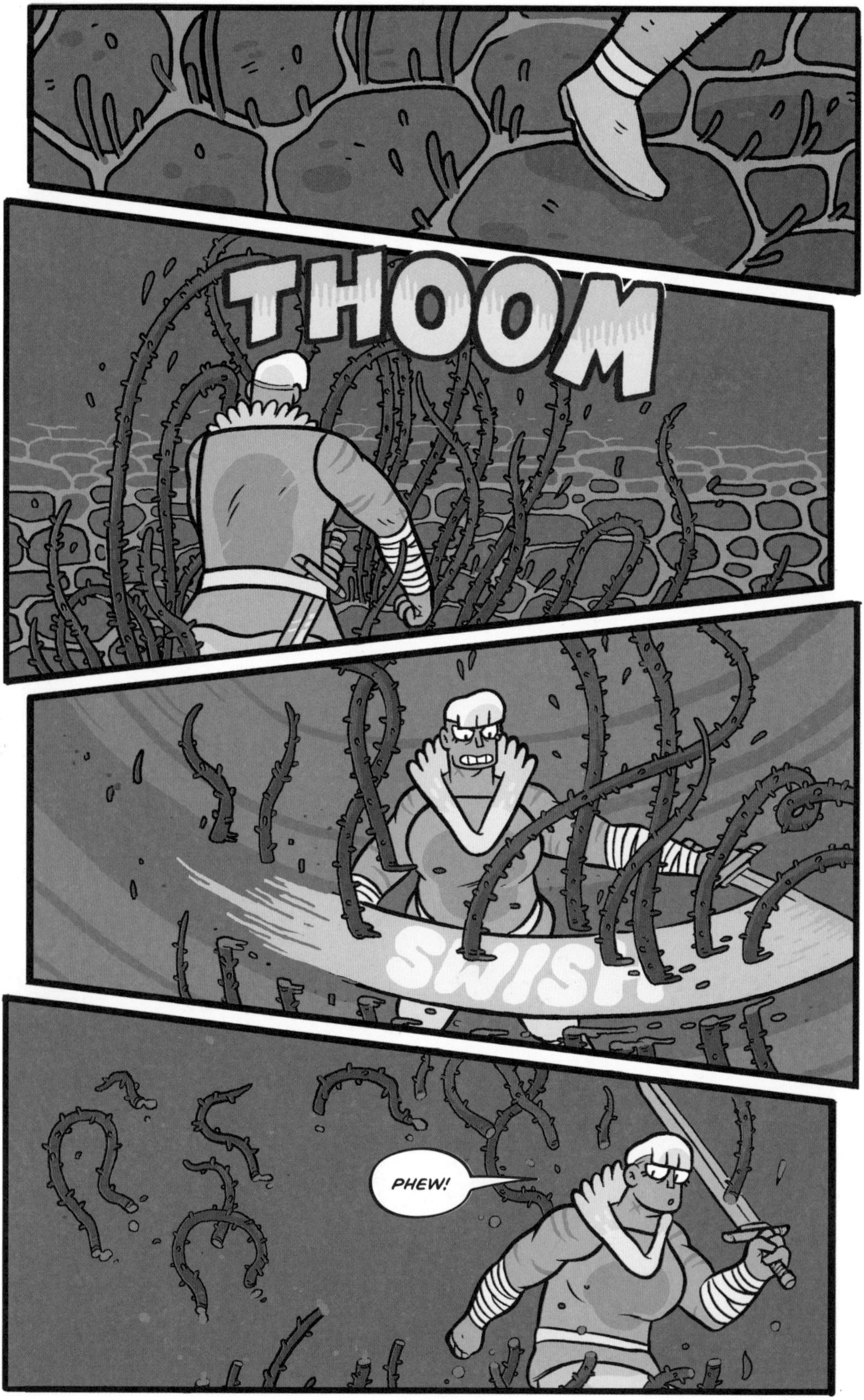
THOOM
SWISH
PHEW!

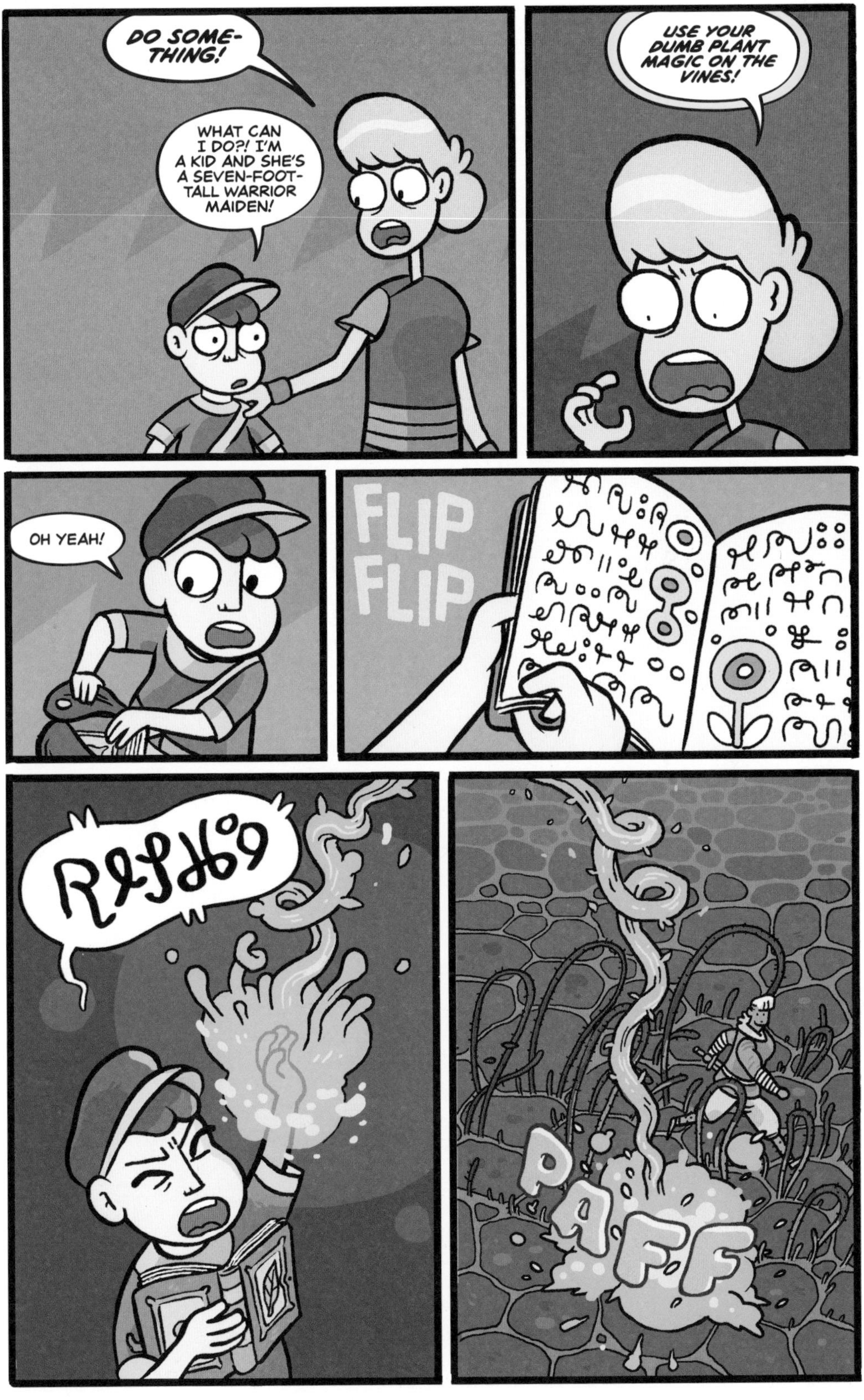
DO SOME-THING!
WHAT CAN I DO?! I'M A KID AND SHE'S A SEVEN-FOOT-TALL WARRIOR MAIDEN!
USE YOUR DUMB PLANT MAGIC ON THE VINES!
OH YEAH!
FLIP
FLIP
PAFF

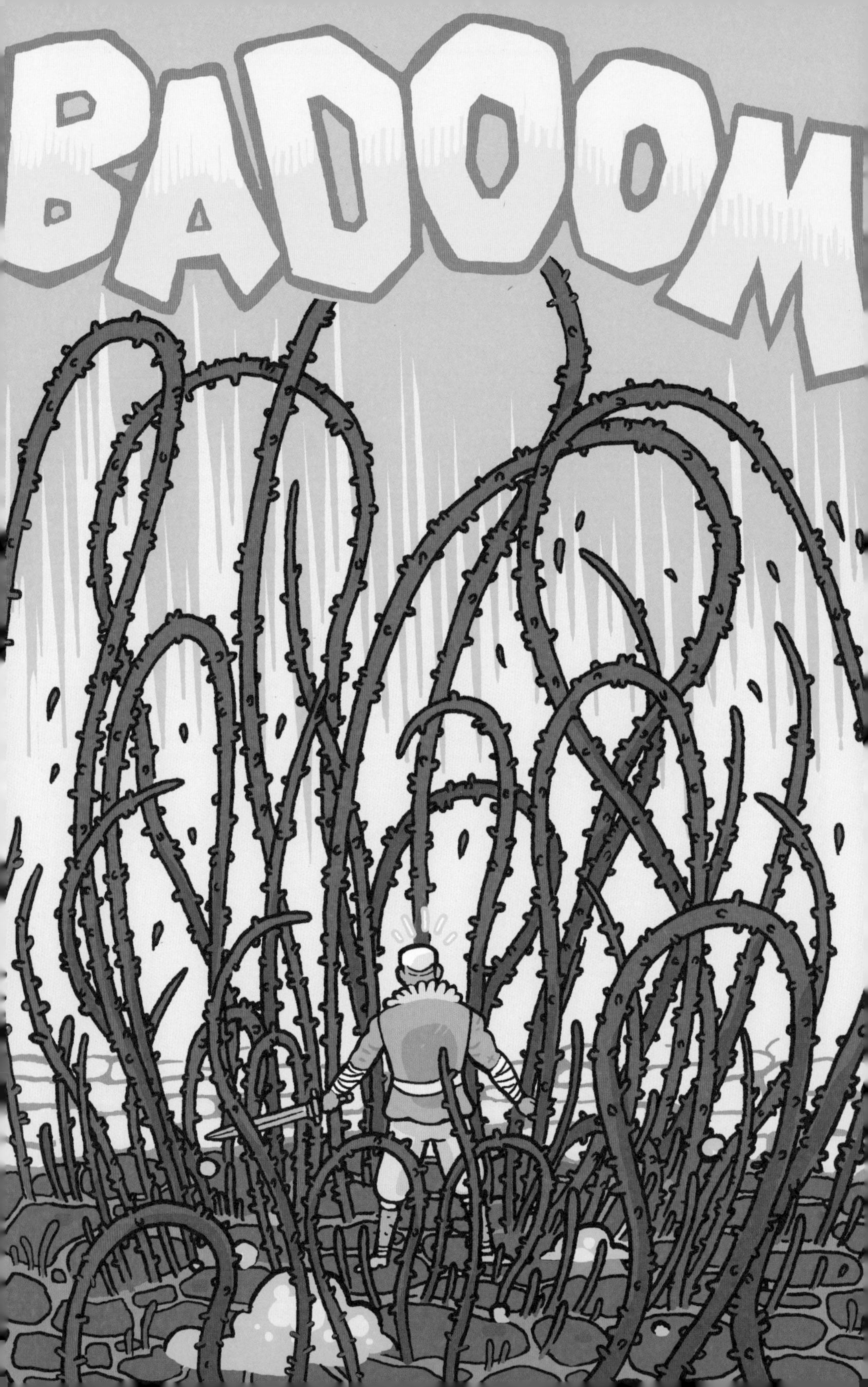
BADOOM

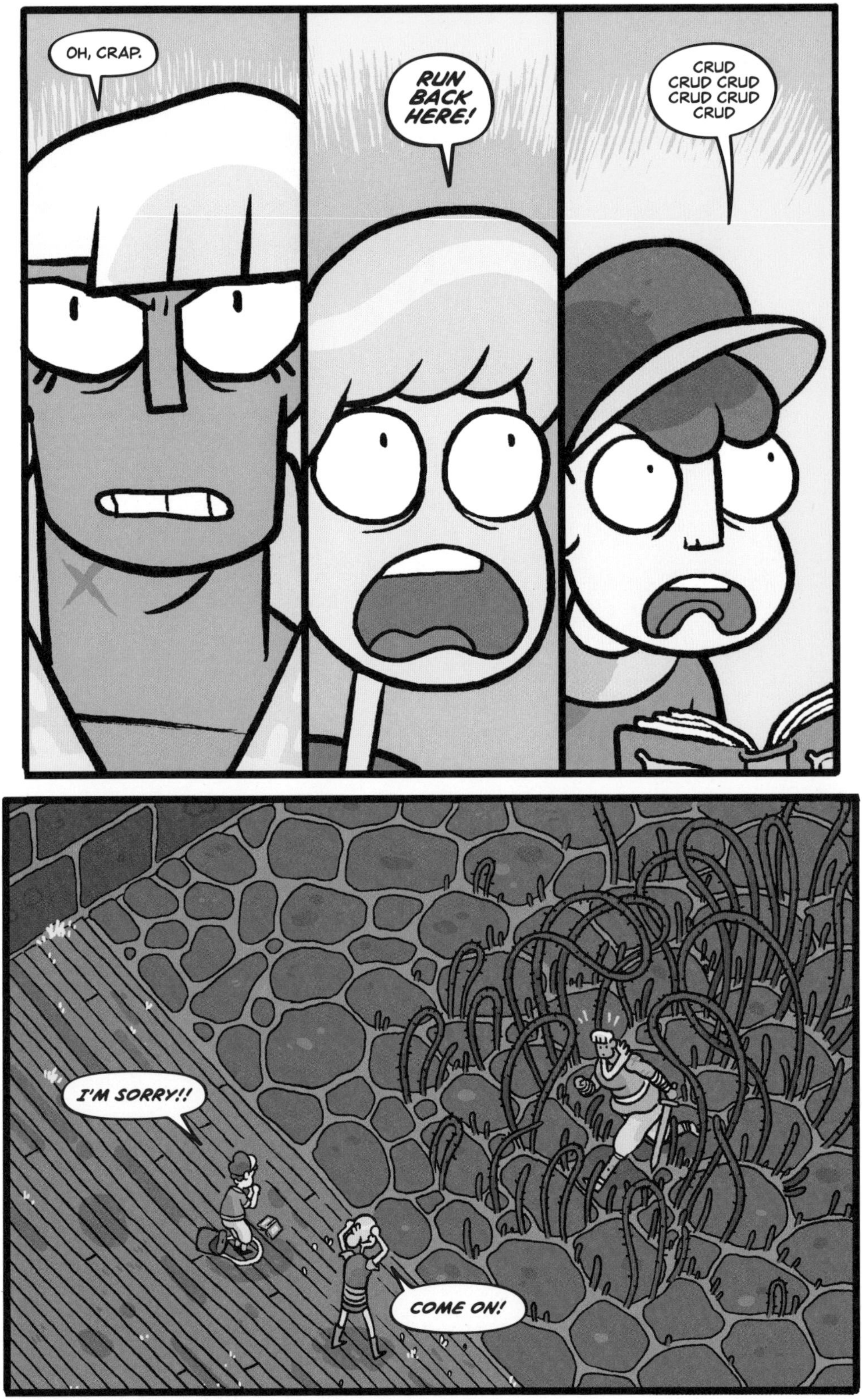
OH, CRAP.
RUN BACK HERE!
CRUD CRUD CRUD CRUD CRUD CRUD
I'M SORRY!!
COME ON!

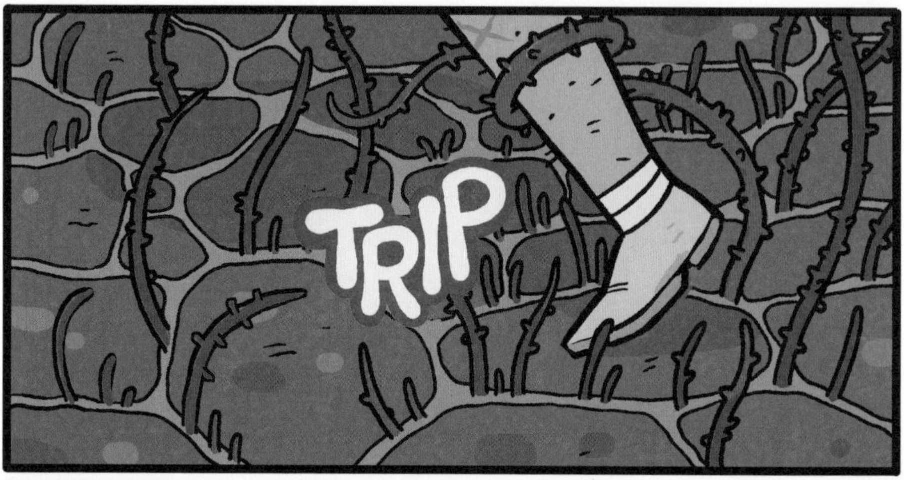
TRIP

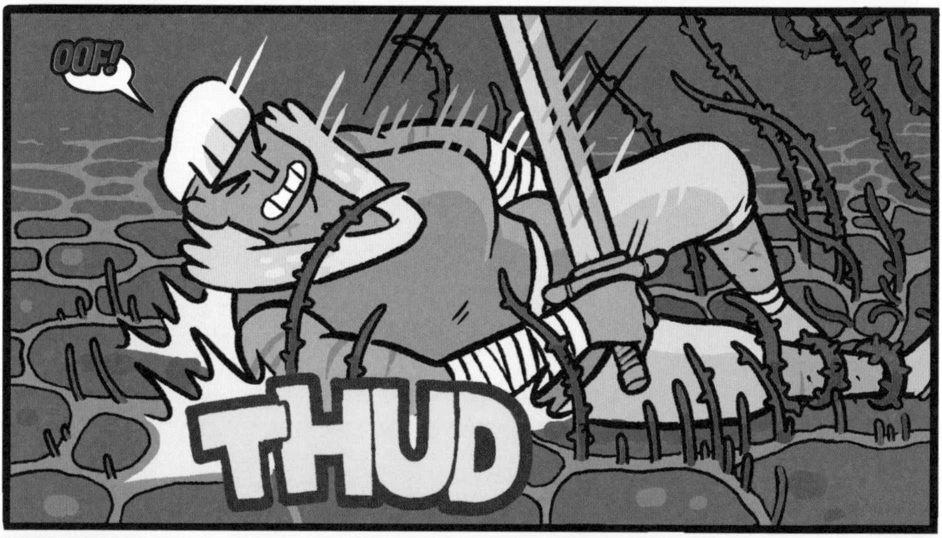
OOF!
THUD

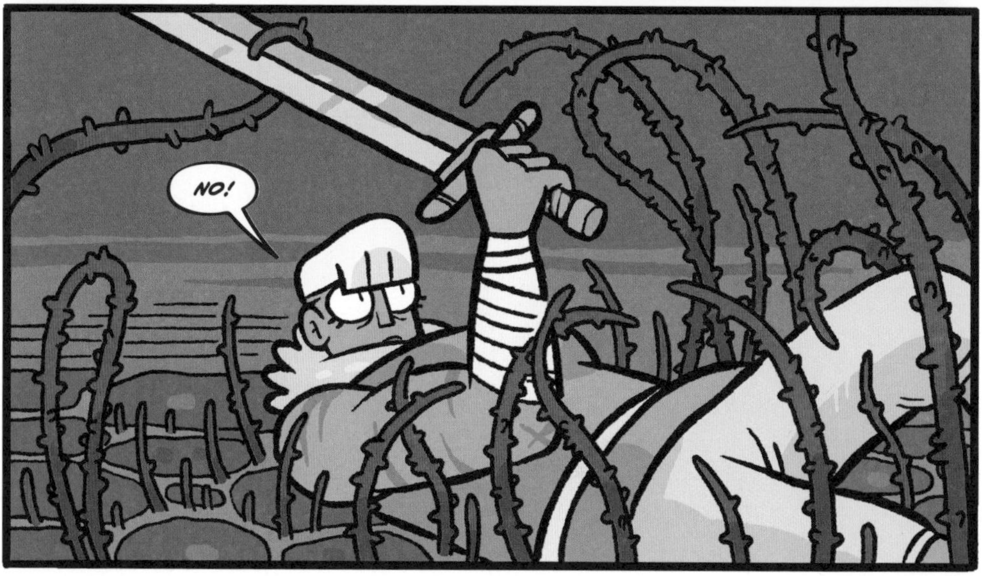
NO!

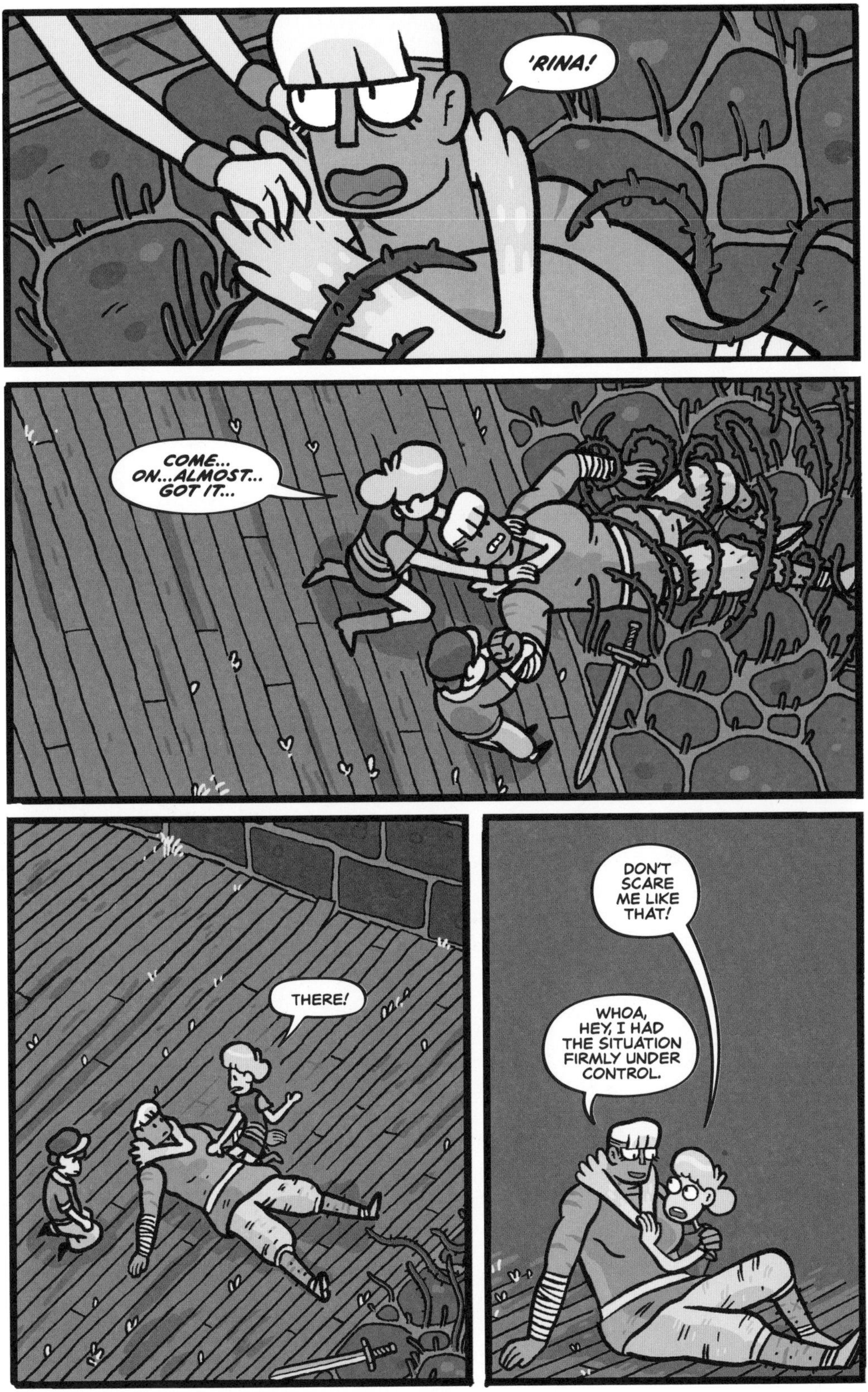

'RINA!
COME... ON...ALMOST... GOT IT...
THERE!
DON'T SCARE ME LIKE THAT!
WHOA, HEY, I HAD THE SITUATION FIRMLY UNDER CONTROL.

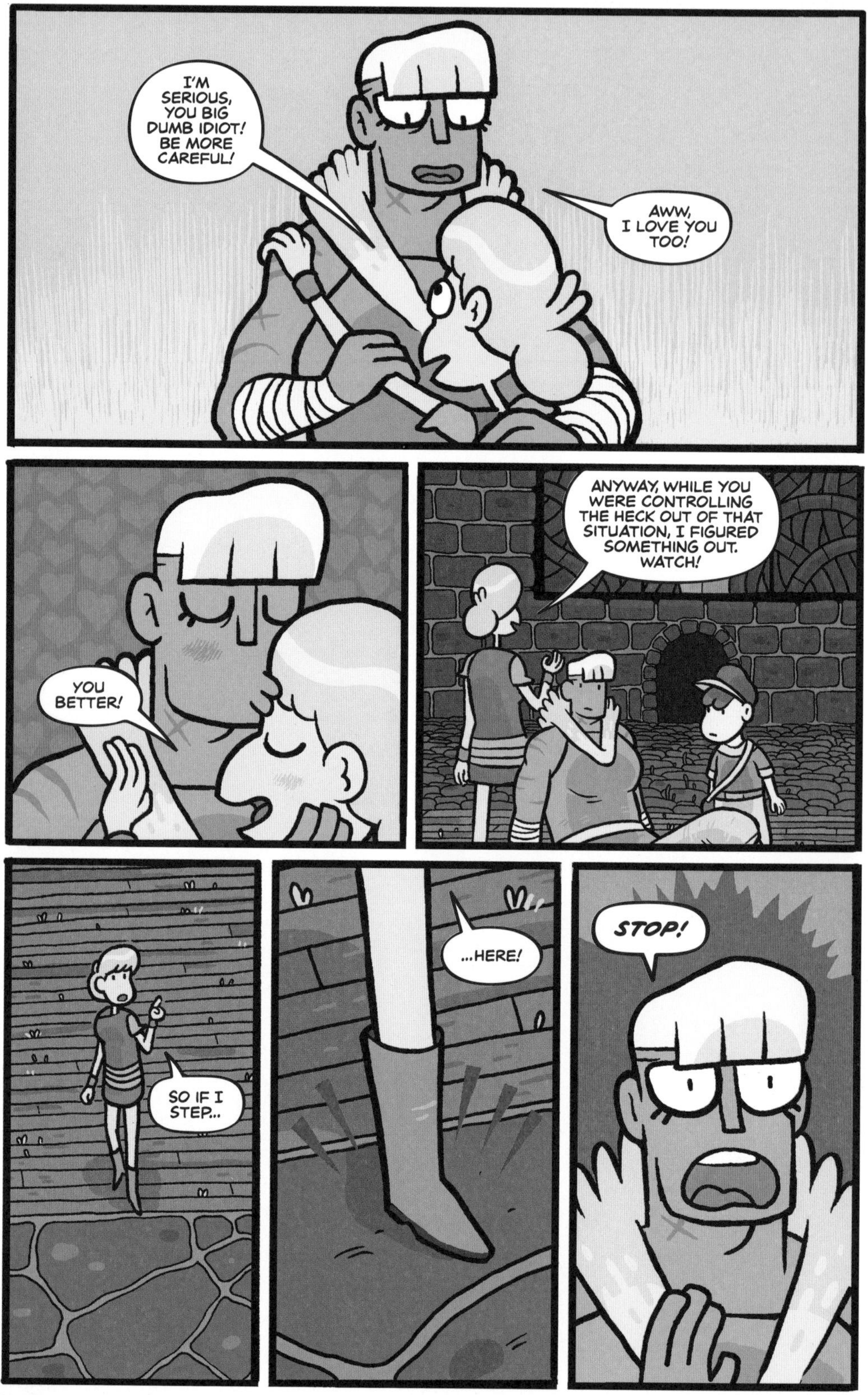
I'M SERIOUS, YOU BIG DUMB IDIOT! BE MORE CAREFUL!
AWW, I LOVE YOU TOO!
YOU BETTER!
ANYWAY, WHILE YOU WERE CONTROLLING THE HECK OUT OF THAT SITUATION, I FIGURED SOMETHING OUT. WATCH!
SO IF I STEP...
...HERE!
STOP!

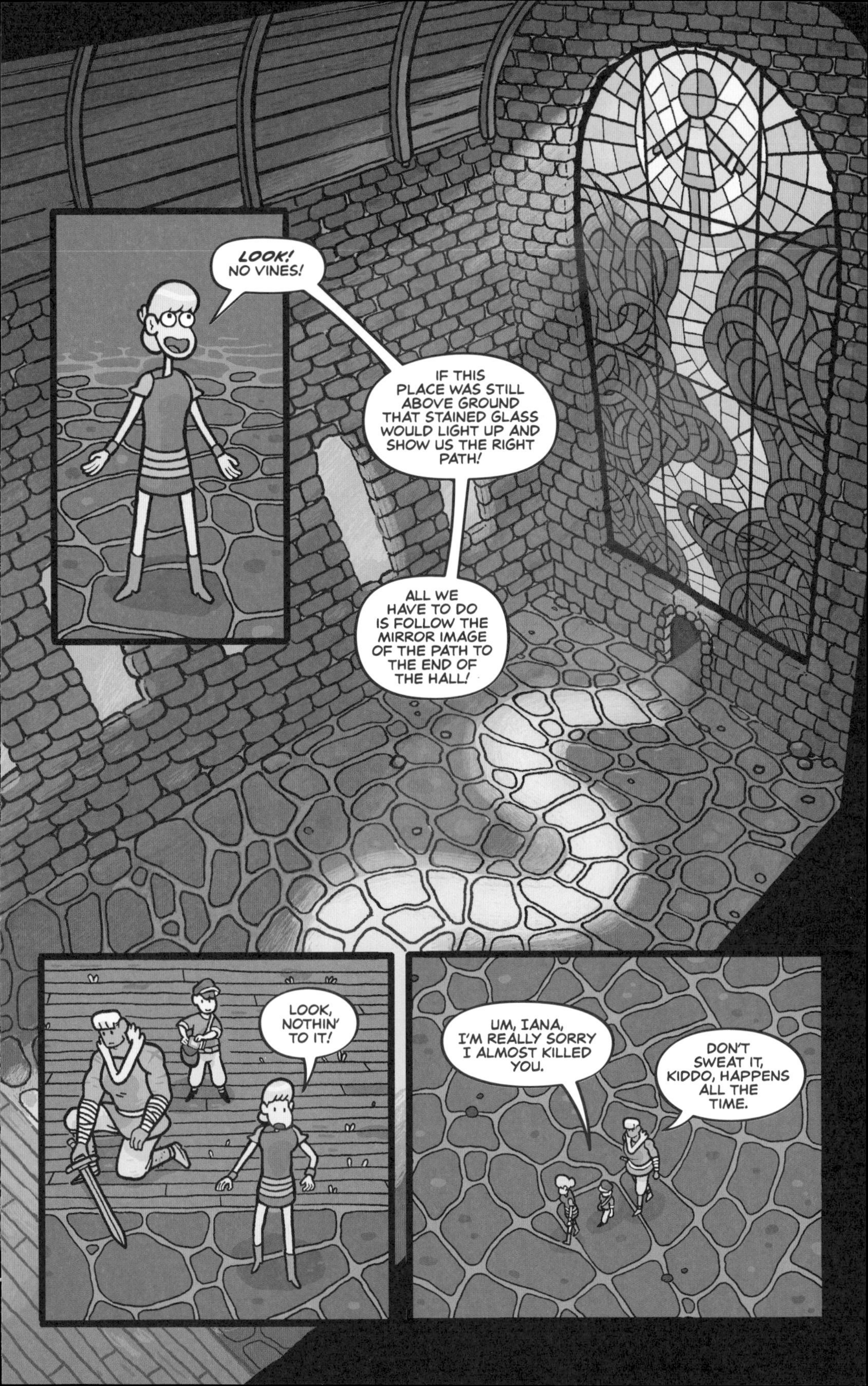
LOOK! NO VINES!
IF THIS PLACE WAS STILL ABOVE GROUND THAT STAINED GLASS WOULD LIGHT UP AND SHOW US THE RIGHT PATH!
ALL WE HAVE TO DO IS FOLLOW THE MIRROR IMAGE OF THE PATH TO THE END OF THE HALL!
LOOK, NOTHIN' TO IT!
UM, IANA, I'M REALLY SORRY I ALMOST KILLED YOU.
DON'T SWEAT IT, KIDDO, HAPPENS ALL THE TIME.

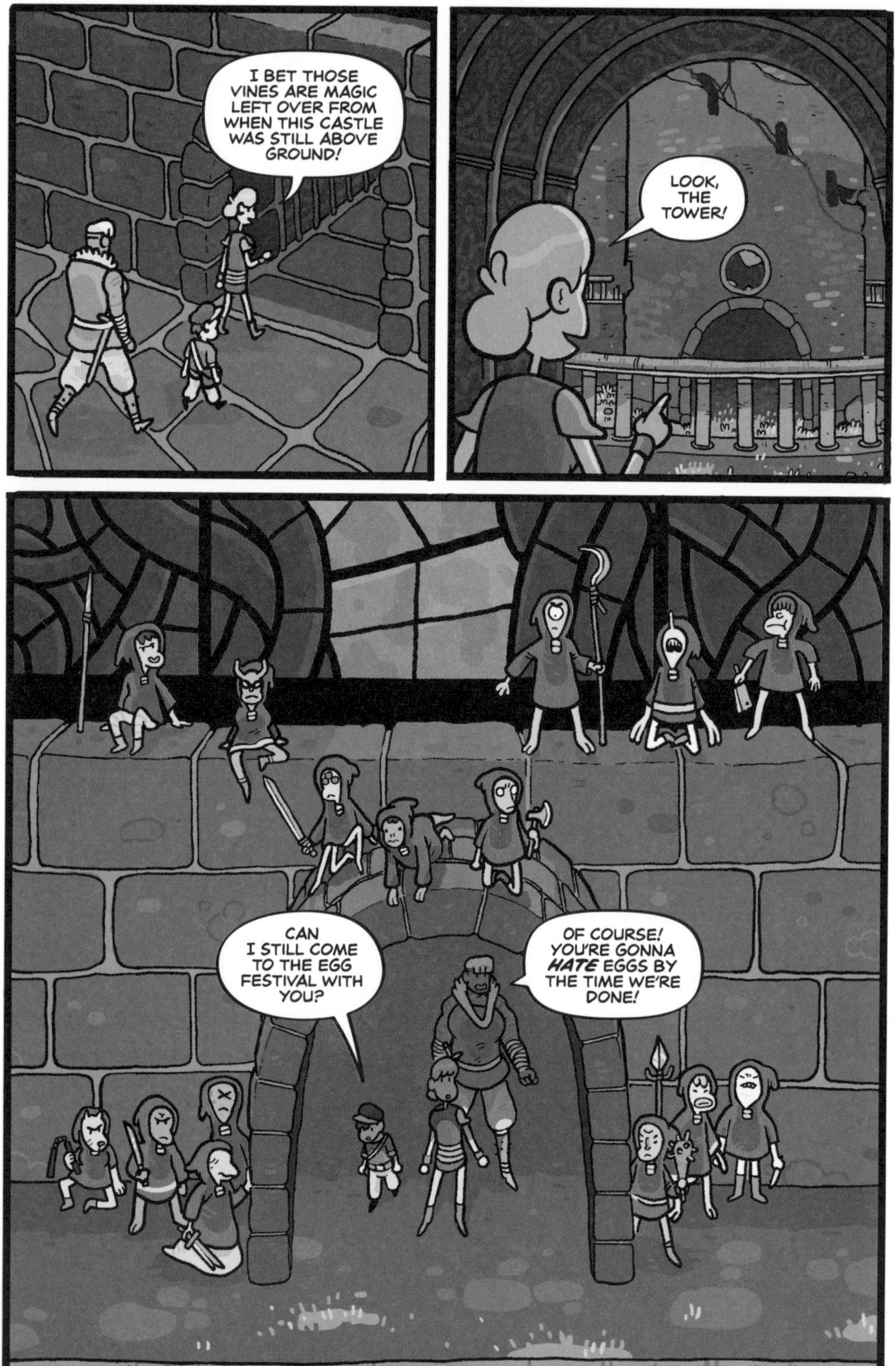
I BET THOSE VINES ARE MAGIC LEFT OVER FROM WHEN THIS CASTLE WAS STILL ABOVE GROUND!
LOOK, THE TOWER!
CAN I STILL COME TO THE EGG FESTIVAL WITH YOU?
OF COURSE! YOU'RE GONNA **HATE** EGGS BY THE TIME WE'RE DONE!

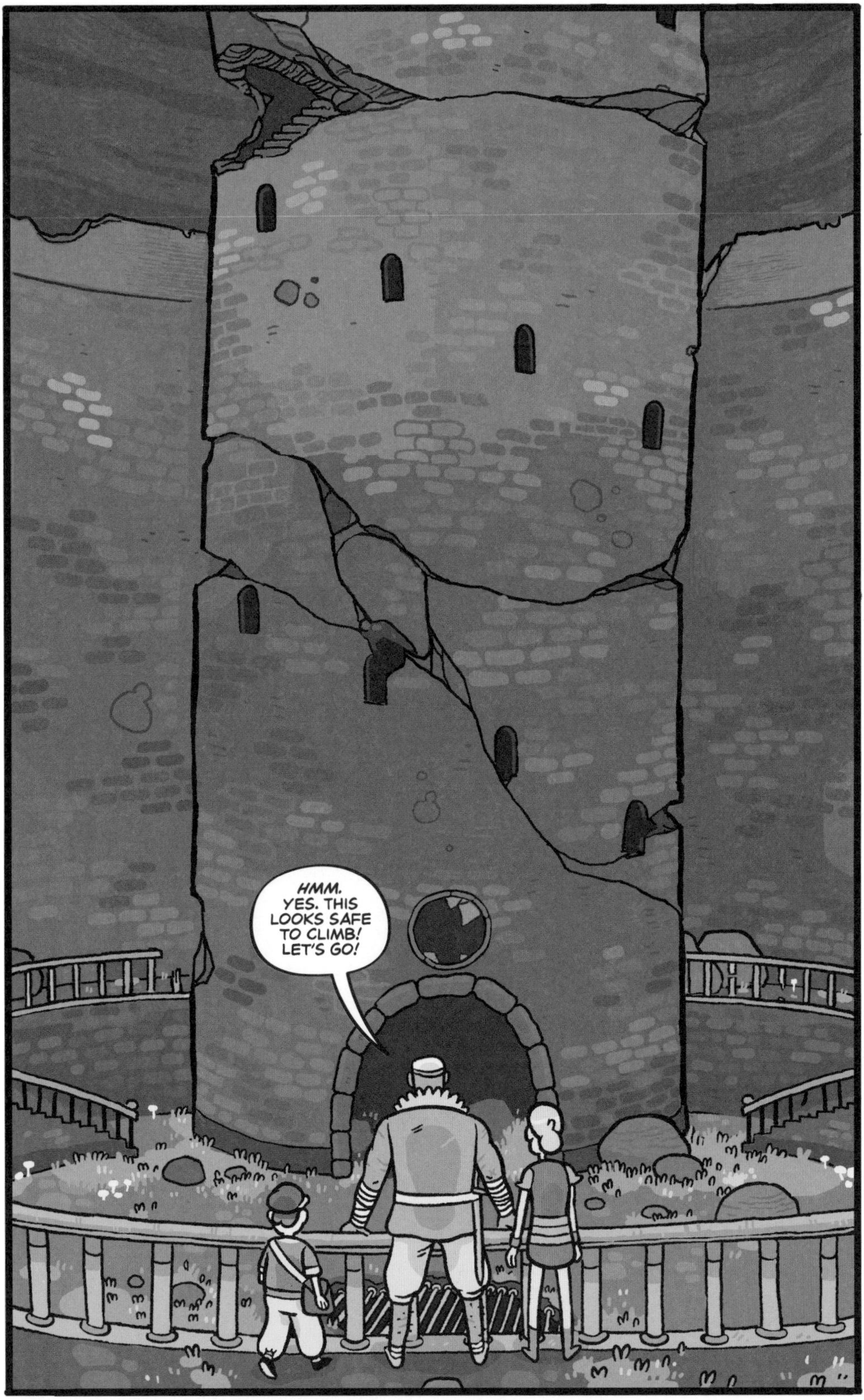
HMM. YES. THIS LOOKS SAFE TO CLIMB! LET'S GO!

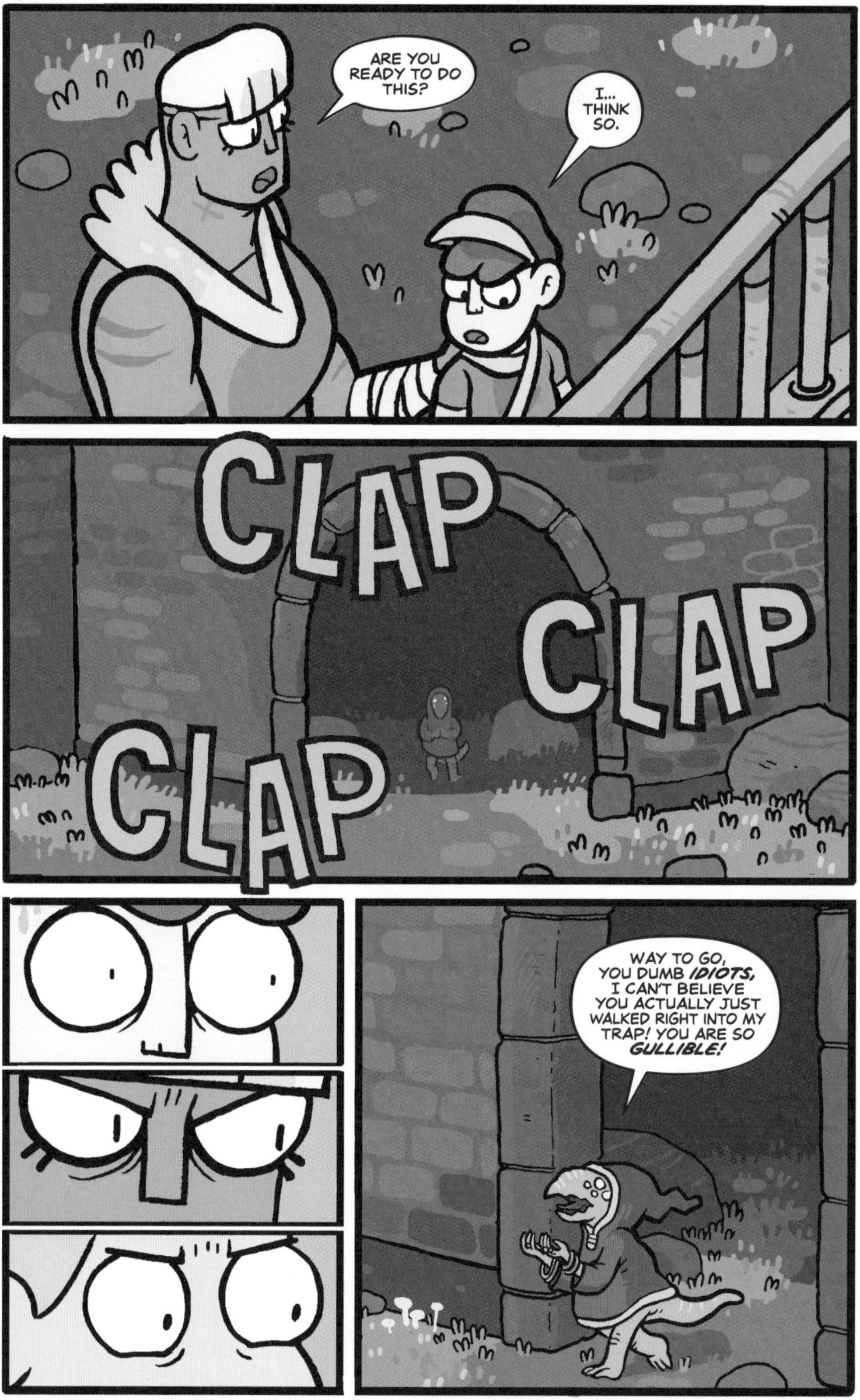
ARE YOU READY TO DO THIS?
I... THINK SO.
CLAP
CLAP
CLAP
WAY TO GO, YOU DUMB *IDIOTS,* I CAN'T BELIEVE YOU ACTUALLY JUST WALKED RIGHT INTO MY TRAP! YOU ARE SO ***GULLIBLE!***

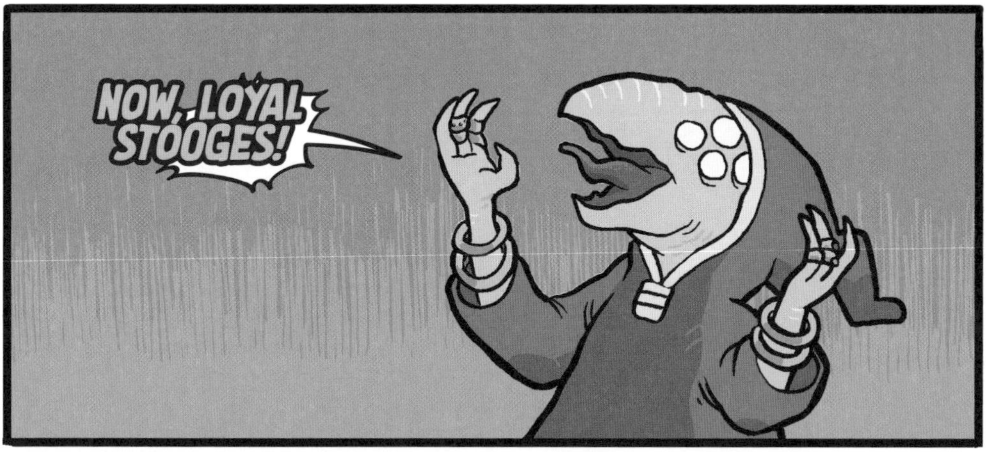
NOW, LOYAL STOOGES!

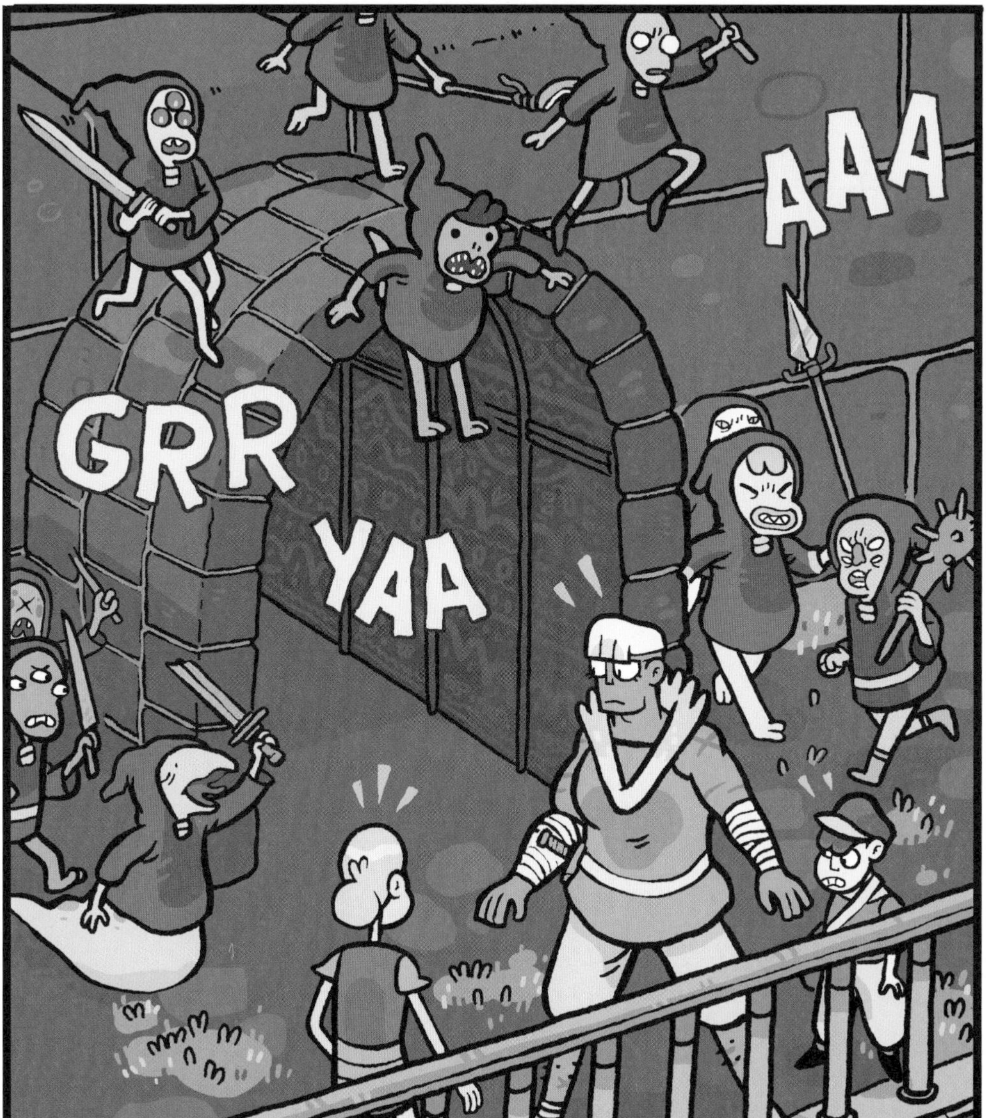
AAA
GRR
YAA

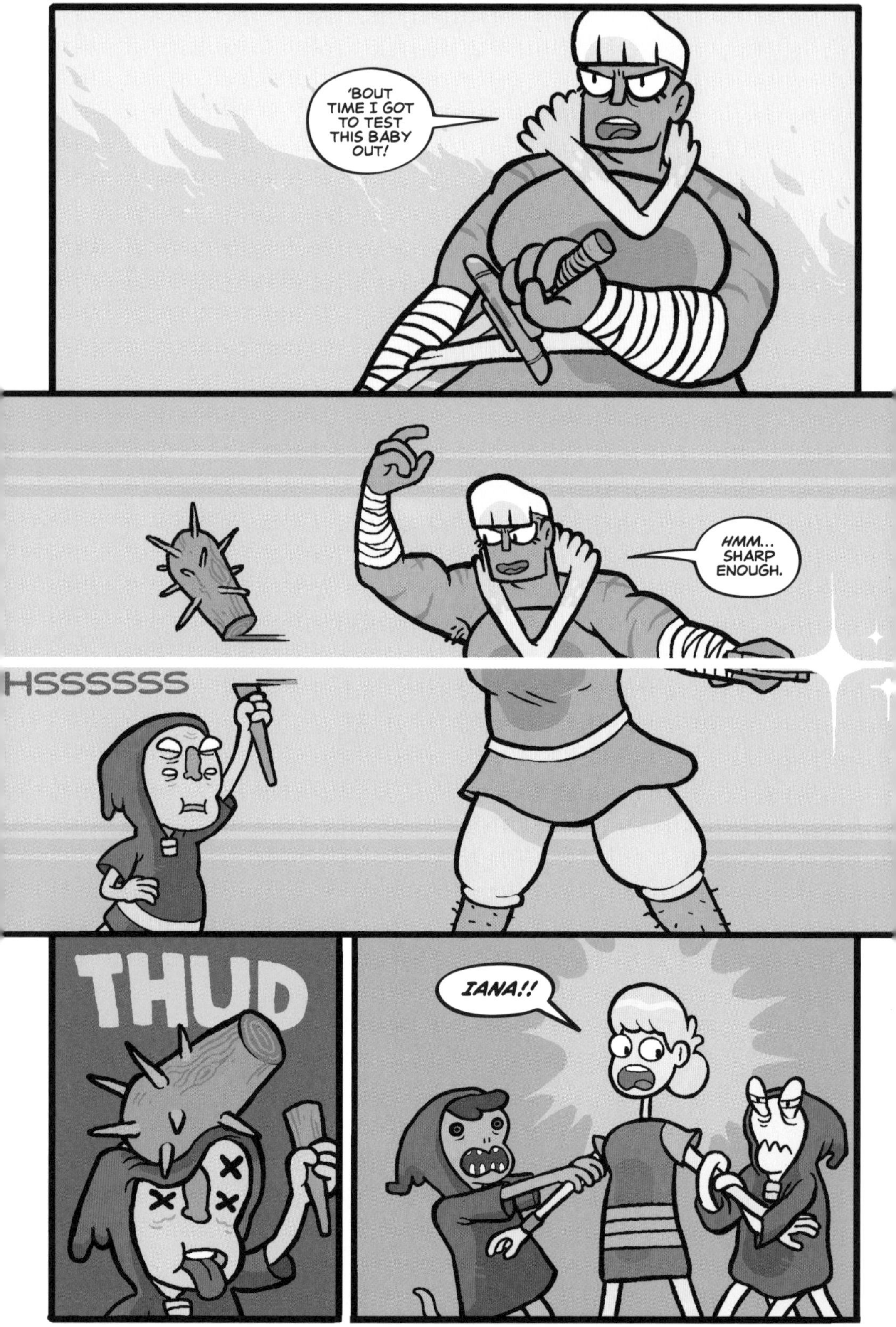
'BOUT TIME I GOT TO TEST THIS BABY OUT!
HMM... SHARP ENOUGH.
HSSSSSS
THUD
IANA!!

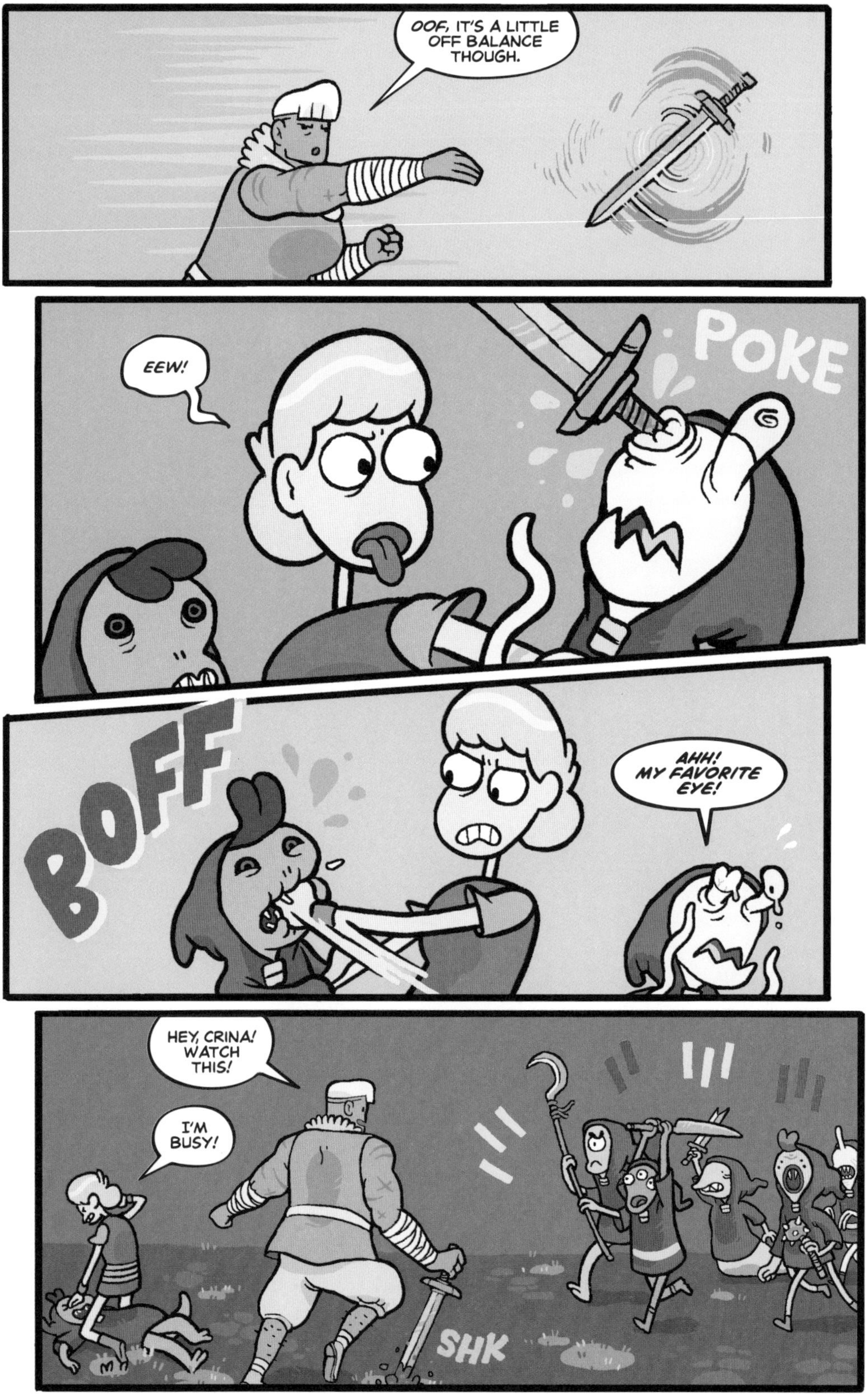
OOF, IT'S A LITTLE OFF BALANCE THOUGH.
EEW!
POKE
BOFF
AHH! MY FAVORITE EYE!
HEY, CRINA! WATCH THIS!
I'M BUSY!
SHK

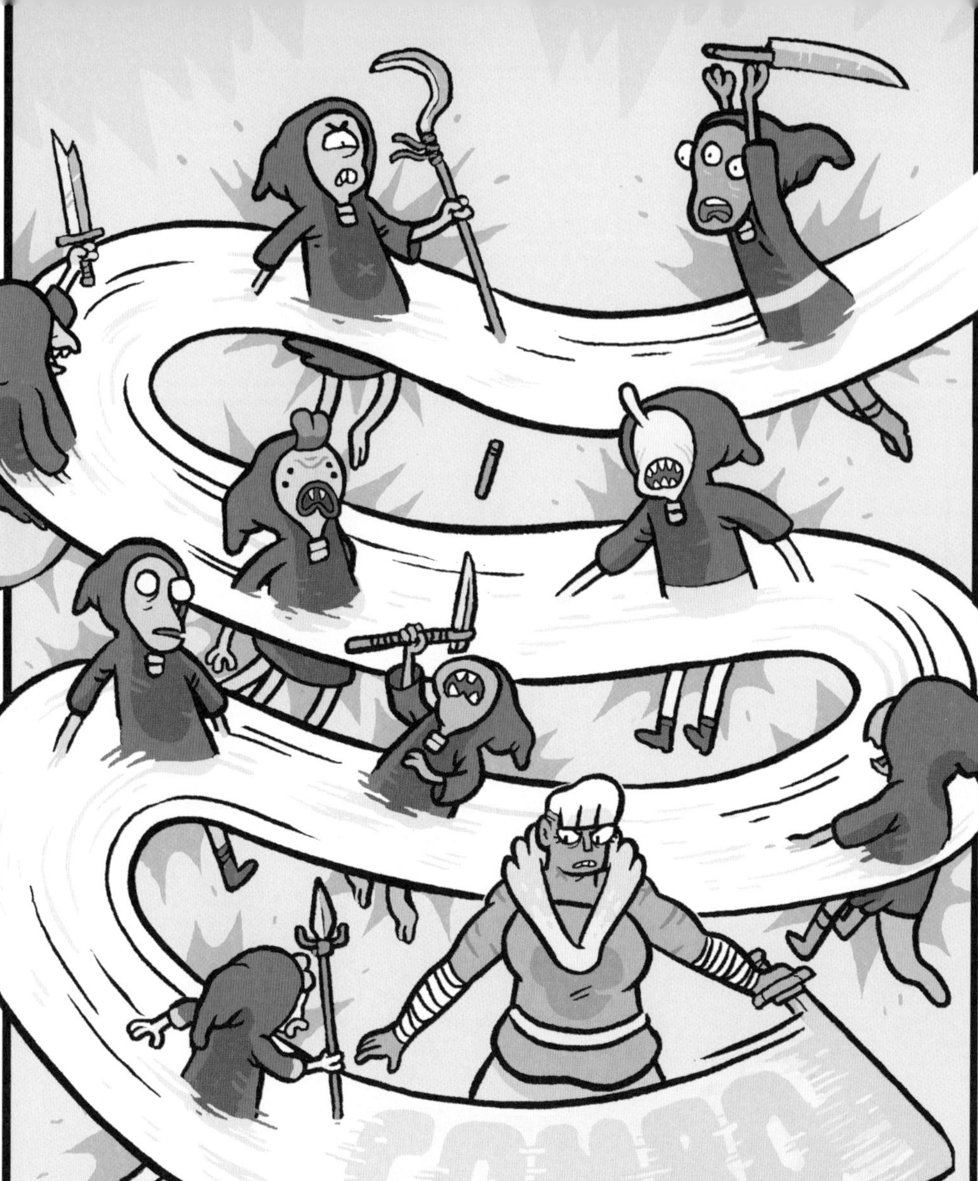
COMBO
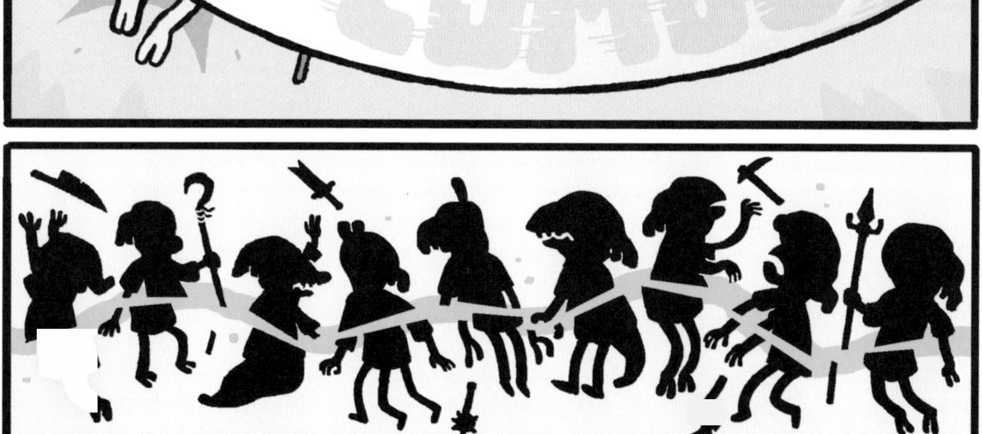

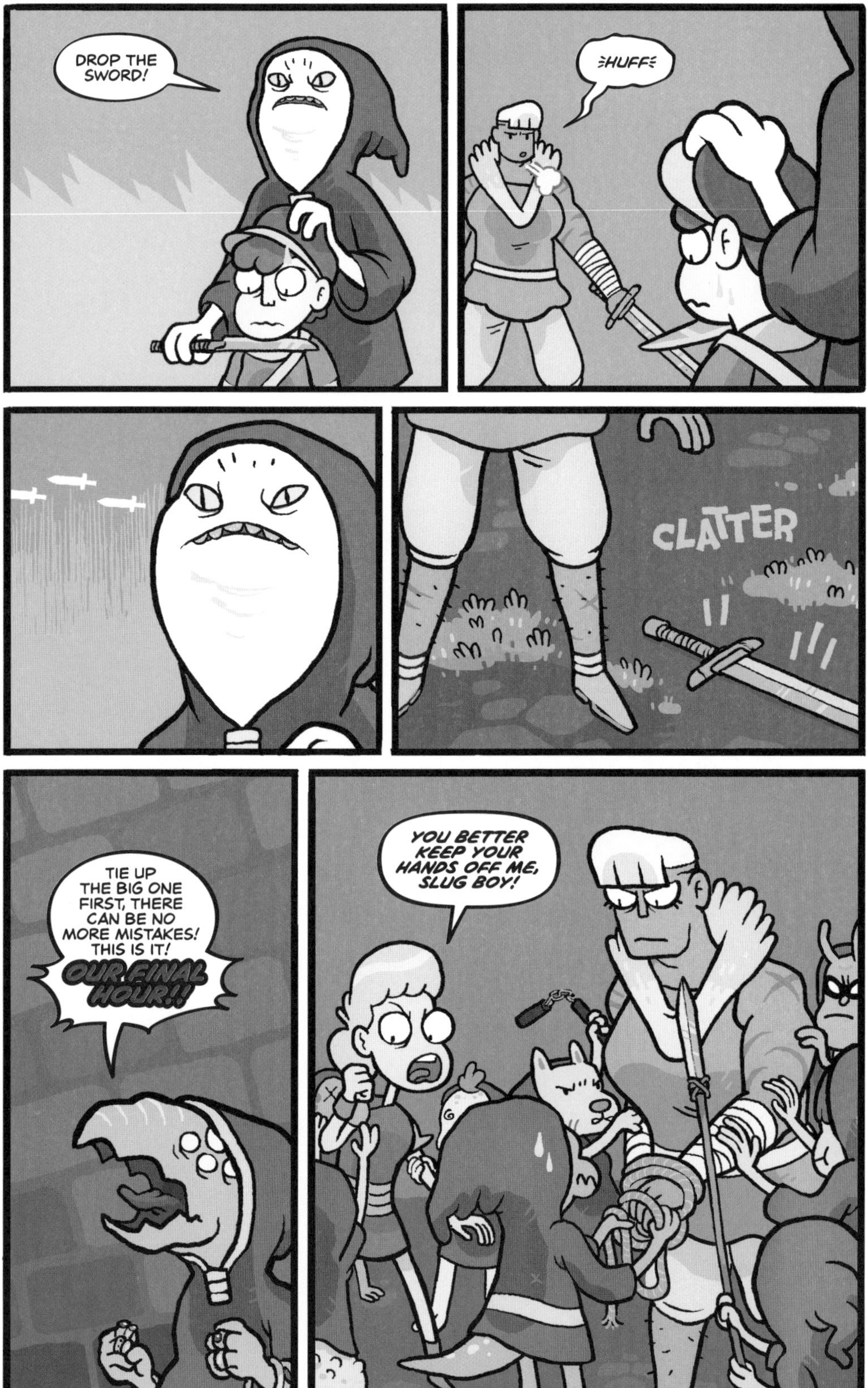
DROP THE SWORD!
HUFF
CLATTER
TIE UP THE BIG ONE FIRST, THERE CAN BE NO MORE MISTAKES! THIS IS IT!
OUR FINAL HOUR!!
YOU BETTER KEEP YOUR HANDS OFF ME, SLUG BOY!

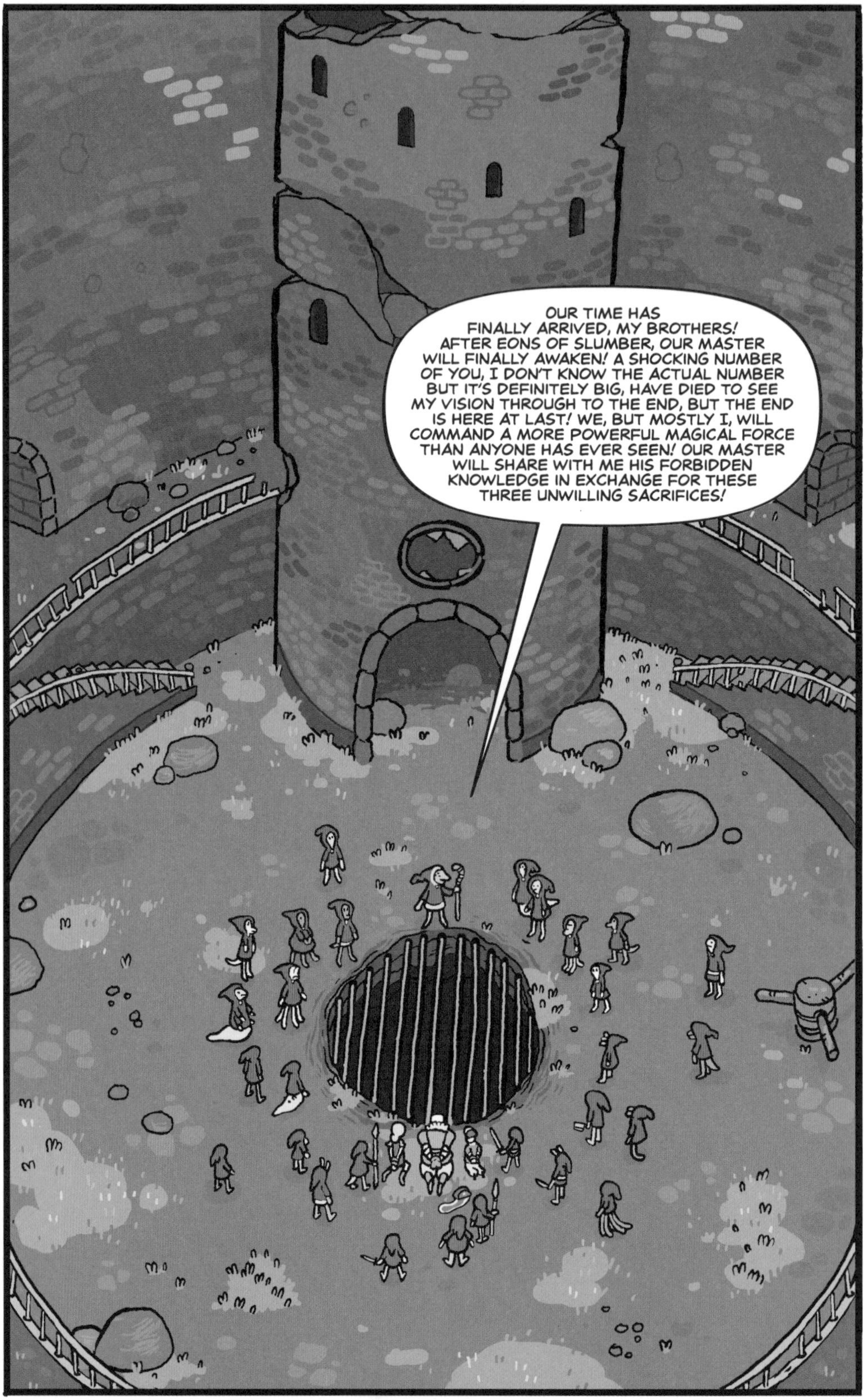
OUR TIME HAS FINALLY ARRIVED, MY BROTHERS! AFTER EONS OF SLUMBER, OUR MASTER WILL FINALLY AWAKEN! A SHOCKING NUMBER OF YOU, I DON'T KNOW THE ACTUAL NUMBER BUT IT'S DEFINITELY BIG, HAVE DIED TO SEE MY VISION THROUGH TO THE END, BUT THE END IS HERE AT LAST! WE, BUT MOSTLY I, WILL COMMAND A MORE POWERFUL MAGICAL FORCE THAN ANYONE HAS EVER SEEN! OUR MASTER WILL SHARE WITH ME HIS FORBIDDEN KNOWLEDGE IN EXCHANGE FOR THESE THREE UNWILLING SACRIFICES!

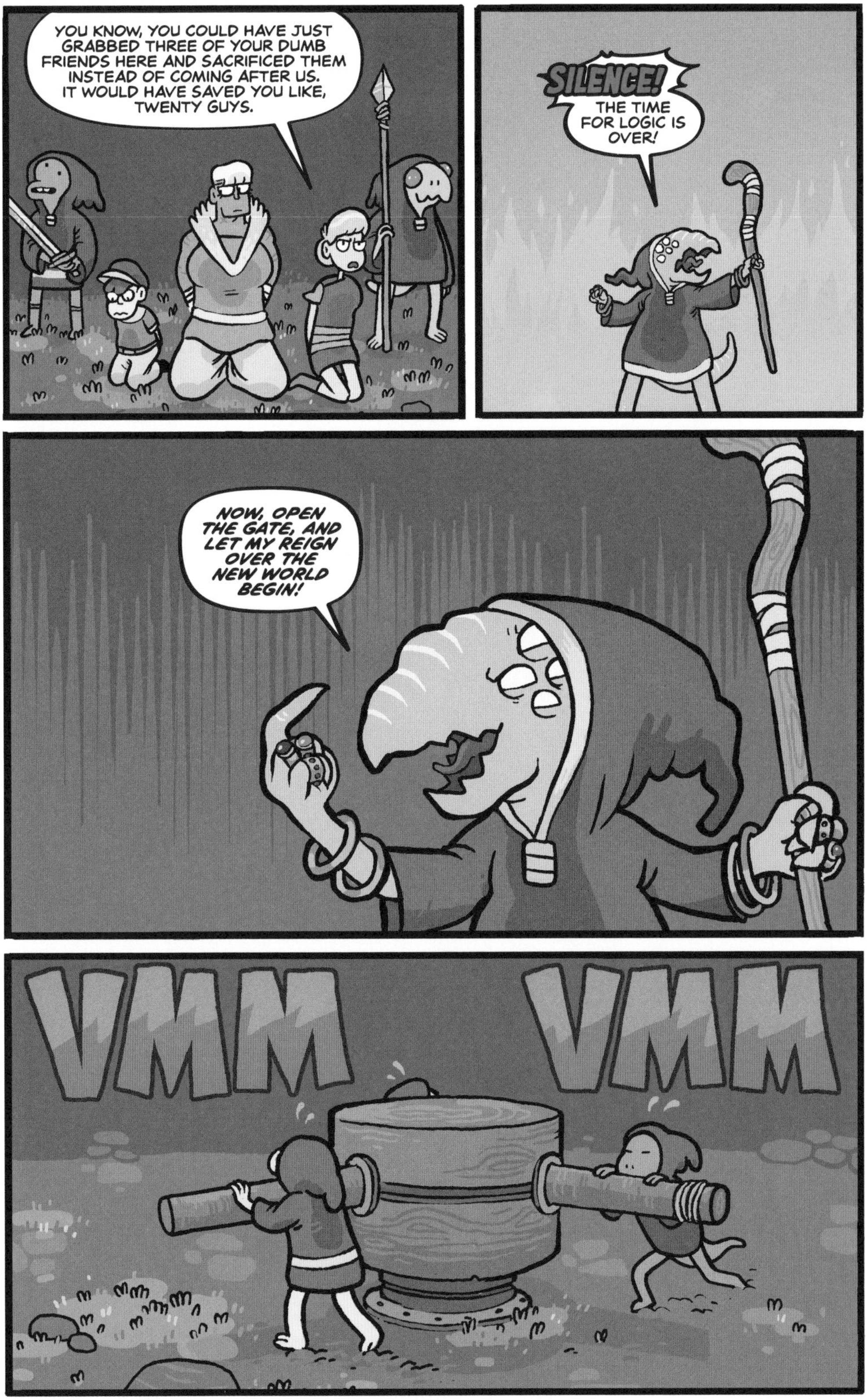
YOU KNOW, YOU COULD HAVE JUST GRABBED THREE OF YOUR DUMB FRIENDS HERE AND SACRIFICED THEM INSTEAD OF COMING AFTER US. IT WOULD HAVE SAVED YOU LIKE, TWENTY GUYS.
SILENCE!
THE TIME FOR LOGIC IS OVER!
NOW, OPEN THE GATE, AND LET MY REIGN OVER THE NEW WORLD BEGIN!
VMM VMM

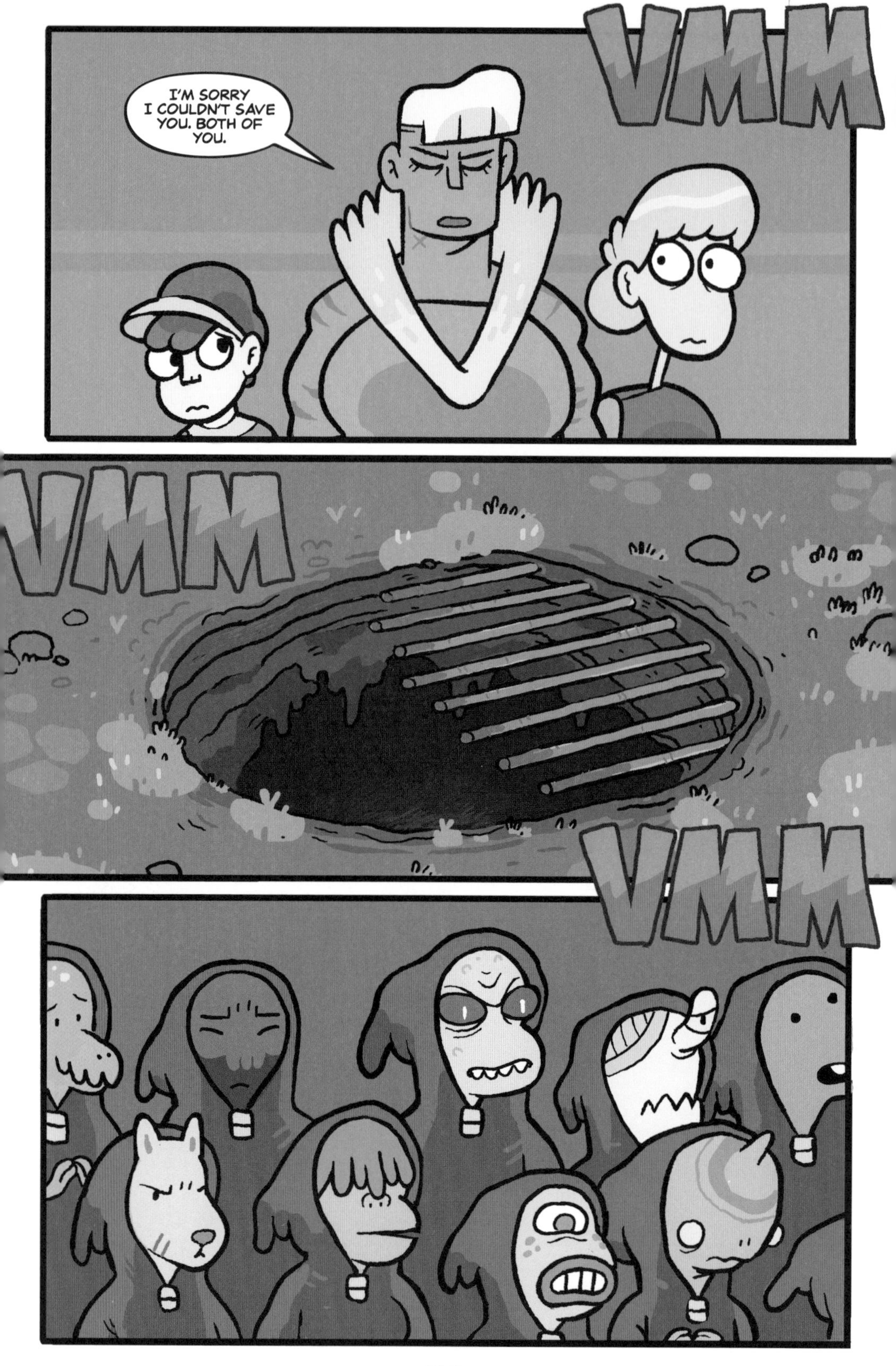
I'M SORRY I COULDN'T SAVE YOU. BOTH OF YOU.
VMM
VMM
VMM
VMM

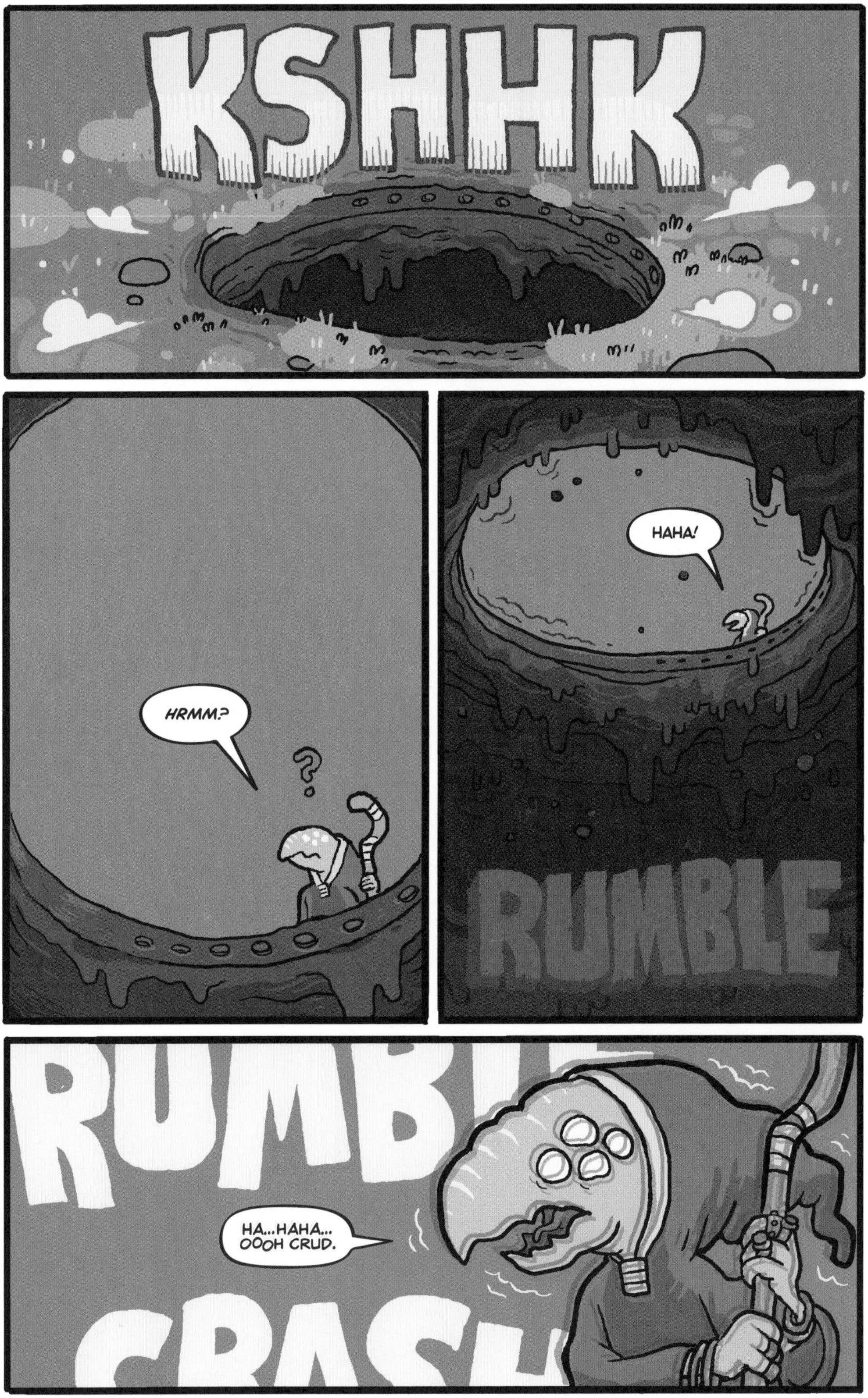
KSHHK
HRMM?
HAHA!
RUMBLE
HA...HAHA...
OOOH CRUD.

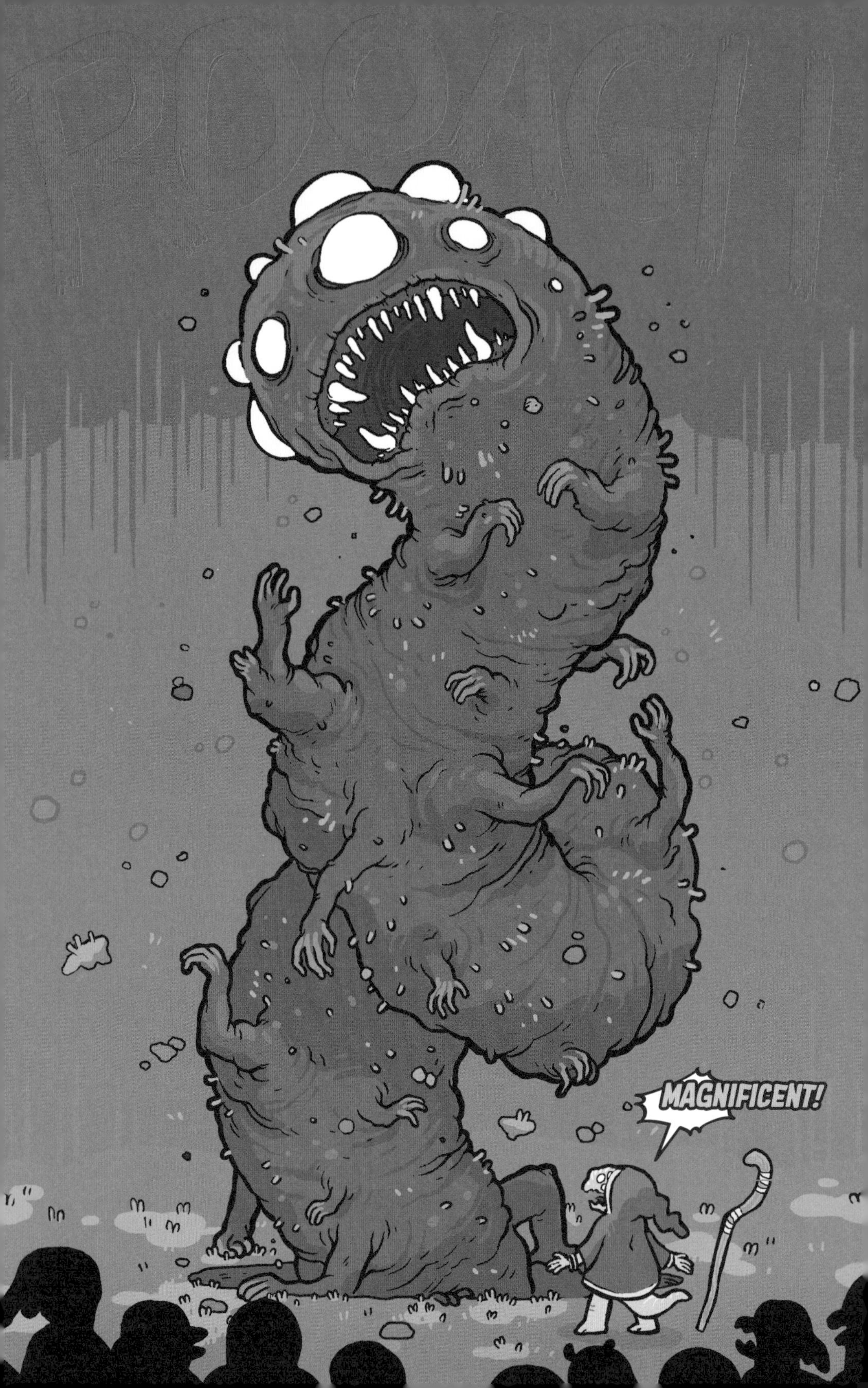
MAGNIFICENT!

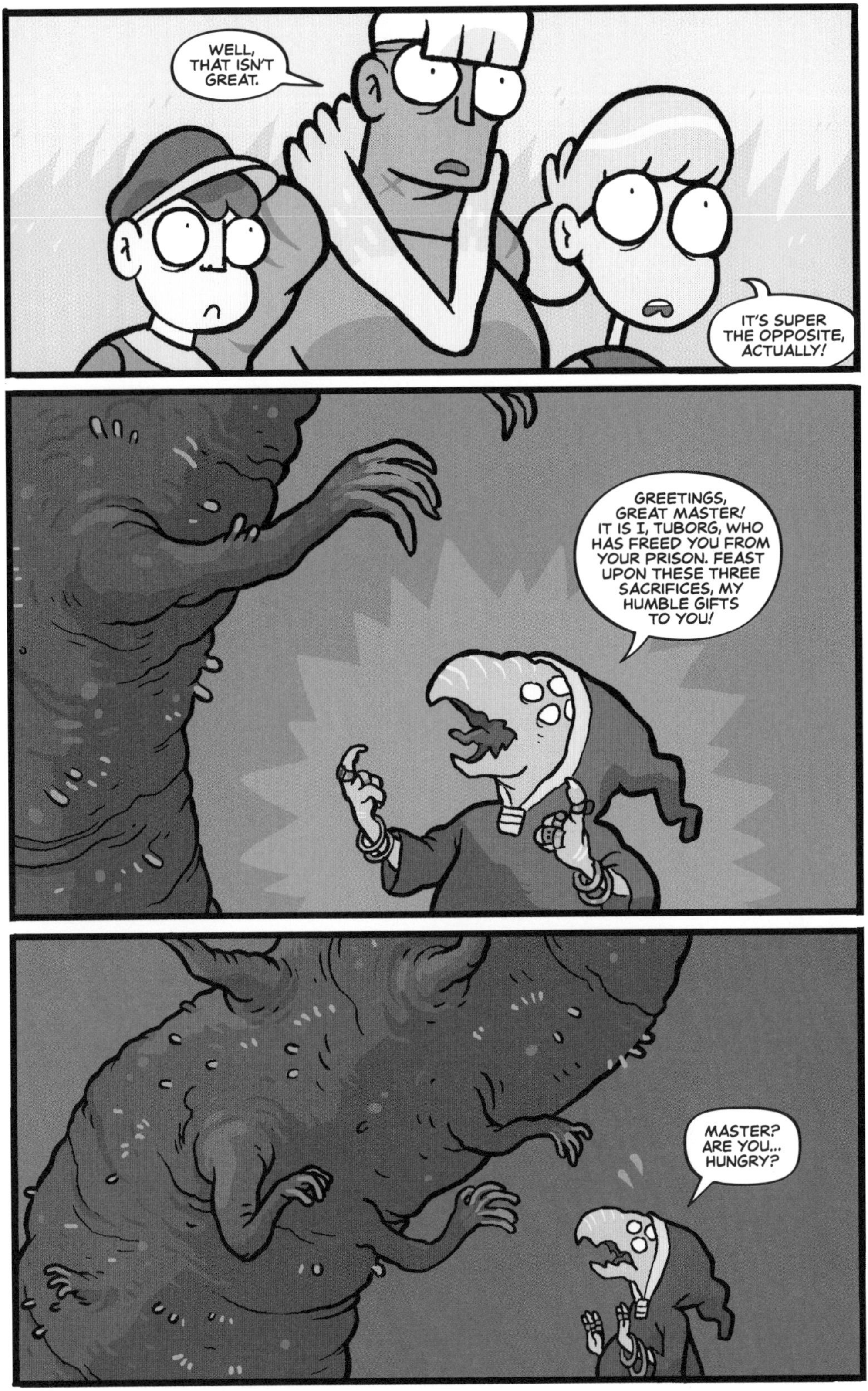
WELL, THAT ISN'T GREAT.
IT'S SUPER THE OPPOSITE, ACTUALLY!
GREETINGS, GREAT MASTER! IT IS I, TUBORG, WHO HAS FREED YOU FROM YOUR PRISON. FEAST UPON THESE THREE SACRIFICES, MY HUMBLE GIFTS TO YOU!
MASTER? ARE YOU... HUNGRY?

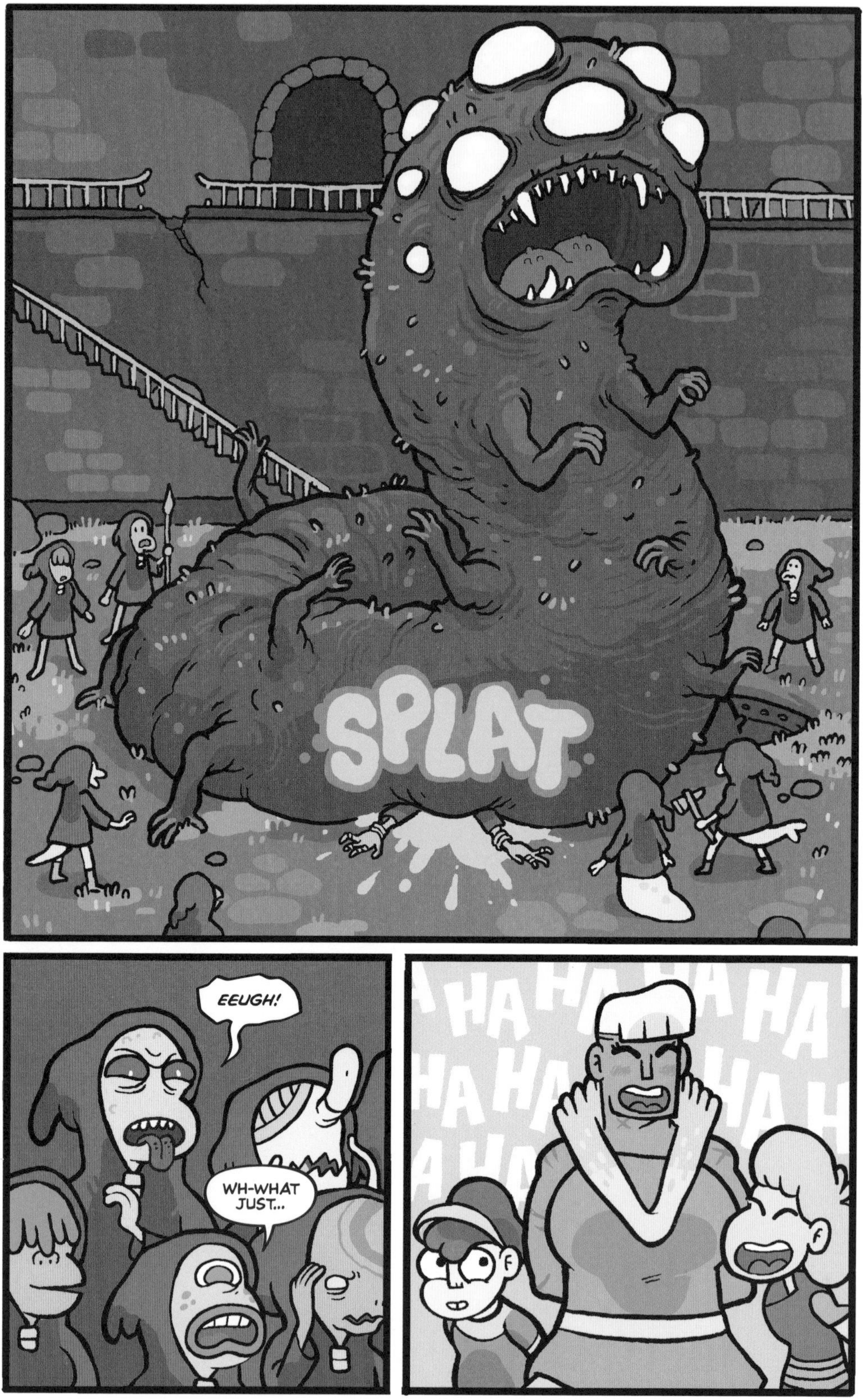
SPLAT
EEUGH!
WH-WHAT JUST...
HA HA HA HA HA HA HA HA HA HA HA HA HA HA

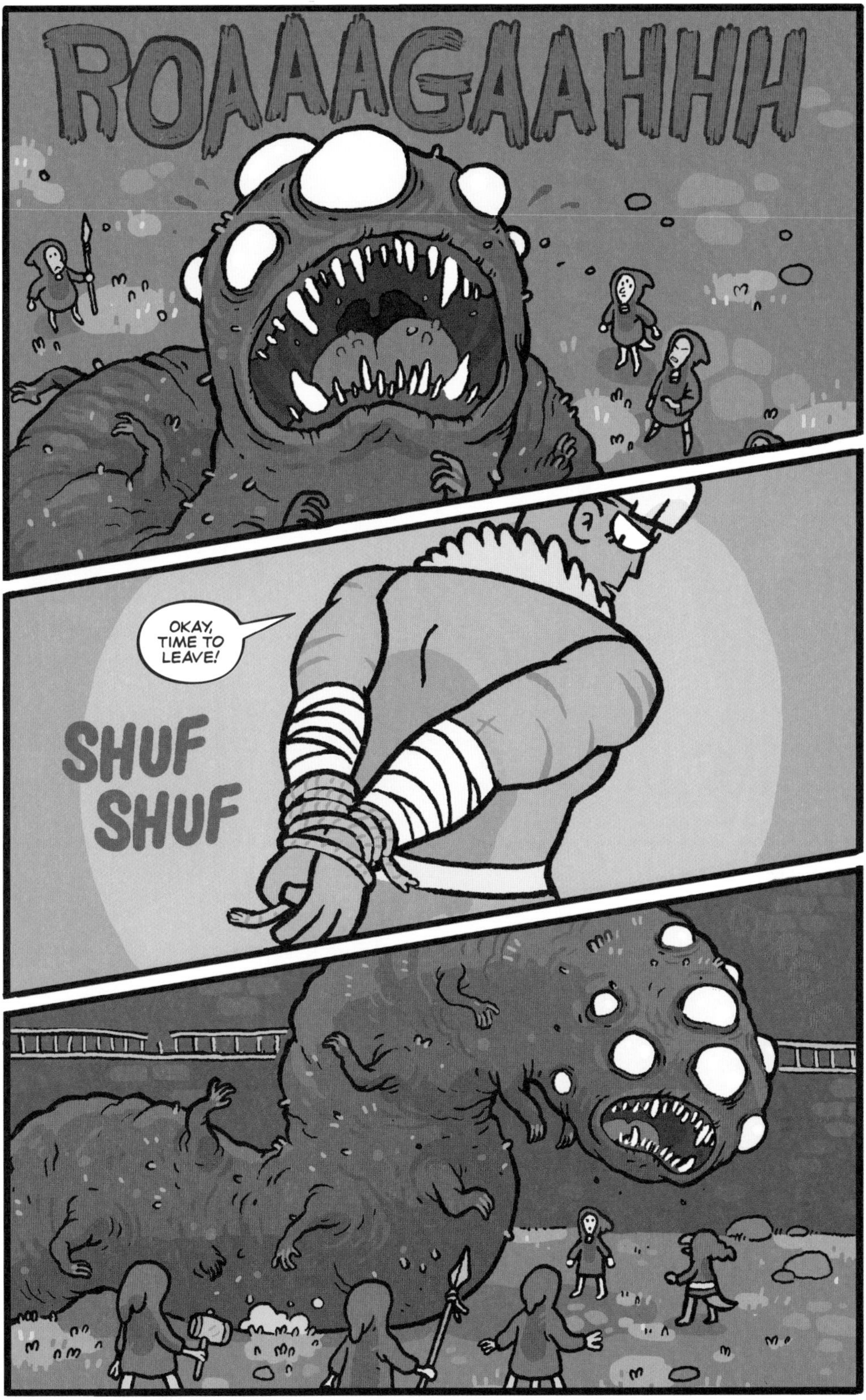
ROAAAGAAHHH
OKAY, TIME TO LEAVE!
SHUF SHUF

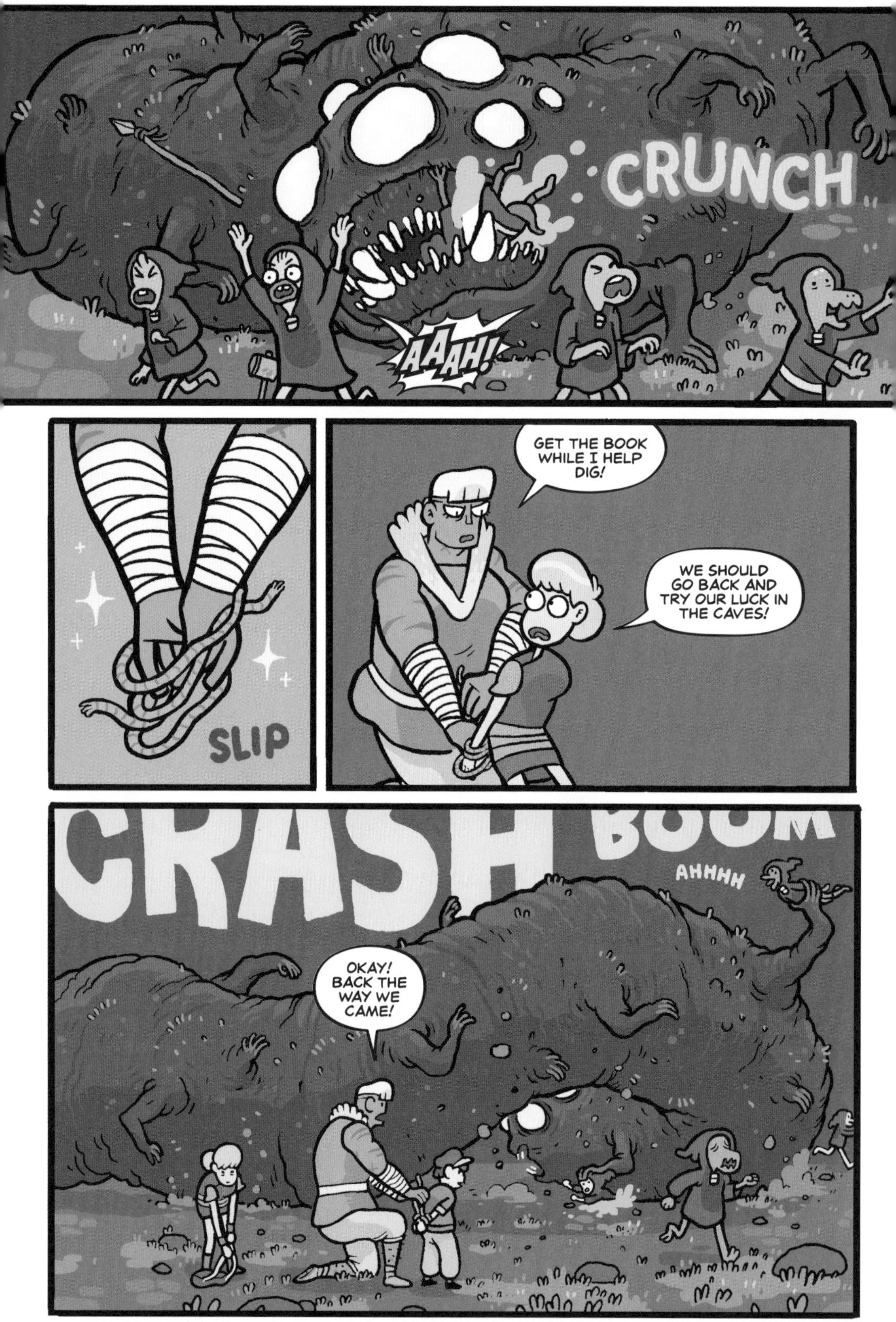
CRUNCH
AAAH!
SLIP
GET THE BOOK WHILE I HELP DIG!
WE SHOULD GO BACK AND TRY OUR LUCK IN THE CAVES!
CRASH
BOOM
AHHHH
OKAY! BACK THE WAY WE CAME!

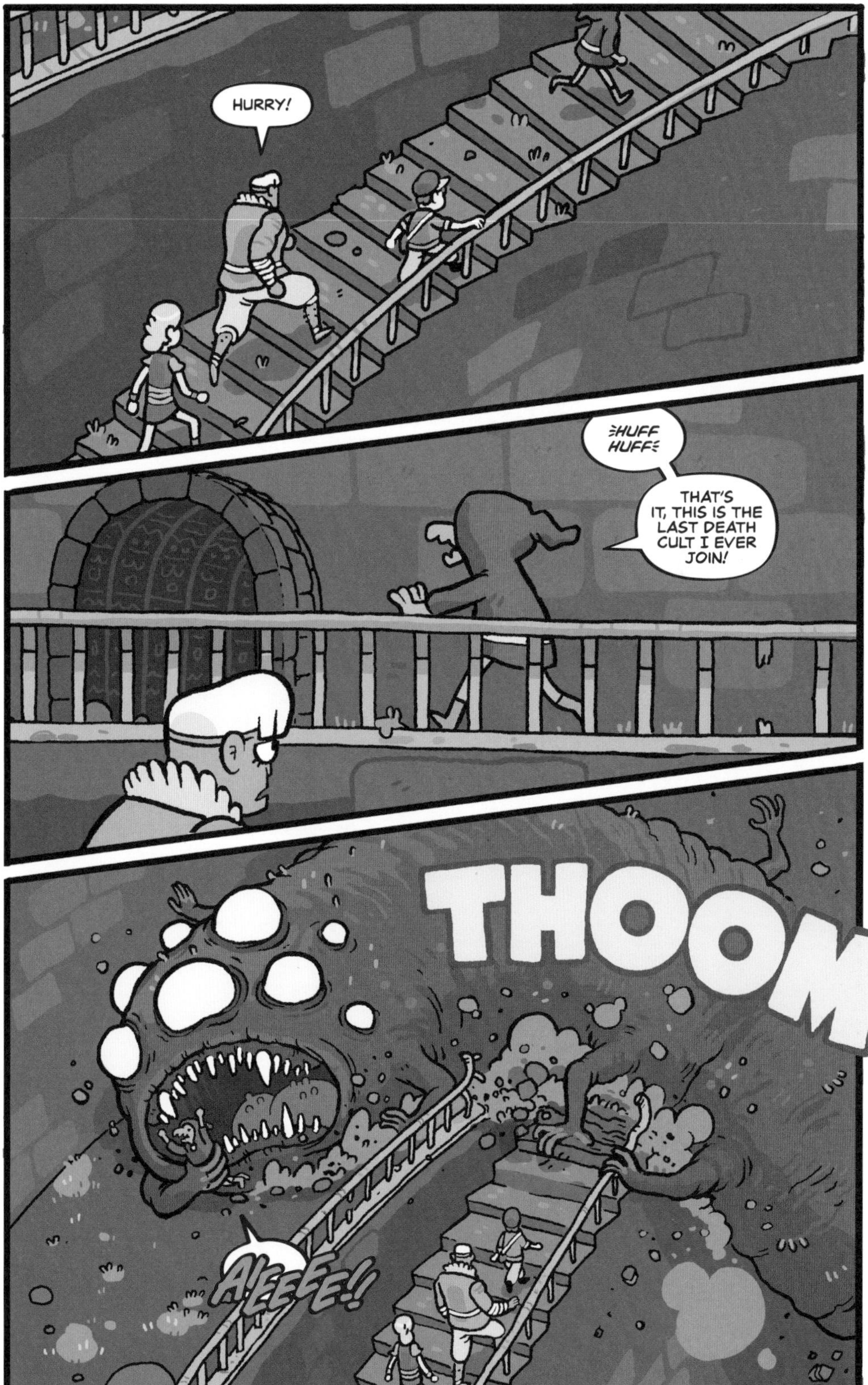
HURRY!
≡HUFF HUFF≡
THAT'S IT, THIS IS THE LAST DEATH CULT I EVER JOIN!
THOOM
AIEEEEE!!

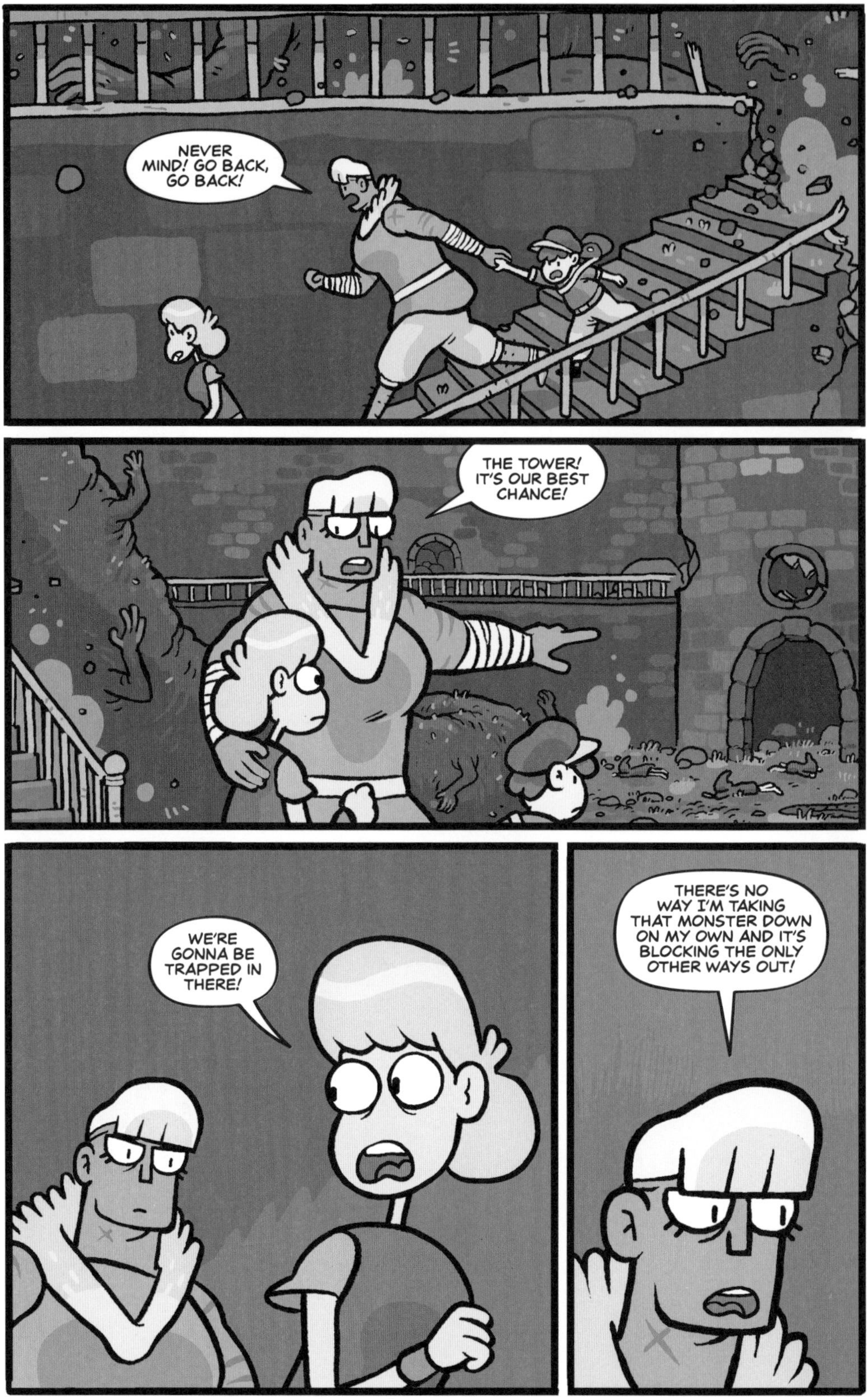
NEVER MIND! GO BACK, GO BACK!
THE TOWER! IT'S OUR BEST CHANCE!
WE'RE GONNA BE TRAPPED IN THERE!
THERE'S NO WAY I'M TAKING THAT MONSTER DOWN ON MY OWN AND IT'S BLOCKING THE ONLY OTHER WAYS OUT!

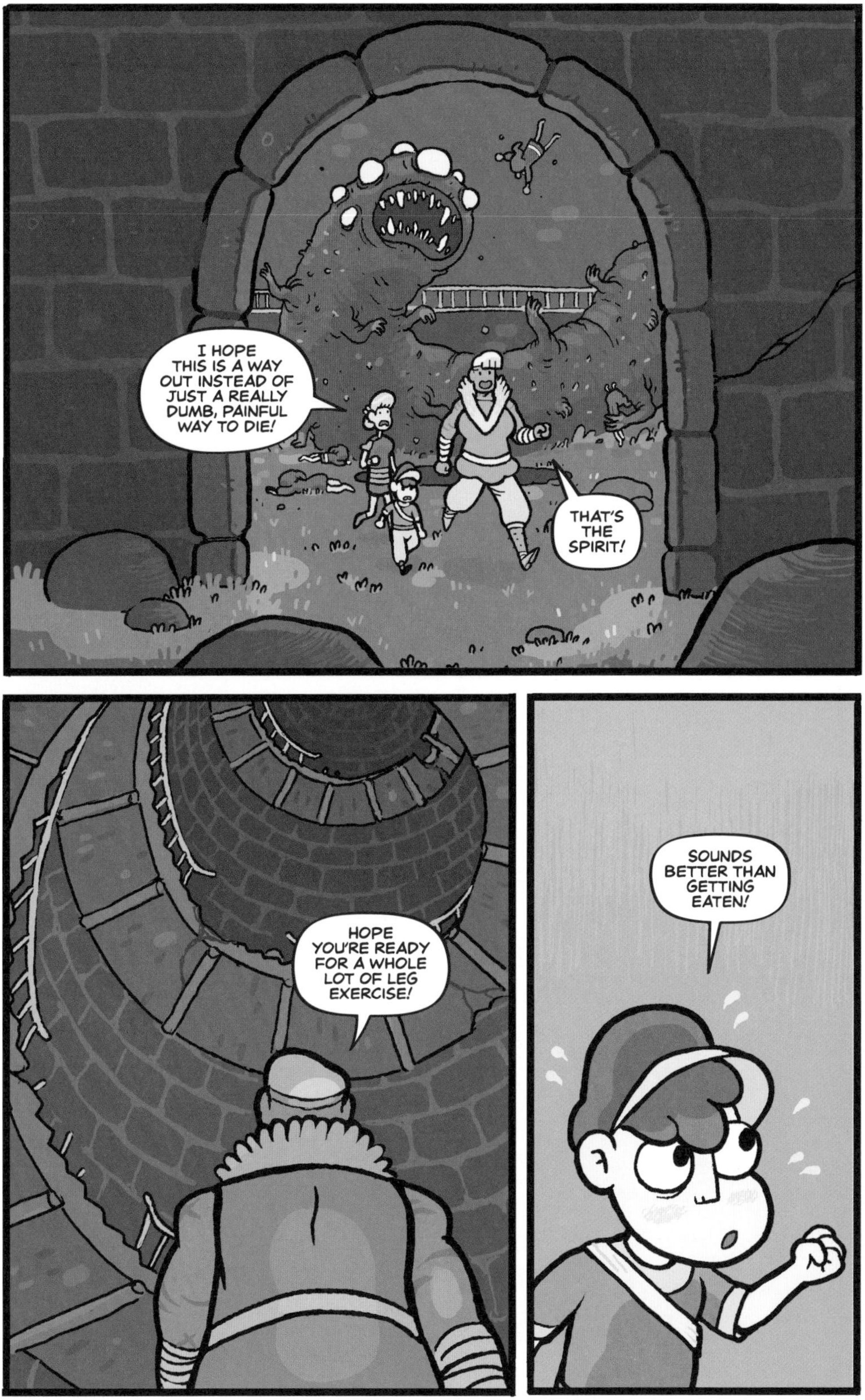
I HOPE THIS IS A WAY OUT INSTEAD OF JUST A REALLY DUMB, PAINFUL WAY TO DIE!
THAT'S THE SPIRIT!
HOPE YOU'RE READY FOR A WHOLE LOT OF LEG EXERCISE!
SOUNDS BETTER THAN GETTING EATEN!

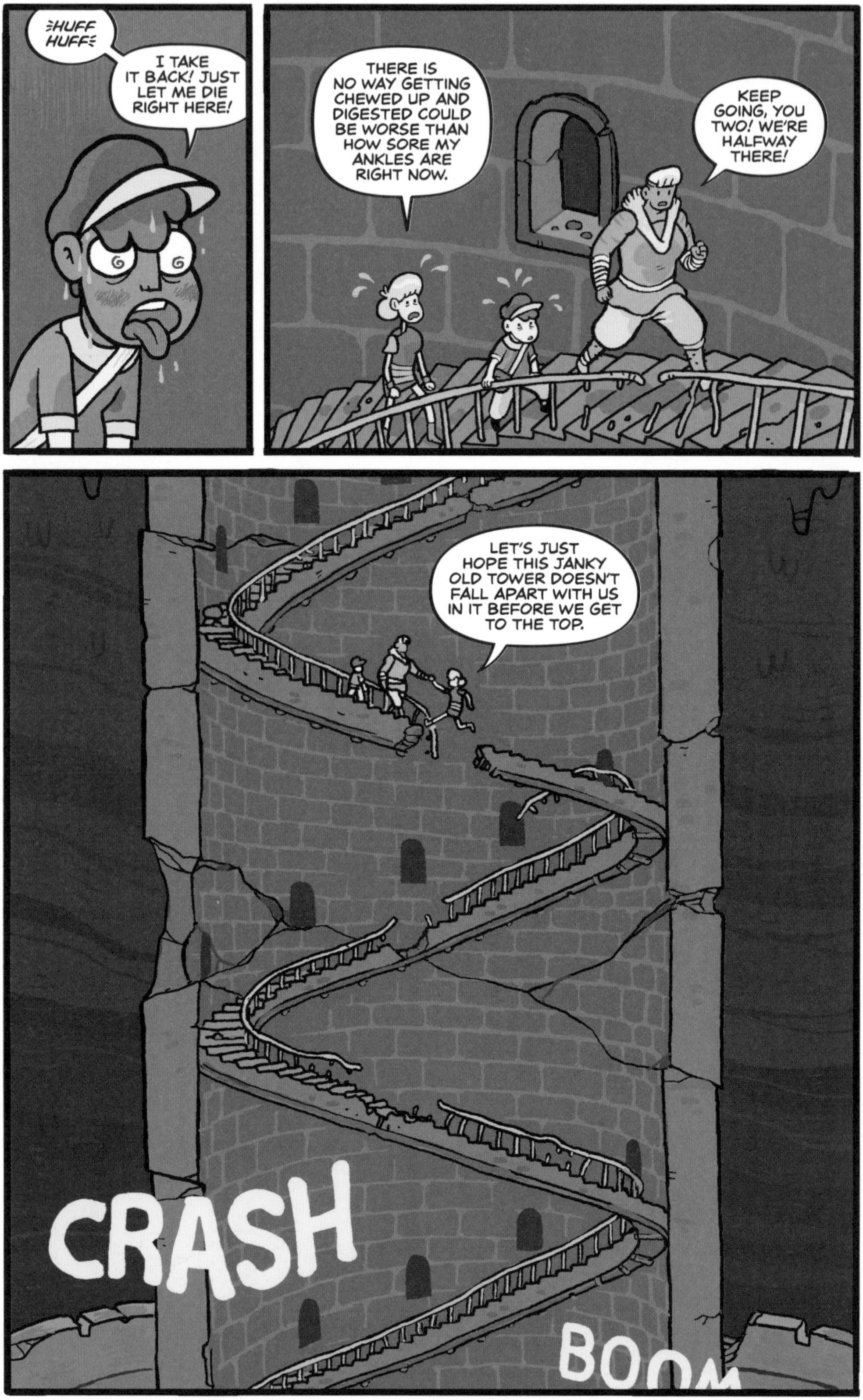

HUFF HUFF
I TAKE IT BACK! JUST LET ME DIE RIGHT HERE!
THERE IS NO WAY GETTING CHEWED UP AND DIGESTED COULD BE WORSE THAN HOW SORE MY ANKLES ARE RIGHT NOW.
KEEP GOING, YOU TWO! WE'RE HALFWAY THERE!
LET'S JUST HOPE THIS JANKY OLD TOWER DOESN'T FALL APART WITH US IN IT BEFORE WE GET TO THE TOP.
CRASH

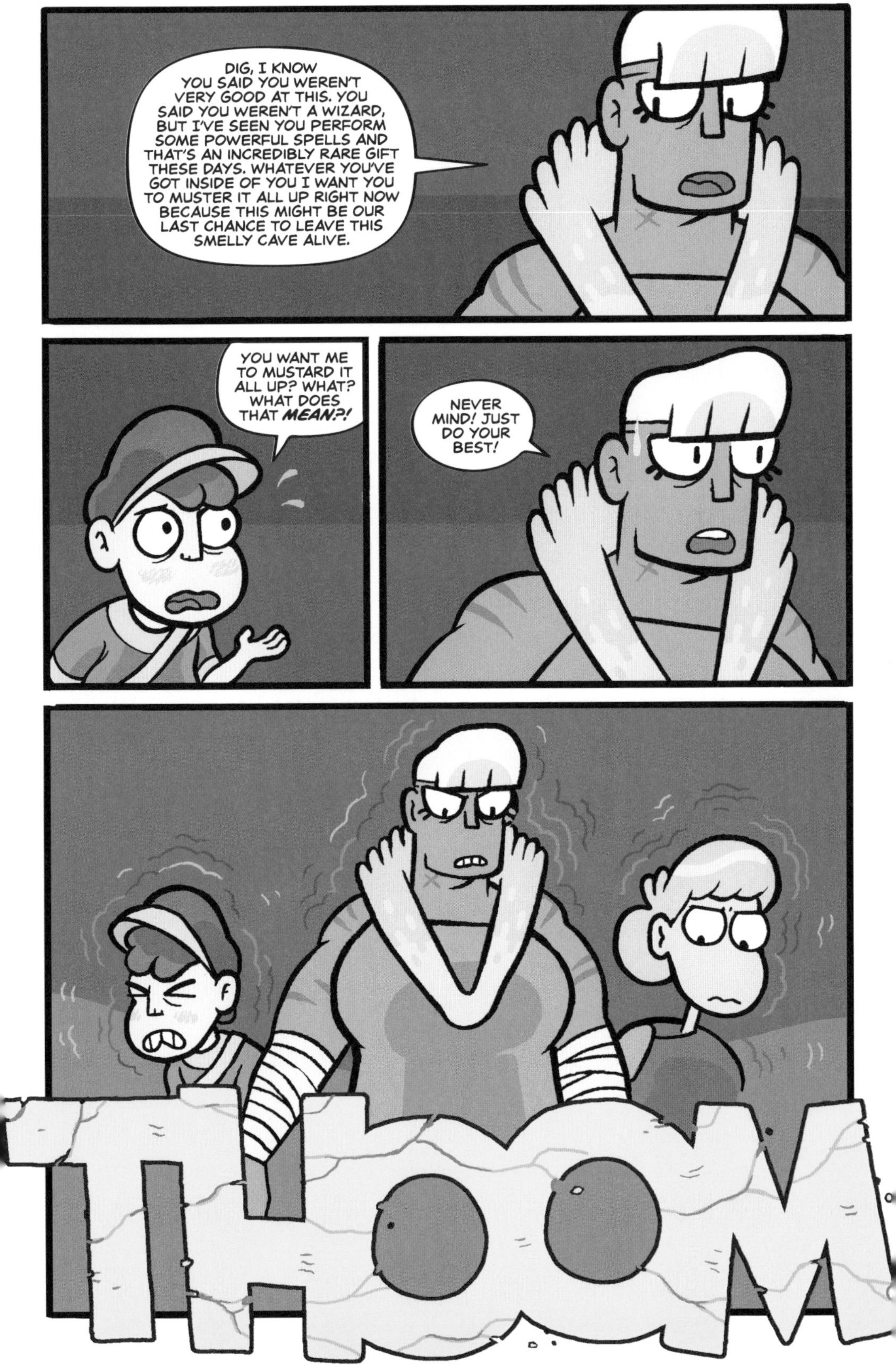
DIG, I KNOW YOU SAID YOU WEREN'T VERY GOOD AT THIS. YOU SAID YOU WEREN'T A WIZARD, BUT I'VE SEEN YOU PERFORM SOME POWERFUL SPELLS AND THAT'S AN INCREDIBLY RARE GIFT THESE DAYS. WHATEVER YOU'VE GOT INSIDE OF YOU I WANT YOU TO MUSTER IT ALL UP RIGHT NOW BECAUSE THIS MIGHT BE OUR LAST CHANCE TO LEAVE THIS SMELLY CAVE ALIVE.
YOU WANT ME TO MUSTARD IT ALL UP? WHAT? WHAT DOES THAT *MEAN?!*
NEVER MIND! JUST DO YOUR BEST!
THOOM

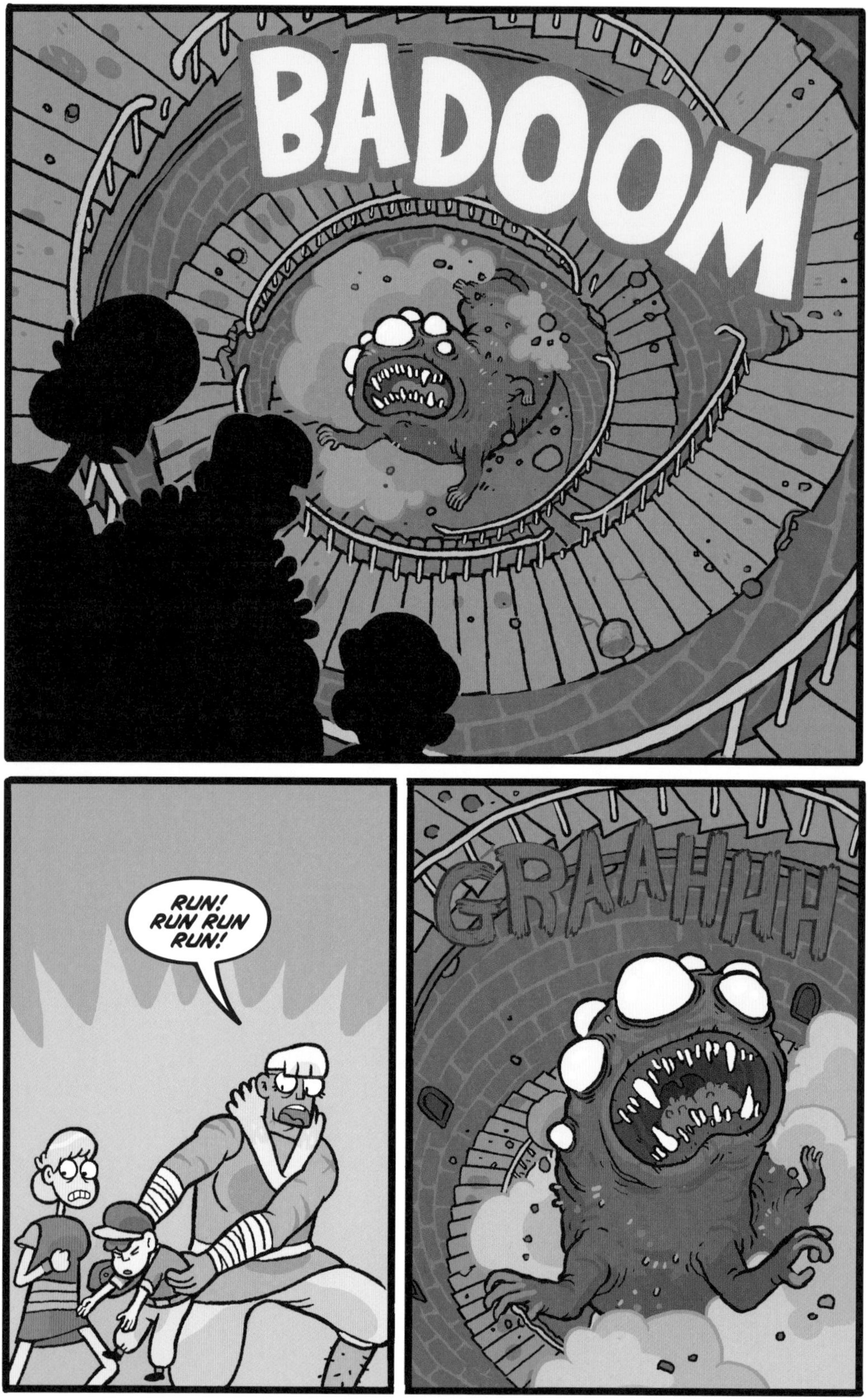
BADOOM
RUN! RUN RUN RUN!
GRAAHHH

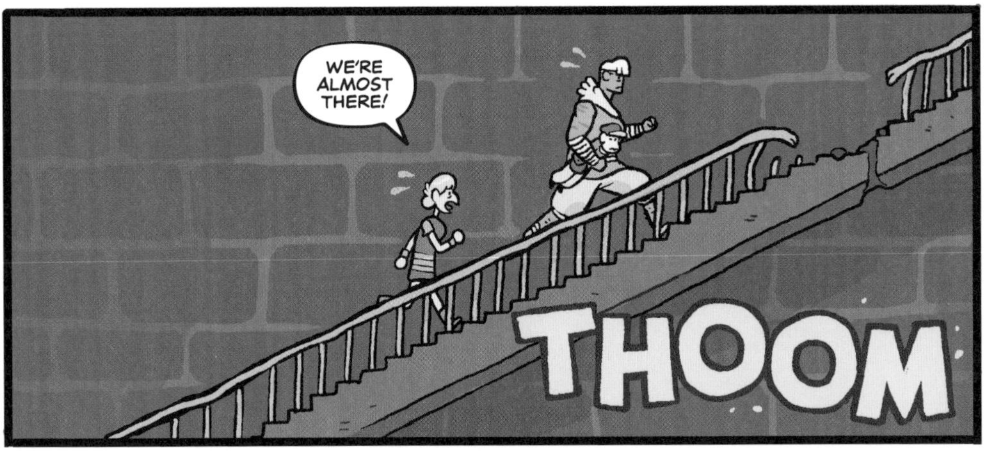
WE'RE ALMOST THERE!
THOOM
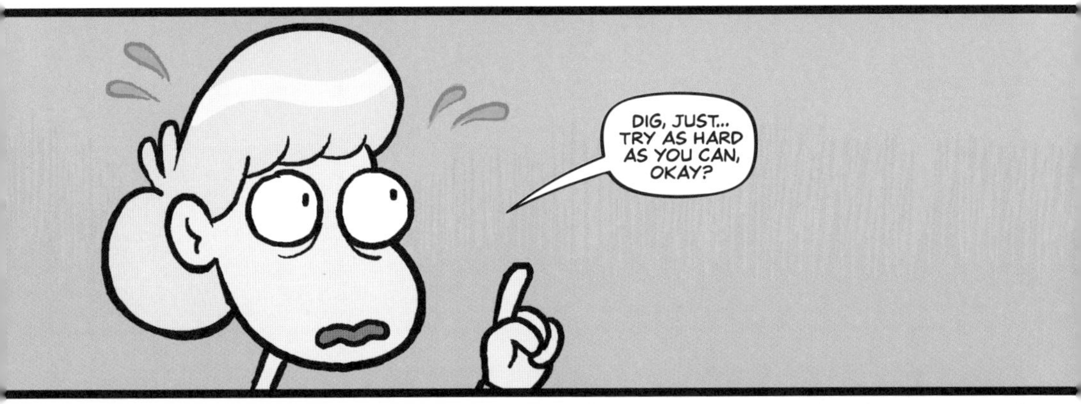
DIG, JUST... TRY AS HARD AS YOU CAN, OKAY?
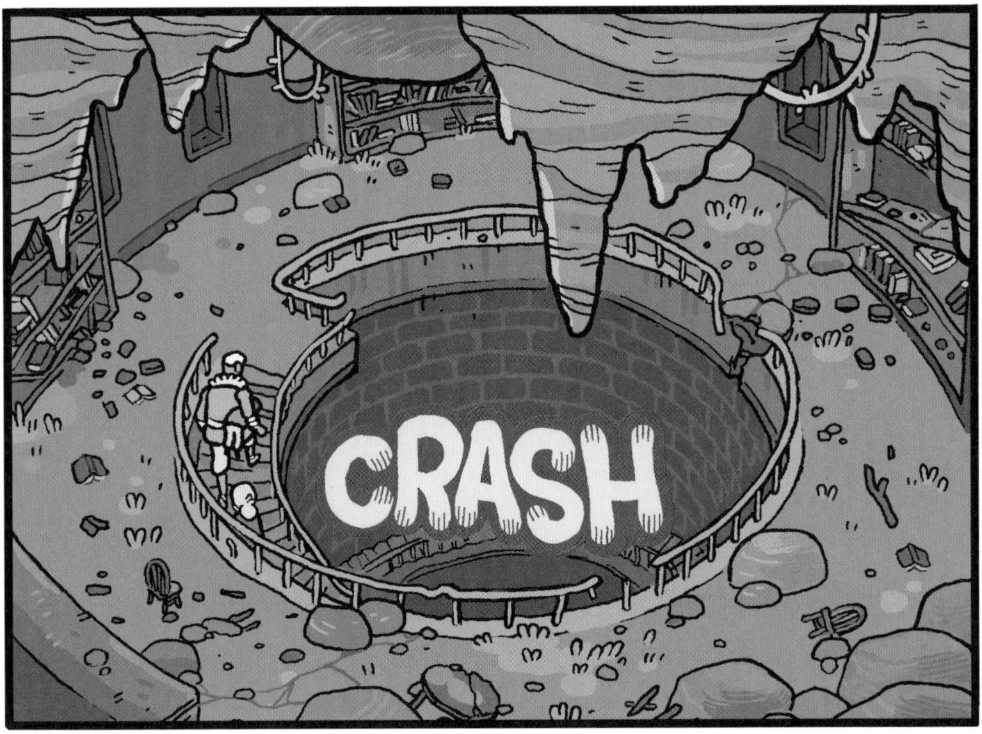
CRASH

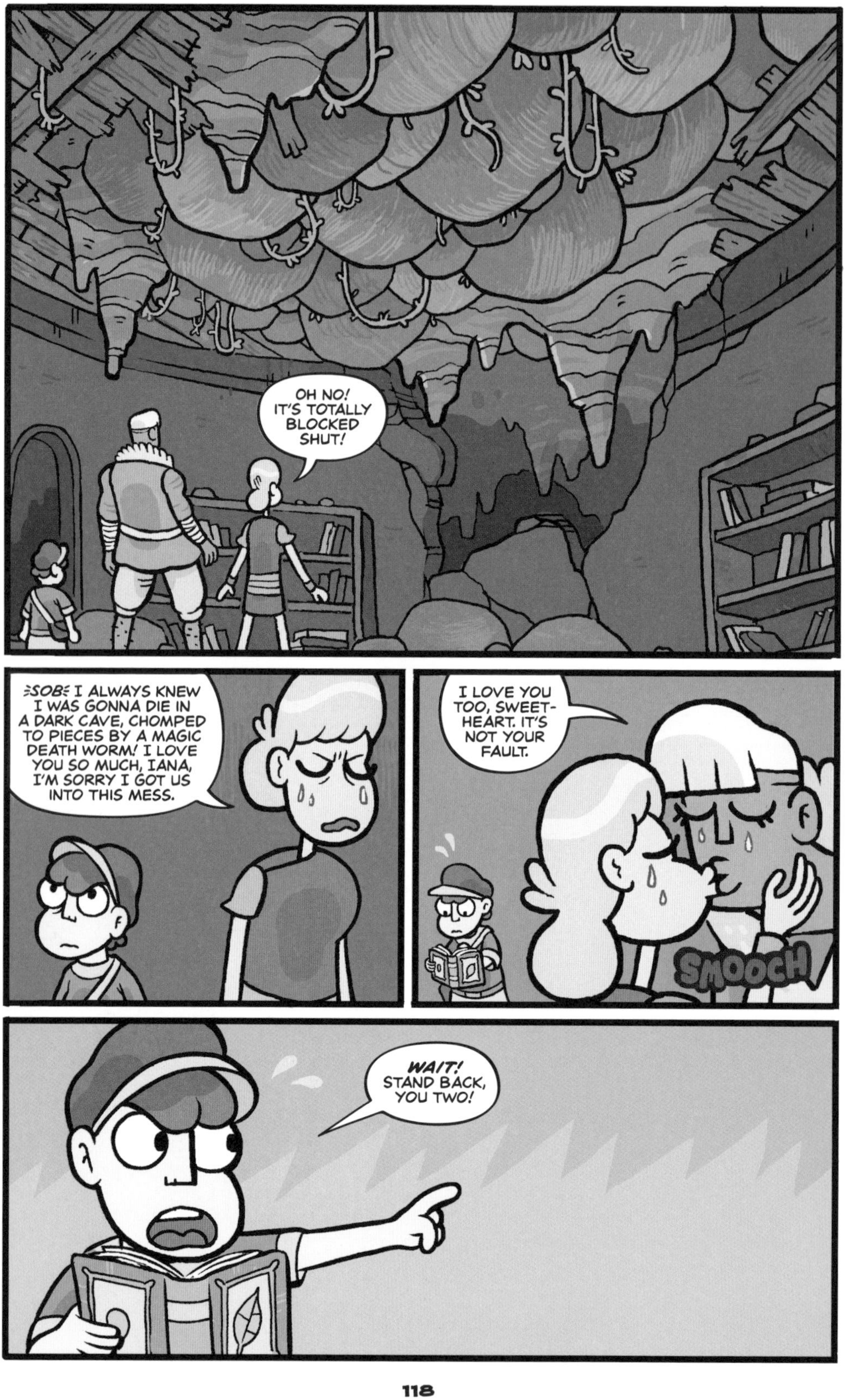
OH NO! IT'S TOTALLY BLOCKED SHUT!
SOB I ALWAYS KNEW I WAS GONNA DIE IN A DARK CAVE, CHOMPED TO PIECES BY A MAGIC DEATH WORM! I LOVE YOU SO MUCH, IANA, I'M SORRY I GOT US INTO THIS MESS.
I LOVE YOU TOO, SWEET-HEART. IT'S NOT YOUR FAULT.
SMOOCH
WAIT! STAND BACK, YOU TWO!

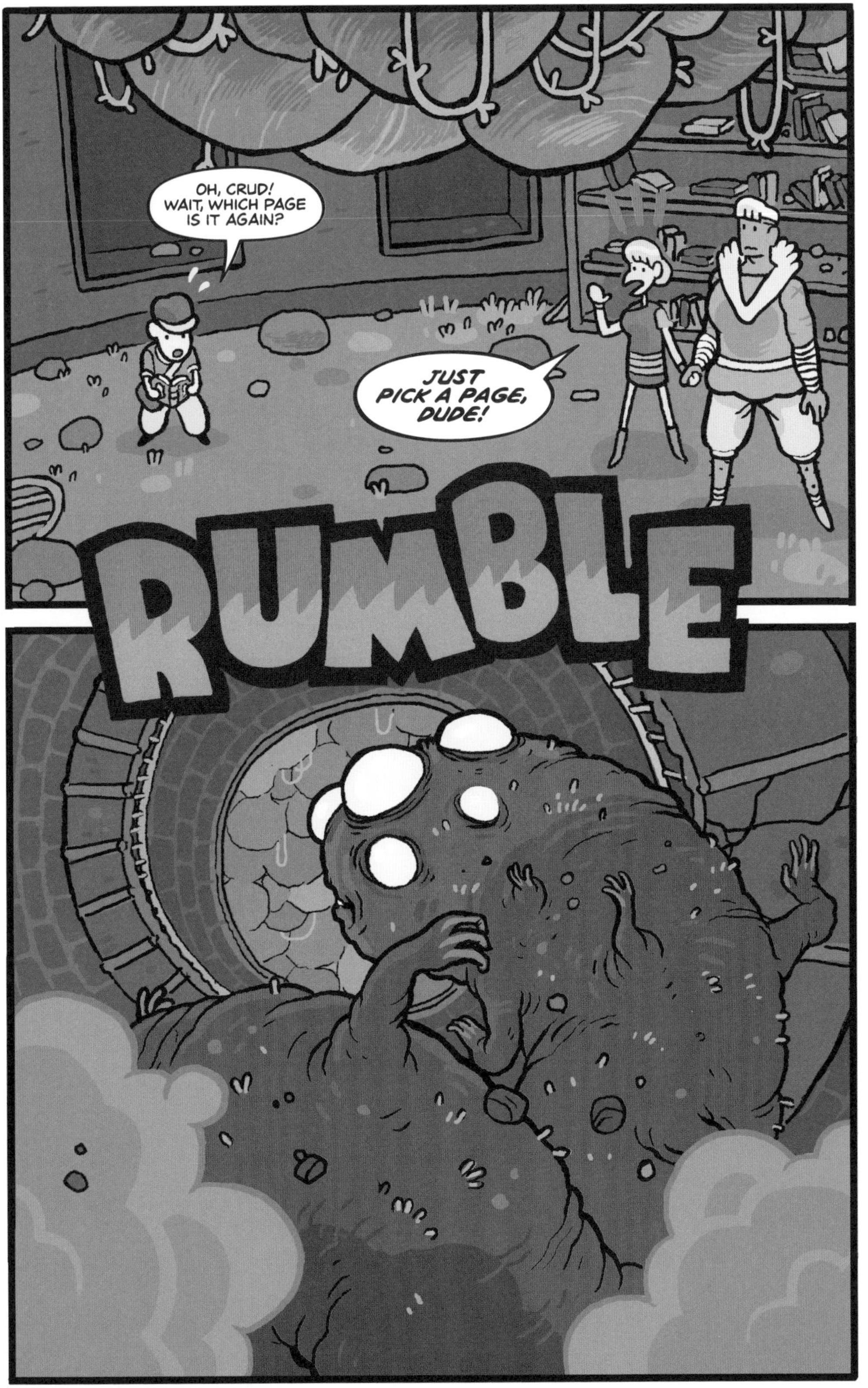
OH, CRUD! WAIT, WHICH PAGE IS IT AGAIN?
JUST PICK A PAGE, DUDE!
RUMBLE

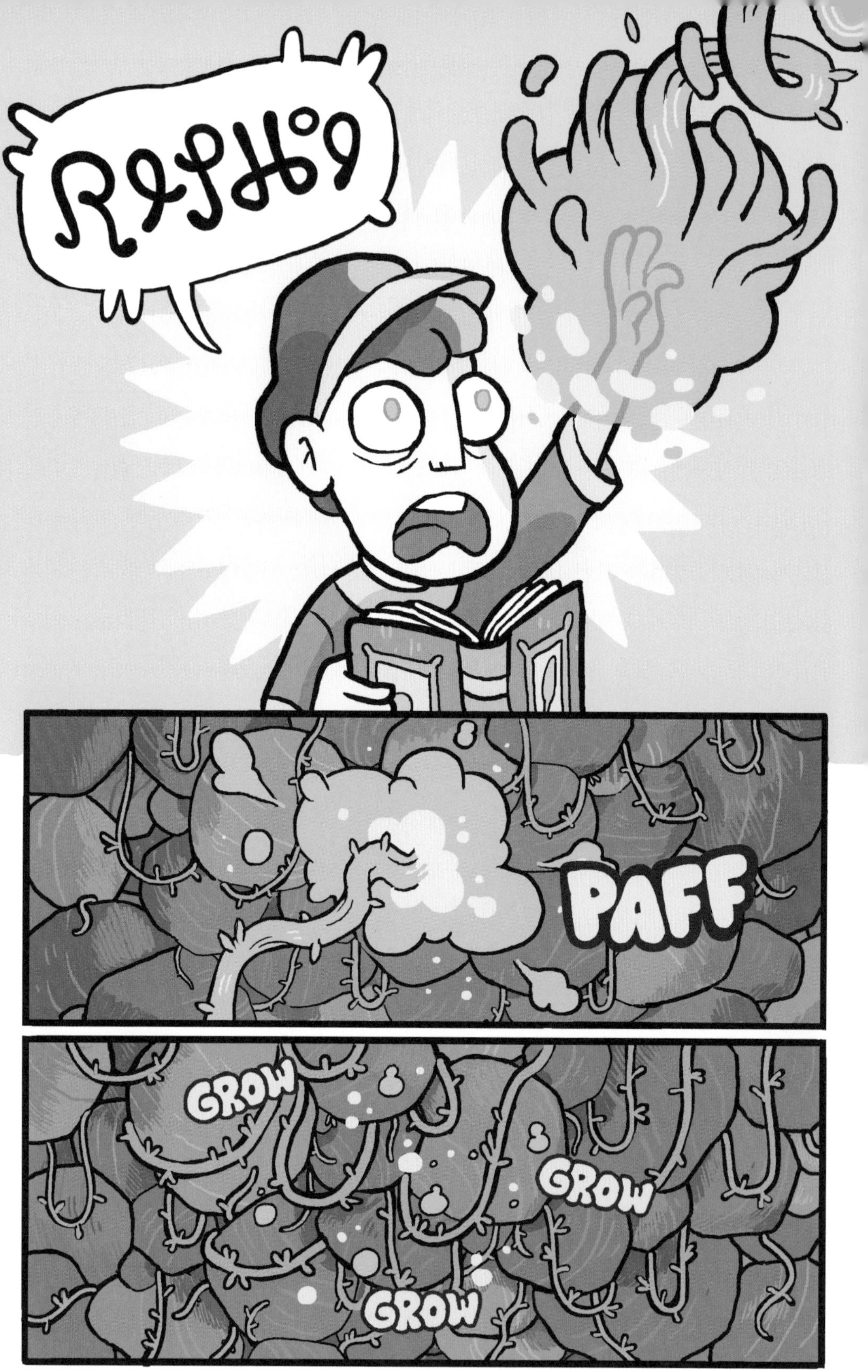
PAFF
GROW
GROW
GROW

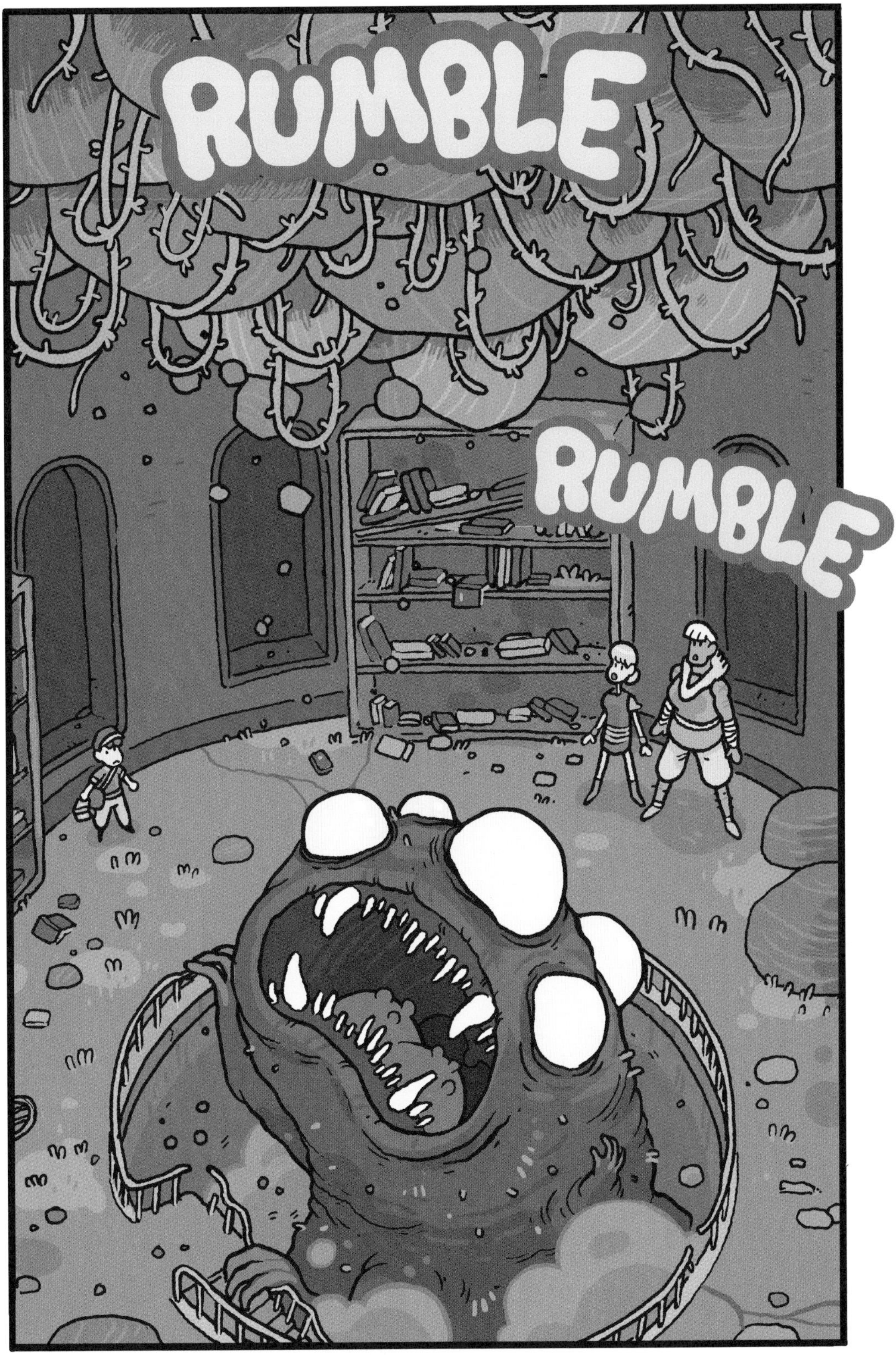
RUMBLE
RUMBLE

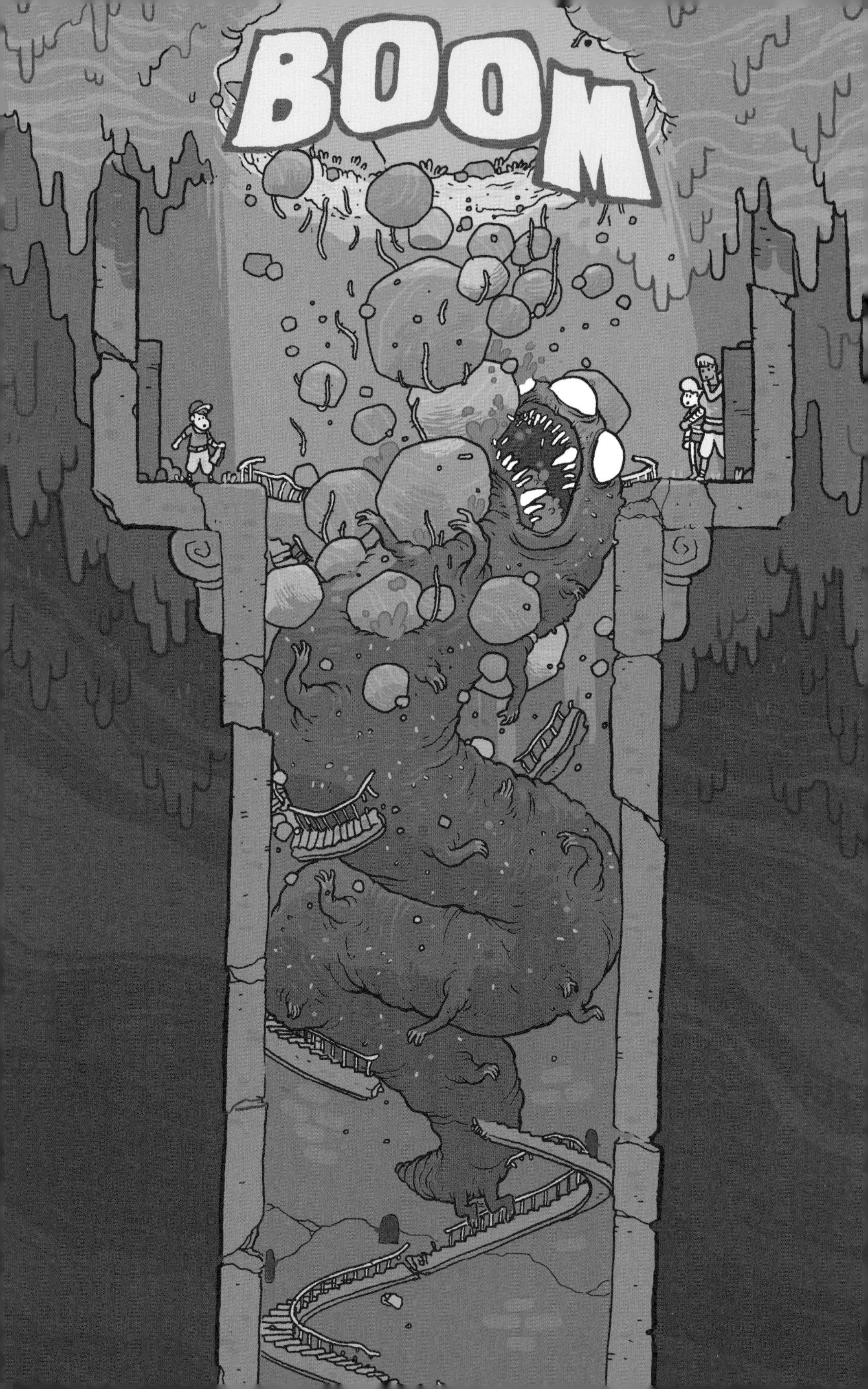
BOOM

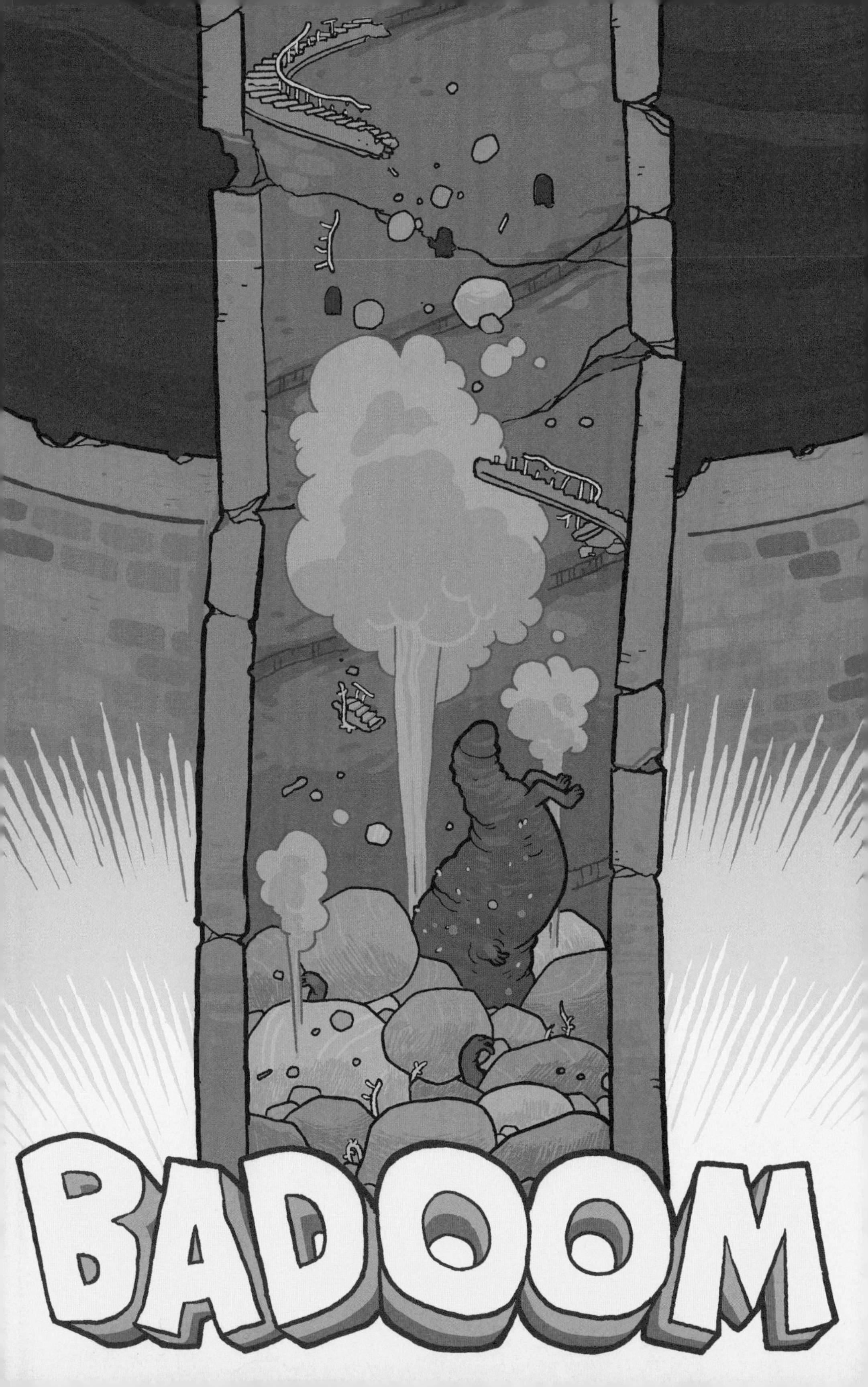
BADOOOM

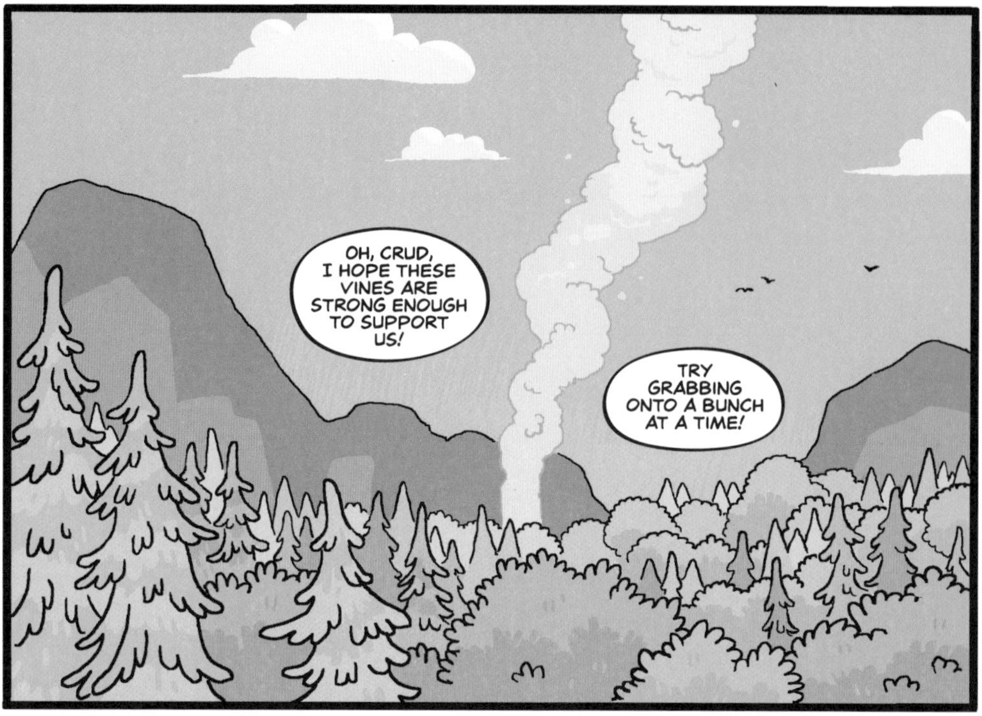
OH, CRUD, I HOPE THESE VINES ARE STRONG ENOUGH TO SUPPORT US!
TRY GRABBING ONTO A BUNCH AT A TIME!

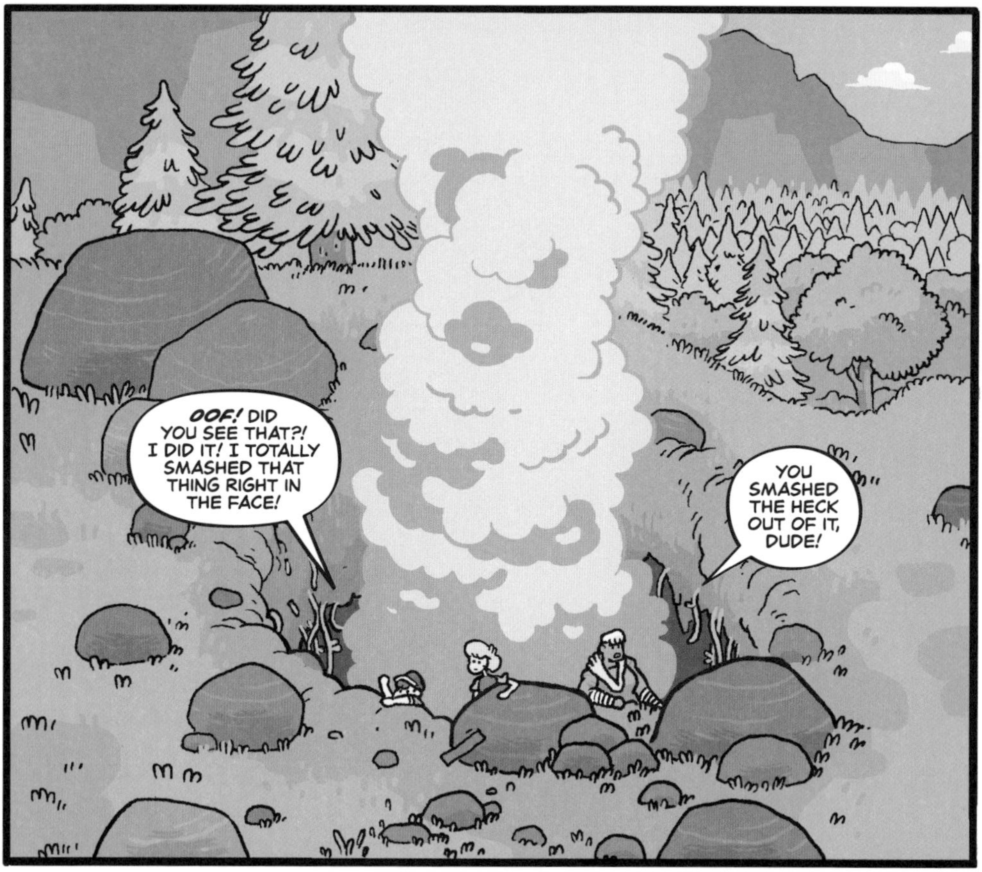
OOF! DID YOU SEE THAT?! I DID IT! I TOTALLY SMASHED THAT THING RIGHT IN THE FACE!
YOU SMASHED THE HECK OUT OF IT, DUDE!

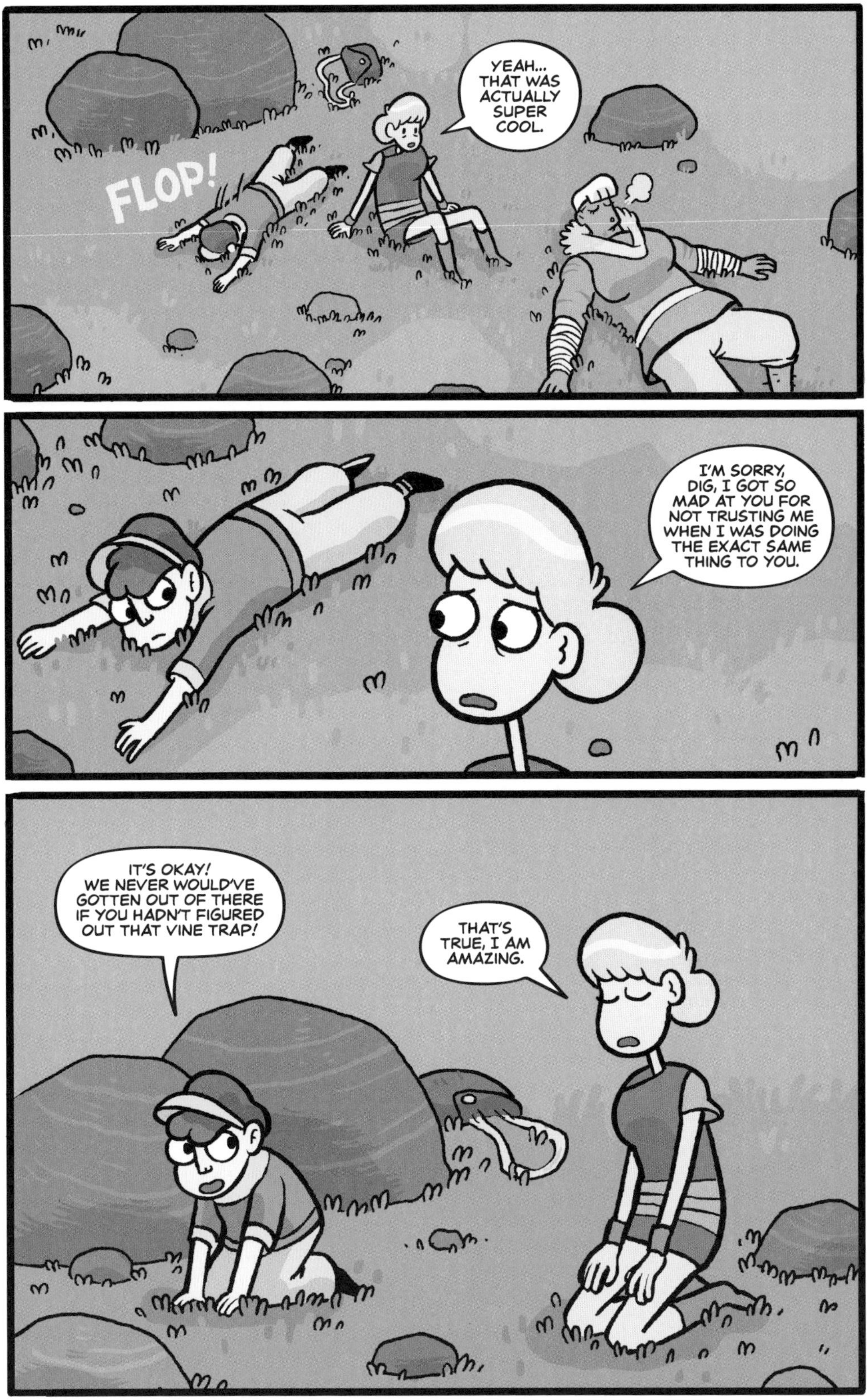
FLOP!
YEAH... THAT WAS ACTUALLY SUPER COOL.
I'M SORRY, DIG, I GOT SO MAD AT YOU FOR NOT TRUSTING ME WHEN I WAS DOING THE EXACT SAME THING TO YOU.
IT'S OKAY! WE NEVER WOULD'VE GOTTEN OUT OF THERE IF YOU HADN'T FIGURED OUT THAT VINE TRAP!
THAT'S TRUE, I AM AMAZING.

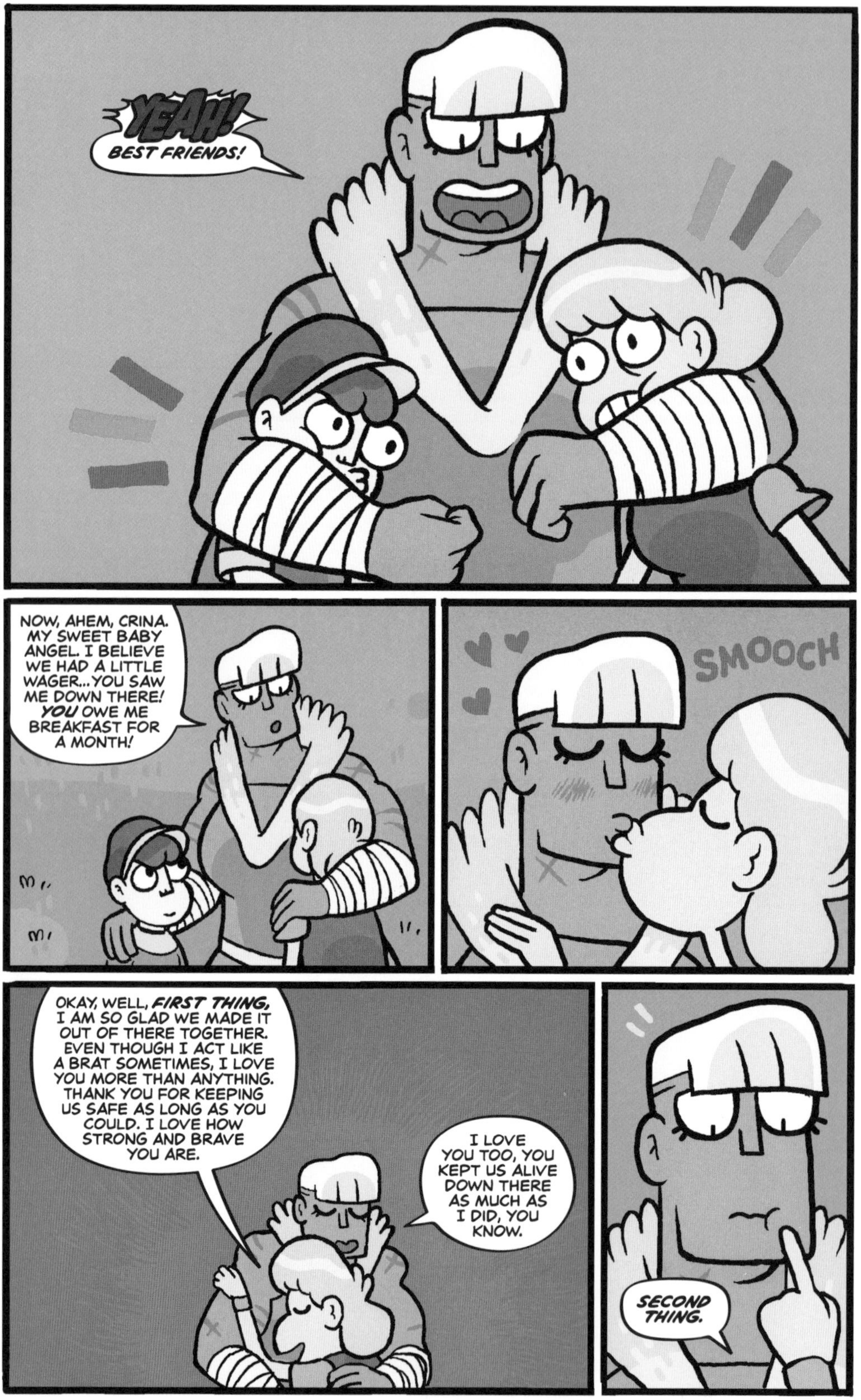
YEAH!
BEST FRIENDS!
NOW, AHEM, CRINA. MY SWEET BABY ANGEL. I BELIEVE WE HAD A LITTLE WAGER...YOU SAW ME DOWN THERE! YOU OWE ME BREAKFAST FOR A MONTH!
SMOOCH
OKAY, WELL, FIRST THING, I AM SO GLAD WE MADE IT OUT OF THERE TOGETHER. EVEN THOUGH I ACT LIKE A BRAT SOMETIMES, I LOVE YOU MORE THAN ANYTHING. THANK YOU FOR KEEPING US SAFE AS LONG AS YOU COULD. I LOVE HOW STRONG AND BRAVE YOU ARE.
I LOVE YOU TOO, YOU KEPT US ALIVE DOWN THERE AS MUCH AS I DID, YOU KNOW.
SECOND THING.

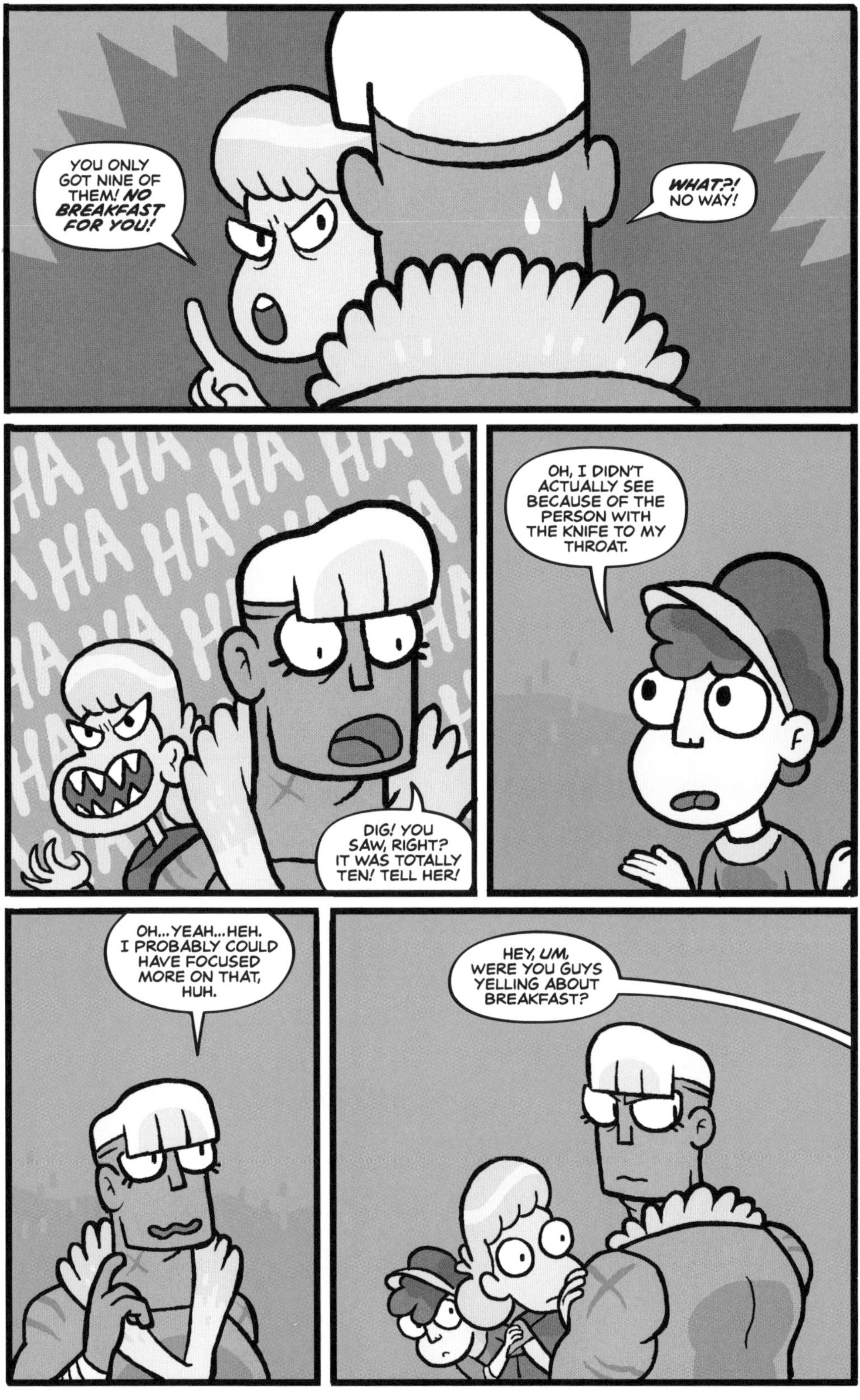
YOU ONLY GOT NINE OF THEM! *NO BREAKFAST FOR YOU!*
WHAT?! NO WAY!
HA HA HA HA HA
DIG! YOU SAW, RIGHT? IT WAS TOTALLY TEN! TELL HER!
OH, I DIDN'T ACTUALLY SEE BECAUSE OF THE PERSON WITH THE KNIFE TO MY THROAT.
OH...YEAH...HEH. I PROBABLY COULD HAVE FOCUSED MORE ON THAT, HUH.
HEY, *UM,* WERE YOU GUYS YELLING ABOUT BREAKFAST?

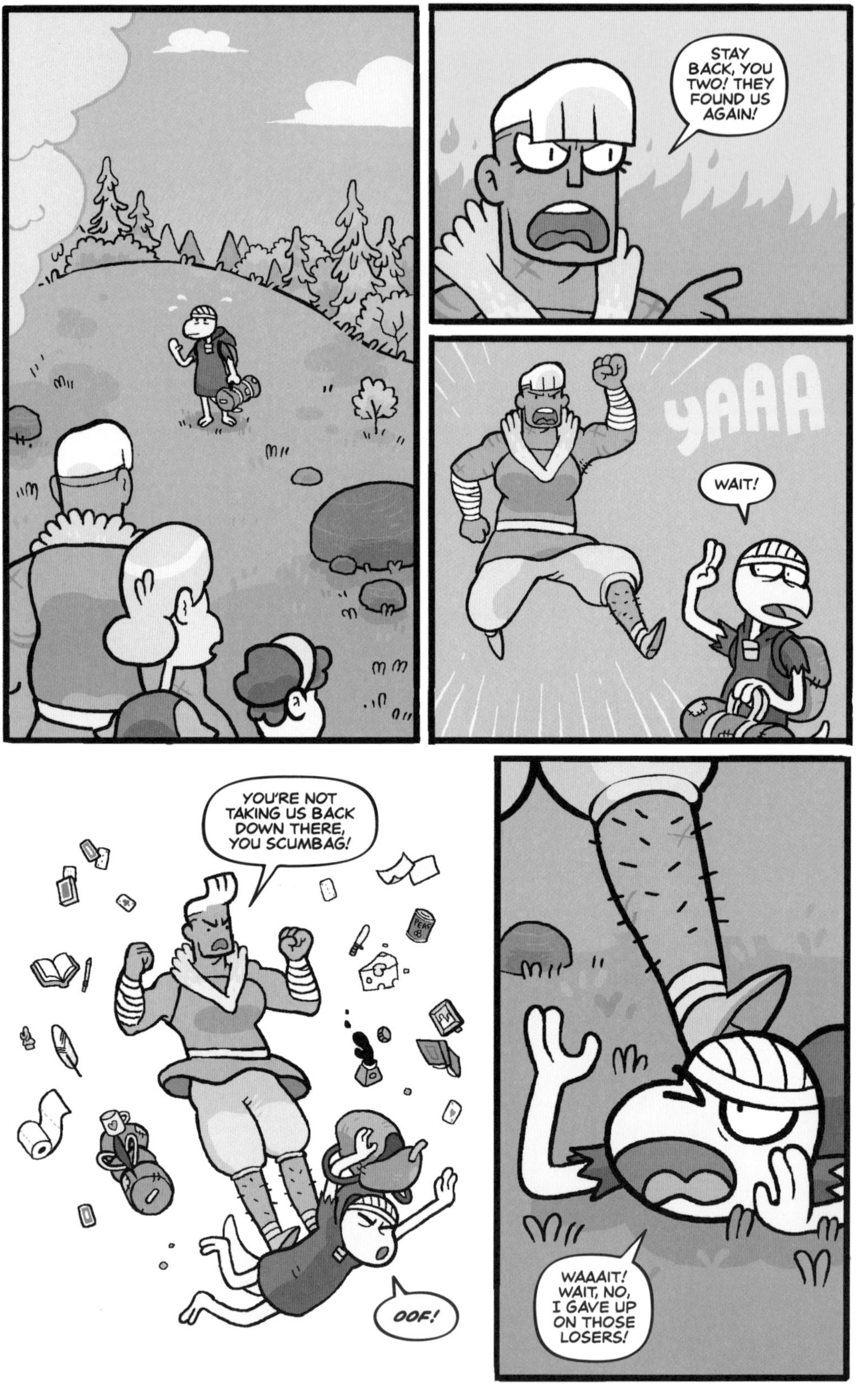
STAY BACK, YOU TWO! THEY FOUND US AGAIN!
YAAA
WAIT!
YOU'RE NOT TAKING US BACK DOWN THERE, YOU SCUMBAG!
PEAS
OOF!
WAAAIT! WAIT, NO, I GAVE UP ON THOSE LOSERS!

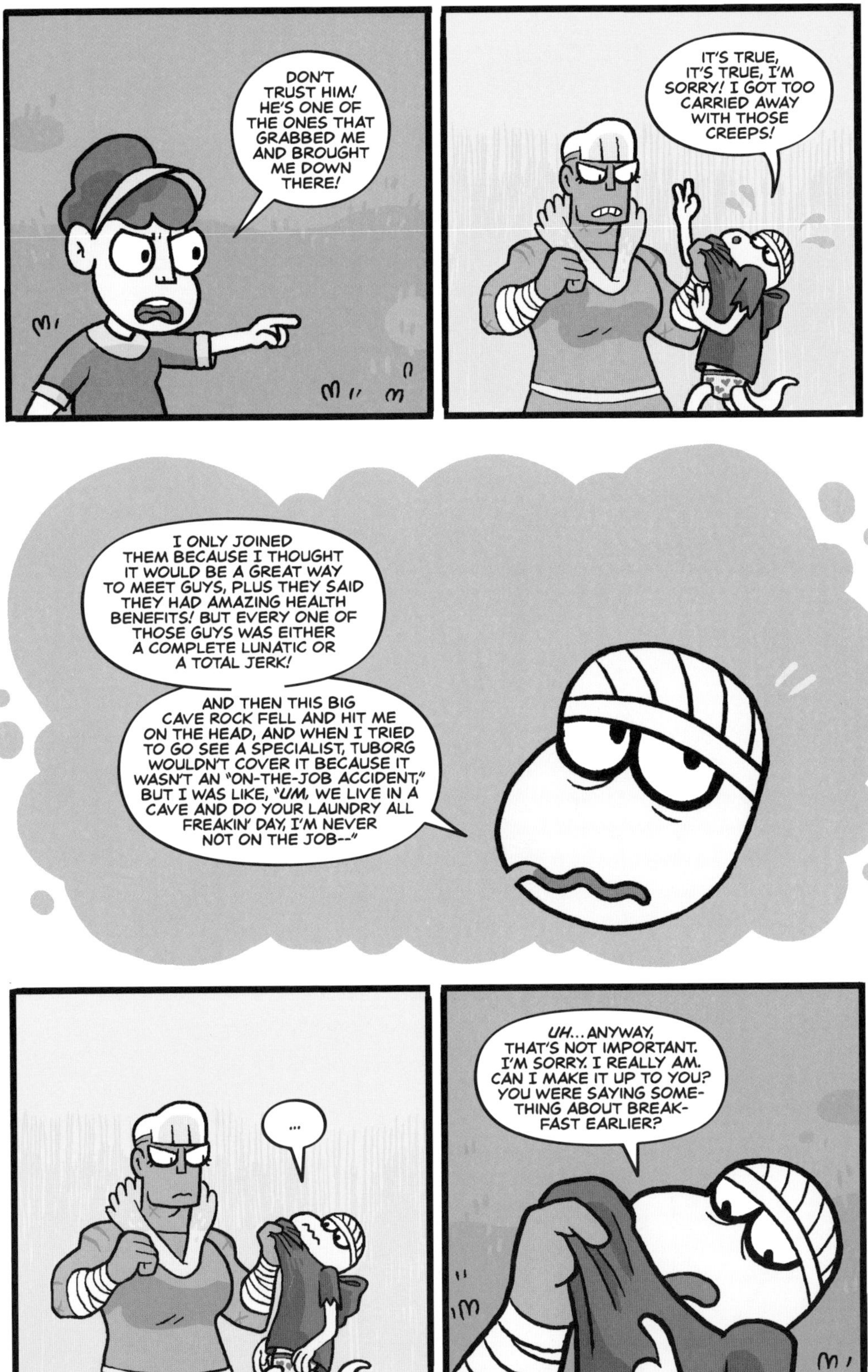
DON'T TRUST HIM! HE'S ONE OF THE ONES THAT GRABBED ME AND BROUGHT ME DOWN THERE!
IT'S TRUE, IT'S TRUE, I'M SORRY! I GOT TOO CARRIED AWAY WITH THOSE CREEPS!
I ONLY JOINED THEM BECAUSE I THOUGHT IT WOULD BE A GREAT WAY TO MEET GUYS, PLUS THEY SAID THEY HAD AMAZING HEALTH BENEFITS! BUT EVERY ONE OF THOSE GUYS WAS EITHER A COMPLETE LUNATIC OR A TOTAL JERK!
AND THEN THIS BIG CAVE ROCK FELL AND HIT ME ON THE HEAD, AND WHEN I TRIED TO GO SEE A SPECIALIST, TUBORG WOULDN'T COVER IT BECAUSE IT WASN'T AN "ON-THE-JOB ACCIDENT," BUT I WAS LIKE, "UM, WE LIVE IN A CAVE AND DO YOUR LAUNDRY ALL FREAKIN' DAY, I'M NEVER NOT ON THE JOB--"
...
UH... ANYWAY, THAT'S NOT IMPORTANT. I'M SORRY. I REALLY AM. CAN I MAKE IT UP TO YOU? YOU WERE SAYING SOMETHING ABOUT BREAKFAST EARLIER?

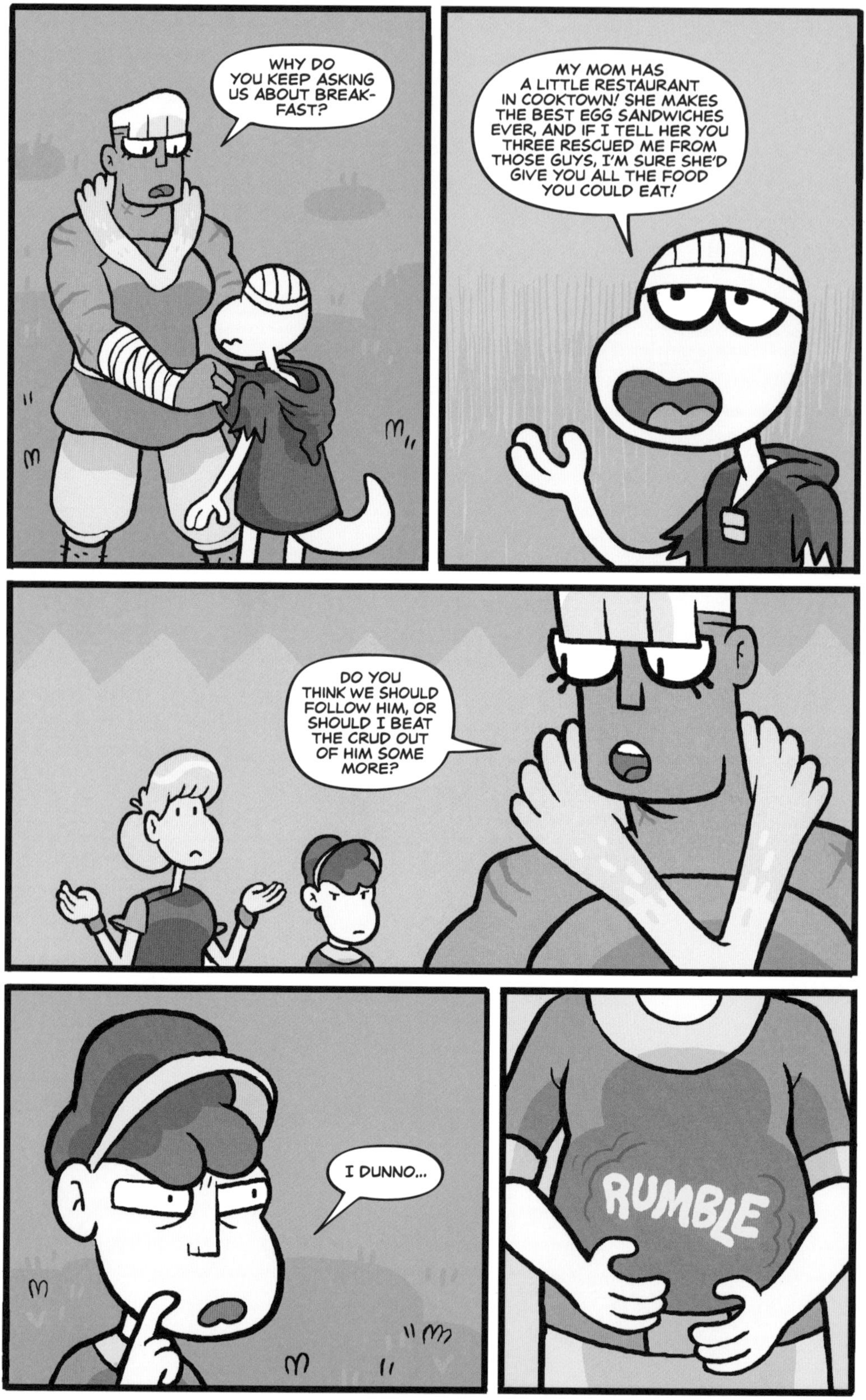
WHY DO YOU KEEP ASKING US ABOUT BREAK-FAST?
MY MOM HAS A LITTLE RESTAURANT IN COOKTOWN! SHE MAKES THE BEST EGG SANDWICHES EVER, AND IF I TELL HER YOU THREE RESCUED ME FROM THOSE GUYS, I'M SURE SHE'D GIVE YOU ALL THE FOOD YOU COULD EAT!
DO YOU THINK WE SHOULD FOLLOW HIM, OR SHOULD I BEAT THE CRUD OUT OF HIM SOME MORE?
I DUNNO...
RUMBLE

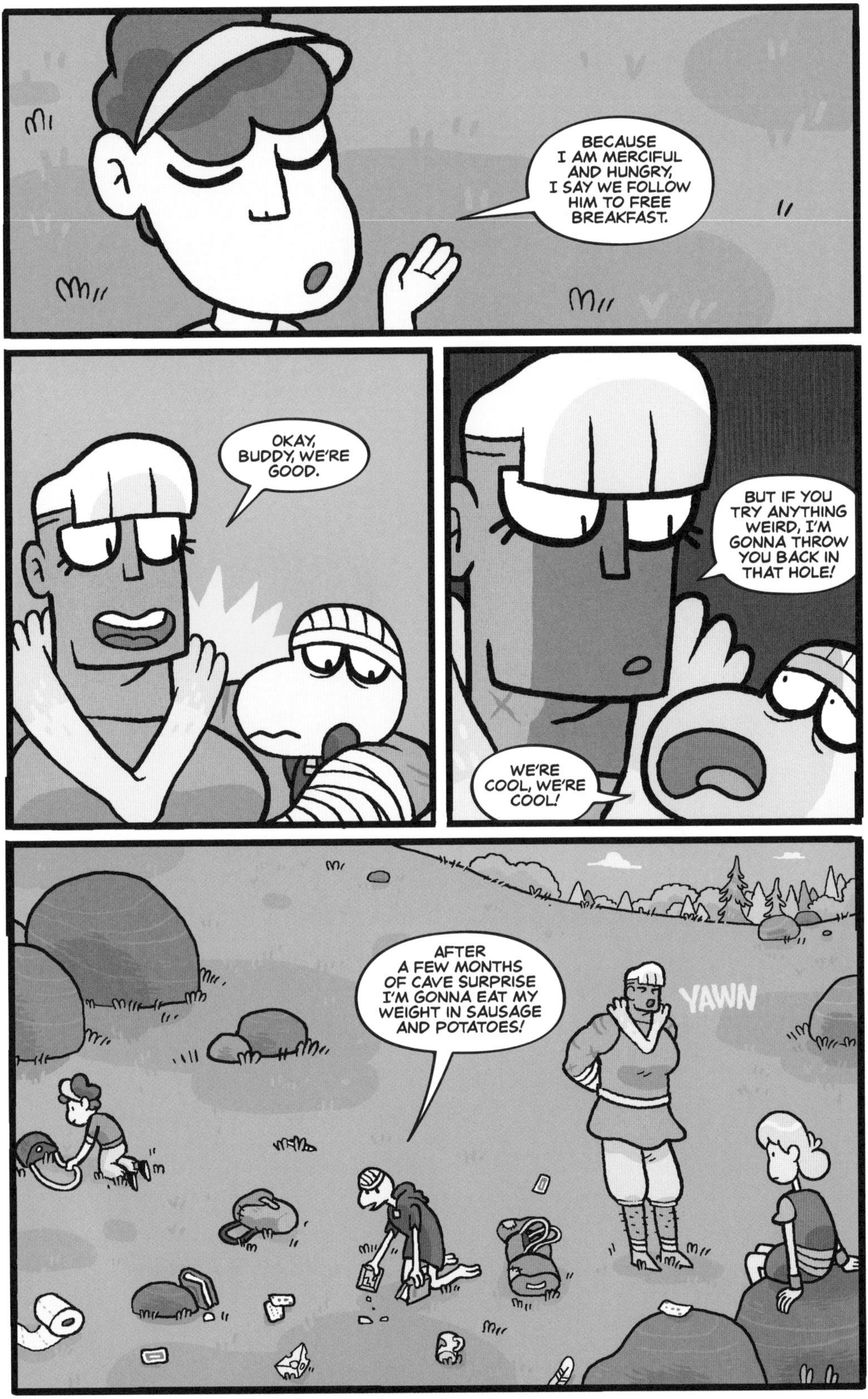

BECAUSE I AM MERCIFUL AND HUNGRY, I SAY WE FOLLOW HIM TO FREE BREAKFAST.
OKAY, BUDDY, WE'RE GOOD.
BUT IF YOU TRY ANYTHING WEIRD, I'M GONNA THROW YOU BACK IN THAT HOLE!
WE'RE COOL, WE'RE COOL!
AFTER A FEW MONTHS OF CAVE SURPRISE I'M GONNA EAT MY WEIGHT IN SAUSAGE AND POTATOES!
YAWN

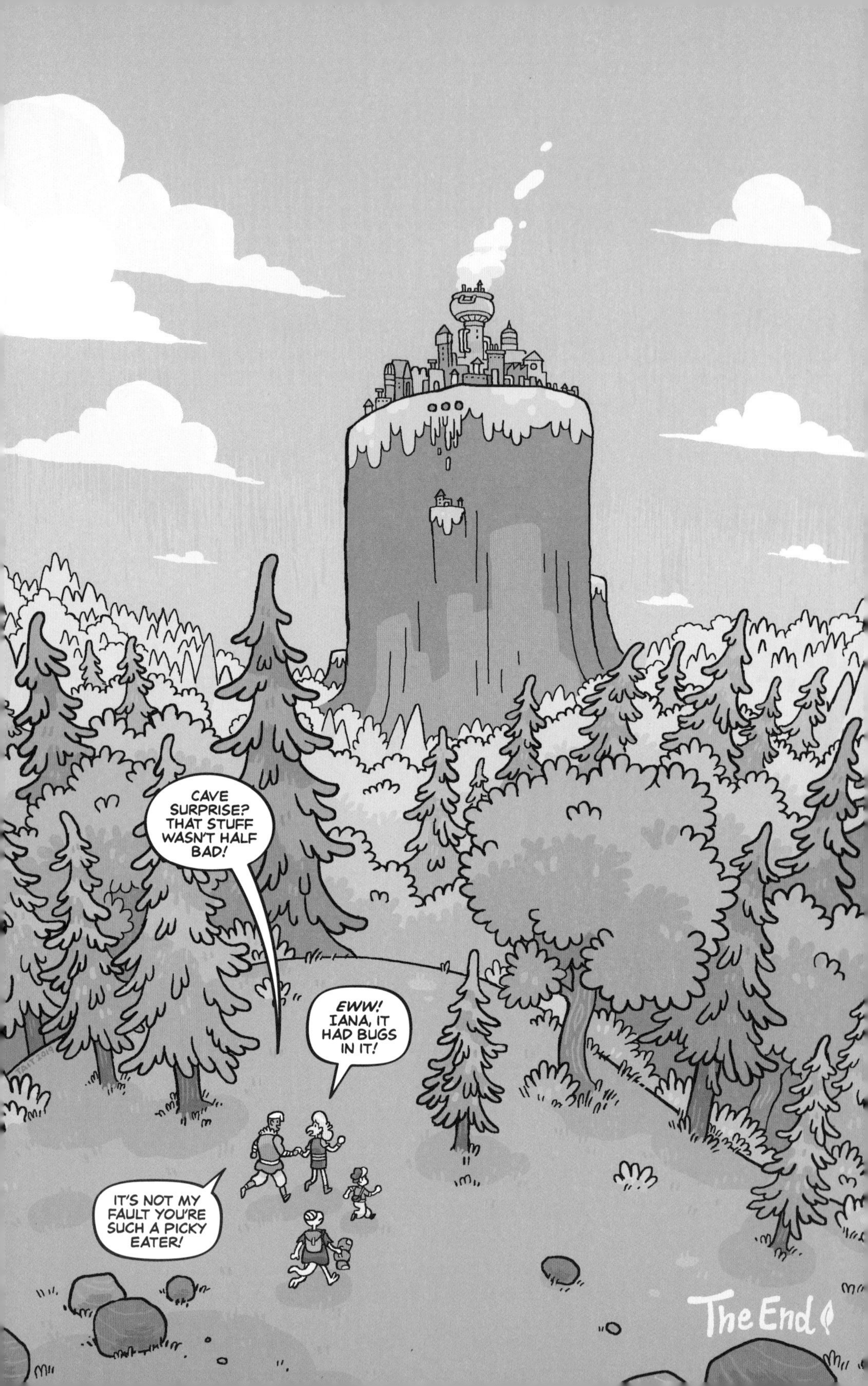
CAVE SURPRISE? THAT STUFF WASN'T HALF BAD!
EWW! IANA, IT HAD BUGS IN IT!
IT'S NOT MY FAULT YOU'RE SUCH A PICKY EATER!
The End

TAIT HOWARD

IS AN ARTIST AND WRITER WHO LIVES IN
THE DREARY, GREY PACIFIC NORTHWEST.
HIS FAVORITE COLOR IS PURPLE, HIS
FAVORITE FOOD IS ORANGES, AND
HE LIKES CATS AND DOGS EQUALLY
BECAUSE THEY'RE ALL AMAZING.

If you liked THE SUNKEN TOWER, you might enjoy...

AQUICORN COVE
KATIE O'NEILL

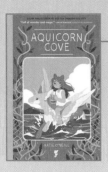

AQUICORN COVE
by Katie O'Neill

A young girl must protect a colony of magical seahorse-like creatures she discovers in the coral reef.

GHOST HOG
by Joey Weiser

Truff, the ghost of a boar killed by a hunter, navigates her new afterlife as she seeks revenge.

GHOST HOG
BY JOEY WEISER

MAI K. NGUYEN
PILU of the WOODS

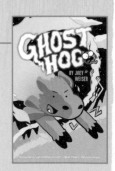

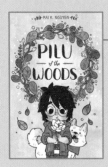

PILU OF THE WOODS
by Mai K. Nguyen

After running away from home, Willow befriends a tree spirit, Pilu, living in the woods near her house.

UNPLUGGED AND UNPOPULAR
by Mat Heagerty, Tintin Pantoja, & Mike Amante

When Erin Song is banned from her phone and computer, she discovers an alien invasion! But will anyone believe her?

MAT HEAGERTY • TINTIN PANTOJA • MIKE AMANTE
UNPLUGGED AND UNPOPULAR

MATT GARDNER
RASHAD DOUCET
ALABASTER SHADOWS

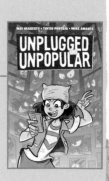

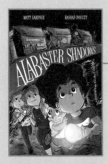

ALABASTER SHADOWS
by Matt Gardner & Rashad Doucet

When Carter moves to a new neighborhood, he finds tears in reality and terrifying monsters.

SPACE BATTLE LUNCHTIME
by Natalie Riess

Peony is a baker with big dreams! Can she make it through the universe's biggest reality cooking show?

SPACE BATTLE LUNCHTIME
VOLUME ONE: LIGHTS, CAMERA, SNACKTION!

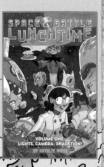

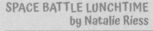

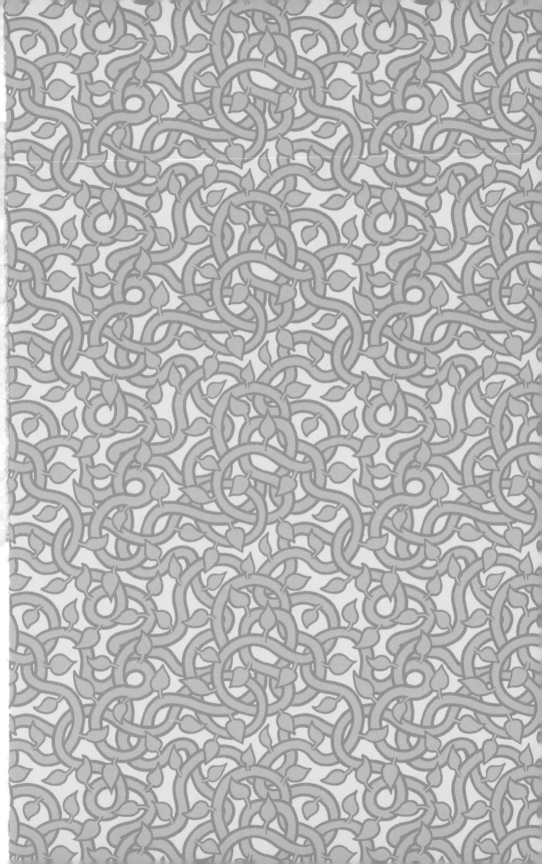

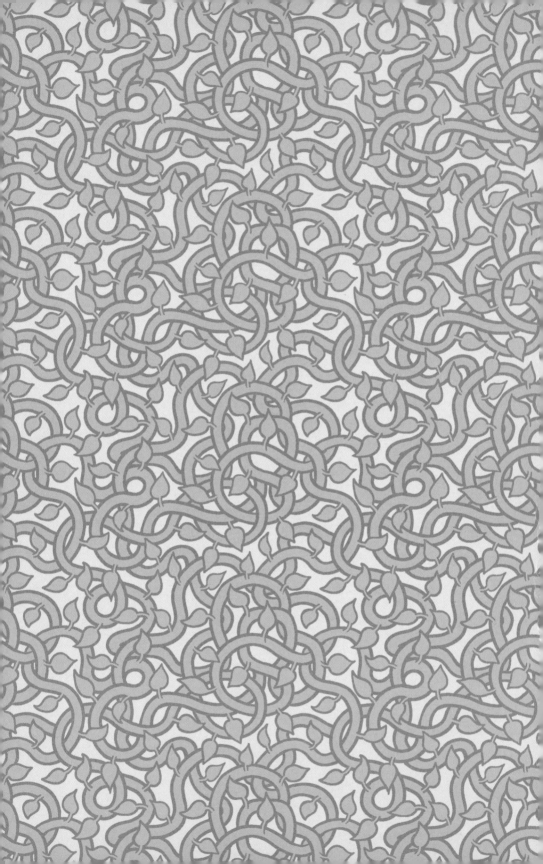